VISIONS OF RELIGION

AMERICAN ACADEMY
of RELIGION

REFLECTION AND THEORY IN THE STUDY OF RELIGION

Series Editor

Theodore M. Vial, Jr., Iliff School of Theology

A Publication Series of The American Academy of Religion and Oxford University Press

Visions of Religion

EXPERIENCE, MEANING, AND POWER

Stephen S. Bush

OXFORD
UNIVERSITY PRESS

OXFORD
UNIVERSITY PRESS

Oxford University Press is a department of the University of Oxford.
It furthers the University's objective of excellence in research, scholarship,
and education by publishing worldwide.

Oxford   New York
Auckland   Cape Town   Dar es Salaam   Hong Kong   Karachi
Kuala Lumpur   Madrid   Melbourne   Mexico City   Nairobi
New Delhi   Shanghai   Taipei   Toronto

With offices in
Argentina   Austria   Brazil   Chile   Czech Republic   France   Greece
Guatemala   Hungary   Italy   Japan   Poland   Portugal   Singapore
South Korea   Switzerland   Thailand   Turkey   Ukraine   Vietnam

Oxford is a registered trade mark of Oxford University Press
in the UK and certain other countries.

Published in the United States of America by
Oxford University Press
198 Madison Avenue, New York, NY 10016

© Oxford University Press 2014

Library of Congress Cataloging-in-Publication Data
Bush, Stephen S., 1974–
Visions of religion : experience, meaning, and power / Stephen S. Bush.
      p.   cm. — (Reflection and theory in the study of religion)
Includes bibliographical references and index.
ISBN 978–0–19–938740–3 (hardcover : alk. paper) — ISBN 978–0–19–938741–0 (ebook) —
ISBN 978–0–19–938742–7 (online content) 1. Religion and sociology.
2. Experience (Religion) I. Title.
BL60.B87 2014
200—dc23
                                                    2014007263

1   3   5   7   9   8   6   4   2

Printed in the United States of America on acid-free paper

For Belinda

Contents

Preface

WHEN PEOPLE WORSHIP, they do so as social actors, embedded in the various institutions and relationships that make up their social context. This means that religion is inextricably intertwined with its larger social setting, a fact that makes describing and explaining religious practices extraordinarily demanding. Over the past hundred or so years, as people have grappled with religion and how best to think about it, they have latched on to one or another feature of religious life and regarded it as prominent. Earlier on, it was common for scholars to think of the experiential dimension of religion as primary. Then they came to think of the symbolic dimension as primary. Now the tendency is to regard social power and materiality as preeminent. Taking any of these three aspects of religion as the basic thing opens up certain insights into religion even as it forecloses others. One's vision of what religion most especially is directs one's attention to see certain things and miss others. The agenda of this book is to find ways to keep all three aspects of religion—experience, meaning, and power—in view and to do so by envisioning religion as a social practice.

This project originated while I was a graduate student in the Department of Religion at Princeton University. First and foremost among those whom I want to thank from Princeton is Jeffrey Stout, my dissertation adviser. Jeff's encouragement, advice, teaching, and critical feedback were essential for my own intellectual development. He was then and still is a model to me for how to be a scholar and teacher. It was his suggestion that led me to broaden my original plan for this book to focus on religious experience and to incorporate meaning and power as co-themes. Eddie Glaude echoed this advice, and I am grateful to him for that but, more important, for his energy and passion for the study of religion and his critical and constructive input into my writing. Eric Gregory is another person whose teaching and scholarship helped shape my own, and I thank him and Leora Batnitzky for their questions and comments on an earlier version of this project. I cannot help but think that Princeton at that time was in a "golden age" of sorts for the study of religion and critical thought, with Cornel West then on the faculty alongside Jeff, Leora, Eddie, and Eric. Cornel's generosity, moral depth, breadth of knowledge, and intellectual rigor inspired me then and continues to do so now.

When I left Princeton, I thought I would never find a department as collegial. Happily, Brown proved me wrong. All of my colleagues in religious studies have been generously supportive and ready with wise counsel, and they have made the Department of Religious Studies at Brown an ideal place to work. I especially want to thank Mark Cladis and Tal Lewis for their good-naturedness, their scholarly excellence, their friendship, and the many pieces of advice that they have readily provided whenever I have needed it. Susan Harvey, too, has especially been helpful with her insightfulness about every aspect of academic life and I have been exceedingly fortunate to have her as a mentor and departmental chair.

Mark Cladis, David Decosimo, Tal Lewis, Wayne Proudfoot, Josh Schenkkan, Jeffrey Stout, Ted Vial, Eric Young, and two anonymous referees have read drafts of this book in part or whole and have provided valuable suggestions. I thank Ted, too, for his expert editorial work. As I was working on the book, I benefited from conversations with Fannie Bialek, Wendell Dietrich, Josh Dubler, Marie Griffith, Kevin Hector, Kevin Schilbrack, Jason Springs, Ian Ward, and many others. I had opportunities to present versions of the book's contents to audiences at Princeton University, Brown University, and the American Academy of Religion annual conference, and I am grateful for the feedback that I received at those places. I have reproduced here excerpts from my essays, "Are Meanings the Name of the Game? Religion as Symbolic Meaning and Religion as Power," *Religion Compass* 6, no. 12 (December 2012): 525–533, and "Are Religious Experiences Too Private to Study?" *Journal of Religion* 92, no. 2 (April 2012): 199–223. I give my thanks to those journals for allowing me to reproduce portions of those articles.

I was fortunate to write much of this book at home. More specifically, I wrote it in shared spaces in various houses, so a good portion of it was written with kids on my lap, kids at my side, and sometimes even kids hanging around my neck. I am tempted to blame these distractions for any errors and lapses in this book! In all seriousness, having their company, distractions and all, proved to be a delightful way to work, and I have loved the energy and joy with which Kara and Mason surrounded me as

I worked. I have learned much from Mason's limitless imagination and Kara's re-
sourceful inventiveness.

I dedicate this book to Belinda. I could not ask for a better partner, friend, and
co-parent.

Introduction

⌒

Religion is experiential. It furnishes people with extraordinary mystical experiences: breathtaking episodes of immediate connectedness, they say, to the most fundamental reality. Religion is also meaningful. It immerses people in constellations of symbols, imbuing their projects, pains, and ambitions with significance. It is infused with power. Religion oppresses, suppresses, and liberates. It is an ideological system of power that buttresses the dominators' control of the dominated, and it just as easily impels heroic resistance against cruel regimes. All three of these factors—experiences, meaning, and power—pervade the practice of religion, sometimes conspicuously, often in subtle and quotidian ways.

These three aspects of religion are significant not just because they play such important roles in religious communities but also because some of the most influential people to grapple theoretically with the nature of religion in the past hundred years have thought that religion was most especially one of these three things. William James, in his classic text, *Varieties of Religious Experience*, construes religion as fundamentally experiential in nature, and such luminaries as Rudolf Otto and Mircea Eliade join him in this vision.[1] Clifford Geertz, a leading figure in both religious studies and anthropology for much of the latter part of the twentieth century, thought of religion as a system of symbols, vehicles of meaning that require interpretation. Talal Asad helped inaugurate an approach in religious studies that emphasizes power when he criticized Geertz's conception of religion. According to Asad, religion is especially a set of power relationships that structure social differences and that shape practitioners into particular types of subjects, that is, into particular patterns of affect, action, desire, and bodily habit. In the hands of James, Geertz, Asad, and many other figures, the experiential, meaning, and power visions of religion predominated, in succession, the landscape of religious studies over the past hundred years.

For those who study religion, it has proved remarkably difficult to attend to all three of these dimensions. A focus on one typically precludes attention to the other two. James, Geertz, and Asad each have a rich account of the element in religion that they regard as preeminent and little to say about the other two. Moreover, proponents of each vision have not always regarded the other visions fondly. On occasion a proponent of one approach does not just neglect but actively disparages the other approaches. One could even get the impression from certain remarks that a commitment to one vision excludes the other two. Mircea Eliade, for example, speaking for the experiential vision of religion, differentiates religion as a creation of the human spirit from matters of power like protest and revolt.[2] Asad pointedly remarks, with Geertz in mind, "Searching for symbolic meanings is not the name of *my* game."[3] Geertz responds that he thinks that Asad is a "power-reductionist."[4] Saba Mahmood insists that her anthropological approach does not focus on the meanings of "utterances, discourses, and practices" but on the "*work* that discursive practices perform in making possible particular types of subjects."[5] Rosalind Shaw and Russell McCutcheon, representing the power approach, charge that Eliade's conception of religion as sui generis is ideological, covertly serving the interests of men, academics, and Europeans.[6] Robert Sharf suggests that we should concern ourselves more with discourse about experiences and the ideological effects of such discourse than with the experiences themselves.[7] And on it goes.

The assumption that guides this book is that the insulation and antagonism among the visions are both regrettable and correctible. The project here is to make a case that each of the three key terms at stake—"experience," "meaning," and "power"—is indispensable for the study of religion. If religions involve all three then it seems that someone who wants to understand a religion adequately would have to attend to all three. We cannot afford to do without any of them, lest we distort and misrepresent religious communities. The student of religion should attend to the experiential dimension of religion, to the meanings of the utterances, actions, and artifacts employed by the practitioners, and to the ways in which religious practices involve power relationships that produce particular types of religious subjects and social differences of gender, class, ethnicity, race, and sexual orientation. If we turn our attention to any religious group without an expectation and awareness that all three of these aspects of religion are occurring, then we will miss something of vital importance.

We need not just to attend to all three dimensions of religious practices; we need to theorize all three categories adequately. So another task that this book undertakes is to bring the three approaches into a single theory of religion. We presently have a difficult time seeing how a single theoretical approach to religion could encompass all three dimensions of religion. In the abstract, accomplishing such a task might seem a straightforward affair. There is nothing conceptually incoherent about the claim that experiences, meaning, and power can coexist in religious practices. However, things are more complicated than they first appear. Each of the three visions has its own history of development and its own theoretical assumptions and methodological orientations. These assumptions do not always fit neatly together, especially since the latter approaches were in important ways developed in reaction against what came before them, and so they are incompatible with their predecessors by design. Power and associated concepts like materiality, practices, and bodies enjoy a certain cachet nowadays. But the status that this vision of religion has gained comes at the expense of the religion-as-meaning approach. And experience is a particularly problematic concept nowadays. Many regard the term as beyond repair: too closely associated with Cartesian notions of interior subjectivity, according to which the mental is a realm thoroughly bifurcated from the public world. Experience is too slippery and difficult to define with any precision, they think.

To reconcile the three visions with each other, we will have to understand the theoretical assumptions of each. Where the assumptions associated with one vision truly are incompatible with one or both of the other two, I will propose adjustments and corrections, guided by the conviction that the three are in principle compatible, even if in their received versions they do not smoothly fit with each other.

It is not just that these three approaches are compatible with each other; all three can be integrated into a single framework, that of social practices. Certain versions of social practice theory, especially those influenced by Ludwig Wittgenstein, give us a way to understand both experiences and meanings as social affairs, which is precisely what we need to counter the Cartesianism that has haunted these matters. Other versions of social practice theory, especially those influenced by people like Michel Foucault, Pierre Bourdieu, and Judith Butler, readily account for power. So between these two brands of social practice theory, we have resources toward a comprehensive theory of religion. We should think of religion not as a special type of experience, or as a system of meanings, or as power relations, but as something that incorporates all three: a social practice. A social practice is a shared pattern of behavior that is conducted according to norms. It is shared in that the participants who occupy a certain role in a practice tend to respond to similar sorts of situations with similar sorts of behavior, and shared norms apply to their performances. Social practices are socially inculcated: people are socialized into them through processes of imitation, explicit instruction, practice, and correction. Social practices endure through time but not in a rigid or inflexible way. They involve habits, so they are relatively stable but not so fixed as to preclude transformation, novelty, reform, or even revolution.

I will turn now to a brief sketch of the theoretical promise and perils of each of the three key terms "experience," "meaning," and "power" in turn, and in doing so, I will indicate some of the interventions that I intend to make in this book. Of all three approaches, experience will require the most attention. Integrating experience into a social practice framework is an especially tricky matter. The notion of social practices indicates a focus on shared attitudes and shared patterns of behavior into which members of a group are socialized. This notion has received much attention in the humanities and social sciences recently in part because it corrects the long-standing bias in the Western intellectual tradition for mind over matter and spirit over body. In their emphasis on the body and its habitual ways of behaving, social practice theorists tend to eschew matters of mind and consciousness. But experiences seem to be precisely a matter of mind and consciousness, events that supposedly occur in a Cartesian realm of interior subjectivity. What, then, could experiences have to do with practices? As things stand, not much.

The experiential conception of religion ascended to prominence in an era when consciousness was a privileged site for inquiry, whether in the phenomenology of Edmund Husserl or the sense-data of Anglo-American empiricist philosophy. Husserl maintained that all philosophical inquiry begins with an investigation into the nature of the inquirer's conscious experience. The empiricists treated our sensations as given but found it more difficult to account for the existence of extra-mental objects. But then the linguistic turn occurred in the humanities and social sciences. As Seyla Benhabib puts it, "*The paradigm of language has replaced the paradigm of consciousness*" and so "the focus is no longer on the epistemic subject or on the private contents of its consciousness but on the public, signifying activities of a collection of subjects."[8] And after the turn to language (to which Geertz was a significant contributor) came the turn to practice, another step removed from the paradigm of consciousness. The category of experience now seems hopelessly antiquated. Scholars of religion describe its present status in the academy as "passé," "widely critiqued," and "beleaguered" or even "totally abandoned as a subject of academic study."[9]

Much of the current skepticism about religious experience has to do with the role that experience played in the thought of an extremely prominent mid-twentieth-century approach to religion known as the phenomenology of religion, closely associated with Eliade. Phenomenologists of religion like Eliade are primary representatives of the religion-as-experience vision, and they have three key views that are important for our purposes: first, they view the essential, most important aspect of religion as something experiential. For Eliade, a special sort of conscious experience, which he calls the sense of the sacred, is what religion most fundamentally is. Second, they think that the particular type of experience that is the essence of religion is cross-culturally universal, present throughout all religious communities regardless of historical era or geographic locale. Third, they think that students of religion can come to an intimate understanding of others' religious practices by empathizing with the practitioner and undergoing the sense of the sacred themselves. Subsequent generations of scholars came to criticize and reject all three of these assumptions. This is not to say that there aren't still vocal and articulate proponents of the phenomenology of religion, but they are the minority now, and the close tie between the concept of experience and the phenomenology of religion leaves experience guilty by association. In a recent development, Sharf has posed a provocative challenge to the experiential approach to religion, wondering whether our words can possibly refer to episodes that are private in nature: "The category experience is, in essence, a mere placeholder that entails a substantive if indeterminate terminus for the relentless deferral of meaning," he says, and, borrowing a turn of phrase from Samuel Beckett, "All attempts to signify 'inner experience' are destined to remain 'well-meaning squirms that get us nowhere.'"[10]

So the category of experience is beset with difficulties. But are the difficulties insurmountable? Might there be a continuing place for the concept of experience in religious studies, and, if so, how should we conceptualize experiences to address the specters of Cartesianism and absolute mental interiority? My attempt to answer these questions first grants a very different status to experience than that found in the phenomenologists of religion. I depart from all three of their key assumptions. In my understanding of religion, experience is not the fundamental essence of religion, rather it is one facet of religious practices among others, such as doctrines, rituals, institutions, texts, and artifacts. In principle it is neither more nor less important than any of these. Further, unlike the phenomenologists, I am not committed to the view that any single experiential state is common across religious traditions. I expect that there are a variety of religious experiences, and it is not important to my view that there be any type of experience that is universal. I quite doubt there is. And third, I do not assume that the outsider can obtain the equivalent of an insider's understanding of religious experiences through the exercise of empathy.

So the place that I assign to experience is not as lofty as the one the phenomenologists of religion do. But I do insist, in contrast to tendencies among some contemporary scholars, that experience deserves to retain a place in the repertoire of scholarly concepts. It will not do, as Ann Taves suggests some would like, to replace the study of experience with the study of discourse about experience.[11] To be sure, discourse about experience is a matter that deserves attention in its own right, and this is a relatively new insight for scholarship on religion. We should, as Sharf and Grace Jantzen suggest, look for all manner of ideological purposes to which such discourse is put, by scholars and practitioners.[12] But experiences are different from talk about experiences, just as having sex is different from discourse about sex and just as the methamphetamine epidemic owes itself to meth use, not discourse about meth use.

In this study, I will use the term "religious experience" in both a narrow and a broad sense. Religious experience, in a narrow sense, speaks of particular episodes of awareness that people report as involving some deity, spirit, other religious entity, or religiously significant state of consciousness. In a broader sense, it speaks of the emotional life of practitioners more generally, their religious affects, emotions, and moods. In both these senses, experiences are pervasive throughout religious practices. Whatever their nature, experiences can and do have real effects in the lives of religious individuals and religious communities and are in turn affected by the religious communities. To account for this, we need to be able to retain experience as a category in the study of religion, not eliminate it in favor of the category of discourse-about-experience, however indispensable that new category may be.

So the role for experience that I propose for religious studies is chastened relative to the phenomenologists but still substantial. If we are to retain it, though, we need to reconceptualize it in such a way that it is not lost to the hidden recesses of a mysterious subjectivity. Such reconceptualization must deal with two primary issues, which I call the problem of privacy and the problem of power. The problem of privacy speaks of the fact that religious experiences typically transpire in the practitioner's mind, not in the publicly observable world. This raises questions of whether experiences are ineluctably Cartesian, belonging to a subjective, private reality that is of an entirely different order than the publicly observable material world. Some have suggested that this problem is so severe that whatever terms we use to refer to experiences cannot properly carry meaning, since meaning is a product of the public and social world.[13] The problem of privacy also involves the question of the degree to which an outsider can come to any understanding about the nature of a religious experience. Otto famously suggested that people who have not themselves had an experience cannot understand anything significant about religious experiences.

I find one helpful resource for addressing the problem of privacy in philosophers of mind who do not bifurcate the mental from the social. Wittgenstein famously claimed that there cannot be a private language. What he meant by this is that individuals cannot invent their own terms to identify the various features of their mental life; rather we are all reliant upon socially employed terminology, even in our most private thoughts.[14] Wilfrid Sellars develops this idea into a criticism of the "myth of the given." The myth of the given is the idea that particular sensations deliver to perceivers particular pieces of knowledge, independently of the perceivers' other beliefs and their social context. Sellars and Robert Brandom following him think that perception is in an important sense historical and cultural in nature.[15] In Brandom's account, perception is a matter that is thoroughly social practical in nature. To perceive something, in the sense that matters, one must have been socialized into a linguistic community so that one acquires the ability to respond to particular types of sensations by applying particular concepts. To grasp any one concept, one must grasp a whole lot of concepts. This account then understands our ordinary perceptual experiences in a non-Cartesian way. My claim is that we can apply the same sort of account to religious experiences. Doing so situates religious experiences thoroughly within social practices and addresses the criticisms of religious experiences that they are essentially, irreparably tainted by Cartesianism. On the basis of this model of religious experience, I claim that we should acknowledge that the insider and the outsider do occupy different statuses in regard to the experience but that the outsider is in principle as capable of coming to understand the nature of the insiders' religious experiences as the experiencers themselves are.

The problem of privacy has received attention in the philosophy of mysticism literature for some time, but the problem of power has only recently emerged as a topic. Particularly relevant is the work of Sharf and Jantzen, both of whom charge that mystical experiences have been conceptualized, by scholars and religious practitioners alike, in such a way as to privilege particular interests. For Jantzen, these interests are male over and against female. For Sharf, the interests are in various cases those of Japanese nationalists, European intellectuals, and particular Buddhist schools. Further, ethnographic and historical studies make clear that experiences themselves can shape and be shaped by people's attitudes toward social differences, as when an African American slave has a vision of God as white or as when people encounter God as male. These sorts of power dynamics have gone almost entirely unremarked in the study of religious experience. Brandom and Sellars are helpful for understanding experiences as transpiring within the social-practical realm, but they have little to say about matters of power. To account for the entanglement of experience in matters of sociopolitical power, I turn to sociologist Marcel Mauss, philosopher of religion Amy Hollywood, social theorist Pierre Bourdieu, and others. They supply resources to understand experiences as episodes that occur in the context of social and bodily practices. Since these social and bodily practices are invested with power, we have a means of understanding the way that experiences relate to societal relations of power and domination. Having addressed the problems of privacy and power, we can see the way forward to a viable use of the category of experience.

Despite my criticisms of the phenomenologists of religion, my theory preserves three of their insights. First is their commitment to the study of the experiential dimension of religion. The second is their insistence that studying religion requires attention to the practitioner's point of view, an idea that was retained and developed by Geertz. The third is the idea that there is a significant asymmetry between the perspective of the practitioner of religion and the outsider. I will develop these insights from the experiential approach in other ways than the phenomenologists themselves did, but I still acknowledge the insights themselves as valuable and lasting contributions of the experiential vision of religion.

Meaning will require significant reenvisioning as well. Meaning became a central matter of philosophical interest through developments in the phenomenological tradition in philosophy (not to be confused with phenomenology of religion, though the two are not entirely unrelated). Husserl, a founding figure in the phenomenological approach, thought that subjectivity involves an aspect that transcends culture and history, the "transcendental ego," but the phenomenologists who followed him came to see human consciousness as thoroughly historical and social in nature. What this implies is that humans do not immediately experience the world in which they live, rather their encounters with the world are mediated by and saturated with meaning: people assign meaning to the objects and events that they experience and respond to the objects and events according to the significance that they accord them. Martin Heidegger is the major figure in inaugurating this type of phenomenology, referred to variously as philosophical hermeneutics, hermeneutic phenomenology, and existential phenomenology. The philosophical hermeneutics of Hans-Georg Gadamer and Paul Ricoeur exercised tremendous influence in the study of religion, and many phenomenologists of religion have drawn from Heidegger, Ricoeur, and Gadamer.

What is of great importance in philosophical hermeneutics is the emphasis on the perspectival and situated character of all knowledge. This means that if you are trying to understand someone else's utterances, two situated perspectives are in play: your own and the other person's. These perspectives interact in dynamic tension, and so comprehension of one person by another is only achieved when a fusion of the two perspectives or horizons (as Gadamer puts it) is realized. Since scholars of religion are often in the position of attempting to understand the texts, utterances, and behavior of people remote from them in time and space, it is valuable to be informed by a philosophy that emphasizes the situatedness of the scholars themselves, as opposed to a view of the scholar as an occupant of a neutral standpoint free from bias and cultural heritage. Further, the hermeneutical philosopher's account shows that understanding a foreigner is possible. The fusion of horizons may involve effort, difficulty, and even the modification of the inquirer's preexisting perspective, but it is in principle possible, so we have a theoretical account of the possibility of success in the scholarly enterprise.

However, the account of meaning that the philosophical hermeneuts promote faces difficulties. Indeed, here we find some of the same difficulties that we find with the category of experience, even if not quite as severe. The category of meaning faces its own versions of the two problems confronting experience: the problem of privacy and the problem of power. If we think of the interpretation of meaning along the lines that Gadamer thought of it, as a fusion of horizons, the question arises as to where exactly the horizons are located and what exactly is occurring when they fuse. One suspicion is that meaning is located in people's heads. Meaning does not seem to be out there in the things themselves, alongside the electrons, protons, and neutrons that constitute matter, but rather in people's mental life. But if this is the case, can we understand meaning in a way that doesn't assume a stark division between the mental and the physical, the interior and the exterior? Further, how do we go about accessing other people's mental lives? It seems that we need something more specific than vague, metaphorical talk of horizons and fusions. Both Ricoeur and Gadamer want to avoid mentalism by appealing to a notion of a world to which meanings and texts refer, but they do not provide a satisfying account of the exact relations among the world, the text, and the interpreting subject. These questions and issues make up meaning's version of the problem of privacy.

Perhaps the most promising place to go to begin to address the problem of privacy in relation to meaning is the work of Geertz. Geertz conceives of religion as a system of cultural symbols and conceives of the study of religion as the interpretation of the meaning of these symbols. While he counts Gadamer and Ricoeur among his influences and even refers at times to his work as phenomenological, what makes his approach especially promising is his appropriation of Wittgenstein. The Wittgensteinian influence constitutes a decisive and productive break from Gadamer, Ricoeur, and also from both phenomenology of religion and hermeneutical phenomenology. Wittgenstein's contribution is the idea of meaning as use. The meaning of the symbol is the social role that it plays, and this role is a public, observable affair, not something sequestered away in some impenetrable, inscrutable mental realm. Meaning, Geertz tells us, is public: "Cultural acts, the construction, apprehension, and utilization of symbolic forms, are social events like any other; they are as public as marriage and as observable as agriculture." [16] For popularizing this notion of meaning, Geertz's place in the pantheon of anthropologists and scholars of religion is well deserved. Even though his influence has waned in the past couple of decades, the central insights in his understanding of religion are as relevant today as ever and deserve a lasting place in the study of religion (and the study of culture generally).

However, several critics of Geertz have thought that even with his explicit avowal of the public nature of meaning, his position does not adequately deal with what I am calling the problem of privacy. Asad has charged that Geertz's approach retains a commitment to meaning as something problematically mentalistic in nature, and Victor Crapanzano and James Clifford suggest that Geertz is overly optimistic about the possibility of accessing other people's meanings. So an attempt to preserve or rehabilitate Geertz's status will have to show that his core insights survive these critics. I will emphasize strands of thought in Geertz according to which meaning is in fact public, not mentalistic, and so we can achieve a significant degree of access to others' understandings of their symbols. To seal this case, however, it is necessary to go beyond Geertz's explicit remarks, which are underdeveloped, and extend and develop his basic position with the help of philosophy. Here again Sellars and Brandom have much to offer. Sellars and Brandom, like Geertz, have a theory of meaning—linguistic meaning in their case—according to which meaning is social and public in nature. They articulate their theory of meaning with far more precision than Geertz does, and so if we extend Geertz's position in the direction of something like the theory of Sellars and Brandom, we can confidently present the ongoing relevance of meaning for those contemporary theorists who are suspicious of it. Indeed, we can go so far as to say that the approaches to religion that appeal to power require some account of meaning, for social power, I will argue, could not operate in any recognizable form without a context of meaning and significance. Meaning requires as sophisticated a theoretical account as power does.

But what about the problem of power as it confronts meaning? Geertz does not fare as well when it comes to power. In fact, the philosophers of meaning typically have ignored power, leaving the impression that the conveyance of meaning transpires in a powerless vacuum. What if Gadamer's horizons do not approach each other on equal terms, but rather certain horizons are advantaged: backed by bigger muscles, bigger guns, ideological supremacy, or more impressive-sounding credentials? How are we to think of the fusion of the horizon of a powerful group with that of a marginalized or suppressed one? For these sorts of questions, Gadamer and Ricoeur do not help, and Geertz does not have convincing answers either. He thinks that the study of religion is the study of symbols and that the meaning of symbols is transparent to the practitioners. To study religion, then, is to come to understand what the practitioners already understand. I agree that this is an essential aspect of the study of religion and one that we must theorize adequately. However, I do not think it is sufficient. To understand how power operates in religious communities, we need an explicit account of various aspects of religious practices of which the practitioners are not aware. Bourdieu helps with this, as he theorizes the way in which bodily habits have unintended and unacknowledged effects in society, effects that establish and perpetuate power disparities within and among groups. So the conclusion to reach while considering Geertz's present-day significance is that his approach or at least key aspects of it are essential to the study of religion but that it requires supplementation by theorists of social power like Bourdieu, Foucault, and Butler.

The third main approach that this book concerns, power, comes to us already far more suited to play a part in a social practice theory of religion than the other two. Indeed, while it is not universally the case, a great many social theorists and philosophers who work with the paradigm of social practices do so precisely because it is a fruitful way to theorize the operations of power in societies. This is certainly true for such major practice theorists as Foucault, Bourdieu, and Butler. Specifically, what is at stake in the religion-as-power approach is the way in which social forms of power, often systemic ones, operate to ensure different social statuses for different groups. In this approach, students of religion are interested in how power functions within and among particular religious groups and how religion is involved in establishing, perpetuating, and resisting various types of oppression, marginalization, and domination. Scholars of power do not just attend to the way that power operates in religious groups, however; they look reflexively at how power operates in scholarship. The idea here is that those who study religion are, in the very work of conducting their study, perpetuating social difference and exclusion in various ways. For example, feminists have shown that scholarship on religion is itself frequently sexist. Postcolonialists argue that religious studies is Eurocentric in a way that legitimates European domination over non-European peoples. The power approach examines the concepts that scholars use—concepts such as religion, experience, and belief—and the way that the application of the concepts privileges contemporary Eurocentric assumptions over competing ones.

It is somewhat strange to say that the power approach is the most recent of the three. Concerns with power have preexisted Mircea Eliade and Clifford Geertz by a long while. Each of the classical social theorists—Karl Marx, Émile Durkheim, and Max Weber—all theorize religion in a way that makes power central to its functioning. Marx's famous remark that religion is the opium of the people reflects his view that religion serves as an illusory form of happiness for those in lower classes who have been denied the happiness that comes with material provision. Weber traces the ways in which religious authorities exercise power over the members of their religious group. Another figure of great importance, Friedrich Nietzsche, sees Judaism and Christianity as the key culprits in the "slave revolt in morality," in which the health and wealth of the aristocratic elite, once regarded as good, became sinfully evil, while the poverty and sickness of the poor went from bad to holy. What's more, feminists have from the start been aware of the way in which religion can be oppressive to women. Elizabeth Cady Stanton's *The Woman's Bible*, for example, reflects a keen awareness of the way in which Christianity has harmed women.[17]

Nevertheless, for much of the twentieth century, the phenomenologists of religion and then the interpretive theorists held sway in religious studies and concerns with power, though hardly absent, tended to be overshadowed. Furthermore, the theory of power that has emerged over the past thirty years has been markedly distinct from Marx's and Weber's in its focus on micropolitics and the body, following Foucault. Traditional conceptions of power often focus on privileged social classes and the occupants of institutional offices and see those individuals and classes as possessing and exercising power over the rest of the population. Foucault's "capillary" conception of power in contrast sees power as exercised throughout the entire social body, by the oppressed and marginalized as well as by elites. For Foucault, modern power is particularly effective in people's bodily habits, and the bodily habits of everyone in the society, not just the rulers, determine the nature of how power operates. Bourdieu and Butler subscribe to a micropolitical view of power, too. This type of theory of power is often combined with post-structuralist accounts of signification, such as that of Jacques Derrida, that view meaning as inherently unstable and so manipulable by power. When we bring these sorts of theories of power to religion what results is a methodology that sees in rituals, sacred texts, institutions, and religious discourse the production of differentiated social identities. These theories' assumptions give rise to research projects that study religions with attention to a variety of social categories, including gender, class, race, sexual orientation, and colonization. Such studies attend to the way that these categories operate both in religious communities and in academic scholarship.

A key moment in the arrival of the power approach to the guild of religious studies occurred when Asad published his criticism of Clifford Geertz's definition of religion in 1983.[18] Asad is influenced by Foucault's methodology of historicizing our concepts and discerning the way in which they developed in the service of particular interests. What Asad says about Geertz is that his approach is tacitly Christian in privileging mentalistic items such as beliefs and that Geertz's attempt to delineate a universal definition of religion is misguided and Eurocentric. In company with Asad, a new constellation of theoretical lenses has emerged for which David Chidester has coined the term "new materialism." Unlike the old materialisms ("naturalist, empiricist, positivist, cultural, historical, dialectical"), this one regards religion as a valid topic of inquiry in its own right, not some epiphenomena of other, nonreligious factors. But in contrast to "dematerialized" conceptions of religion, new materialism rejects anything smacking of the mental (such as ideas, doctrines, beliefs, meanings, and experiences) for tangible things such as bodies (in their manifold differences), social practices, material culture, and artifacts. And though new materialism is not restricted to concerns about power, its attention to power never flags as it sets about "analyzing material relations within political economies of the sacred."[19]

The theorists of power and materiality give us a set of questions and concerns that are vital to the study of religion. It is productive to follow them in thinking of power as something that is not just exercised by certain individuals and offices but that pervades society and transpires in every social relationship. Religions constitute one such network of social relationships, and so attending to religion requires attending to power. Furthermore, scholars, as representatives of a particular social location, often stand in a power relationship with the people whom they are studying. This power relation means that the concepts the scholars utilize and their biases and assumptions are the result of and quite possibly perpetuate a whole host of relations of domination, whether colonialist, sexist, classist, or racist. Scholars should attend to these relations and to the possibility that they are complicit in domination.

However, the theorists of power characteristically overlook matters of meaning and especially experience. When it comes to experience, this means that there is a tendency to treat discourse about experience as a proper matter for investigation but not experiences themselves. When it comes to meaning, the power theorists show far more interest in what religious practices *do*, that is, what sort of subjectivities and power relationships they produce, than what they *mean*. One result of this is that we end up with an impoverished understanding of the motives, desires, and aims of religious practitioners. Someone who stayed close to Bourdieu's perspective would have trouble conceiving religious goods as ends for action in their own right, since Bourdieu's theory treats cultural goods only as the means to perpetuate social group distinctions. Some power and practice theorists treat even the category of belief as nothing more than an ideological device. My strategy will be to retain the insights of the power theorists without sacrificing the insights of the meaning and experience theorists, and I will do this by harmonizing the social practical account of meaning and experience that I develop from Sellars and Brandom with the social practical account of power that I inherit from theorists like Bourdieu, Foucault, and Butler.

PREVIEW OF THE BOOK

Having covered in general terms each of the three approaches and my own strategies in respect to them, I will now provide an overview of the structure of this book. It is organized in two parts. Part 1 provides an initial overview of the experiential, meaning, and power approaches to religion. The aim in these three chapters is to provide, for each approach: (i) a brief historical introduction to the approach, an intellectual history of sorts, designed to describe to the reader the present-day status of the approach in religious studies; (ii) an account of why the approach is, in some form, essential to the study of religion; and (iii) an account of the key problems that presently confront the approach. Part 2 consists of my own constructive proposals as to how best to address the problems facing each approach. I show that the approaches' key insights are still viable in the study of religion and I integrate the three approaches into a single, social practical account of religion.

Chapter 1 takes us from experience to meaning. It gives an intellectual history of the experiential vision of religion and then accounts for the rise of meaning and how the turn to meaning demoted experience. Chapter 2 introduces the power vision. After a brief intellectual history of the approach, I explain the implications of the turn to power for experience and meaning. Although it is hardly the case that everyone subscribes to the power approach, because of its relative novelty (in its present form), there is not as much published criticism of the power approach as there is of the other two. Nevertheless, I will voice some criticisms of this approach, by Robert Orsi, for example. Having introduced each approach, in chapter 3 I make a case for the indispensability of all three. I appeal to historical and ethnographic case studies to show that experience, meaning, and power all transpire in religion and that they are inextricably intertwined. This indicates that all three categories are essential to the study of religion. I end the chapter by highlighting the outstanding theoretical problems with each approach.

Part 2 comprises chapters 4–6, which cover the three approaches in more philosophical detail, with the aim of reconciling them into a common theoretical framework. In chapter 4, I do the work of bringing the power approach and the interpretive approach together in a single theoretical framework. I will criticize certain features of Geertz's understanding of culture, where he seems to drive a wedge between culture and power. I will then turn to an in-depth look at the complicated philosophical issues involved in bringing meaning and power together. One point here is that meaning and power implicate each other: someone who is committed to understanding religion as a matter of power should also understand it as a matter of meaning, and vice versa. Before turning to the theory that I espouse, I will criticize one standard way to account for meaning and power, post-structuralism, arguing that it involves as many mystifications as the previous phenomenological approaches upon which it is supposed to be an improvement. I will then turn for help to the social practice theory of Brandom and Sellars and to standpoint epistemologists. Brandom has a theory of meaning that is social in nature; that is, he subscribes to Hilary Putnam's dictum that "meanings ain't in the head." Meanings are not mysterious mentalistic entities sequestered away between individuals' ears. Rather, they are a product of our social practices, specifically, the way in which our language use depends on our ability to make inferences from the statements that our fellows utter. The idea here is that, as Wittgenstein says, meaning is use: the meaning of an utterance is determined by the role it plays in our social-linguistic and practical context. As Brandom develops this insight, the meaning of a term, such as "cat," is given specifically by its inferential role. The meaning of the term "cat" is determined by the sort of things that one can infer from statements that contain the word. From "Carl is a cat," one can infer that "Carl has fur," "Carl has four legs," "Carl has a heart," "Carl cannot fly," and so on. To grasp the meaning of the word "cat" is to possess the practical ability to make such inferences. Interpretation is the ability to figure out what the proper inferences are from a statement or collection of statements. So Brandom gives us an account of meaning that is faithful to the key representatives of interpretation, including Gadamer and Geertz, but with a greater degree of conceptual precision. The upshot is that we can understand meaning as the result of particular skills: skills of uttering and inferring. Such skills are a pervasive part of our social lives, and so we do not need to worry that a commitment to meaning and interpretation entails a commitment to mysterious mental entities. Brandom is good on these points, but he does not have very much to say about the relation between power and meaning. Feminist standpoint theorists, political theorists, and epistemologists like Miranda Fricker can supplement Brandom and help us make sense of the way that inferring and uttering transpire in a power-laden context, not a neutral sphere that is untainted by interest and domination.

Having argued for the need for incorporating both power and meaning into a single theoretical framework, I will then turn my attention to the topic of experience. My first task, undertaken in chapter 5, will be to discuss the relation between the experiential approach and the meaning approach. In the philosophical study of religious experience, this has been investigated largely under the question of the relation between cultural context and experiences. There is a major divide on this issue, with some, whom I will call perennialists, insisting that religious experiences are acultural. On the opposite side of the debate, the constructivists, especially under the influence of Steven Katz and Wayne Proudfoot, rejoin that experiences are thoroughly determined by the experiencer's cultural context. I find the present status of this debate unsatisfying, because each side has some key unresolved issues. One major source of the lack of resolution is that members of this discussion have not specified precisely enough what they think concepts are and how concepts operate in experiences. The debate between perennialists and constructivists centers on concepts because the constructivists hold that concepts are cultural items. According to constructivists, then, if concepts are involved in experiences, then experiences are cultural in nature. But how do we speak of concepts without being dragged into the recesses of private subjectivity for which the new materialists and others rightly have suspicion? Here again I will draw on the philosophy of Brandom and Sellars, who have not just a theory of meaning but a theory of how perception and meaning interrelate. In this account, concepts are norms that govern our use of linguistic terms and how we use those terms in our inferences, perceptions, and actions. I will treat religious experiences as a special type of perception and argue that the Brandom/Sellars account of perception sheds light on the problems facing the constructivist/perennialist debate by resituating the debate from the mysterious wells of private consciousness to the social statuses that attach to language users when they sense things. Of course, religious experiences aren't exactly like most of the things that we perceive, which are physical objects readily accessible to anyone else who would care to investigate them. There is then a private aspect to religious experiences (though the privacy is not absolute), and this private aspect requires philosophical attention. I argue that the privacy of the experience does entail that the experiencer is in a different situation vis-à-vis the experience than an outsider and that in some ways we can even say the experiencer has a position of privilege in relation to what can be known about the experience. However, it is just as possible that the outsider is in a privileged position, since in many cases an expert can know more about what a person is perceiving and about perception itself than the perceiver herself does (as, for example, a color scientist does).

The final task undertaken in chapter 5 is to attend to a recent and important contribution to the study of religious experience, Ann Taves's *Religious Experience Reconsidered*. I critically examine her ideas about religion, religious experience, and the study of the two. An important facet of her book is its engagement with recent work in neuroscience and cognitive science. I take the occasion of her discussion of these topics to reflect on how cognitive science, neuroscience, and evolutionary psychology might fit with a social practical theory of religion.

In chapter 6, I discuss experience and power. Much of the work in philosophy of religion on mysticism and experience ignores the issue of power altogether. Happily, this has begun to change. Furthermore, it is not as though we are without earlier examples of accounts of experience and power, since Marx, Durkheim, and Weber all subscribed to views that implicitly or explicitly related power to experience. I make the case that experience and power are interrelated by cataloging a number of ways in which experiences have power effects: the concept of experience can be ideological; experience can be a means to personal power; experiences can compensate for deprivation; experience can play a role in cultivating political agency; experiences can foster group solidarity and group identity; experiences can affect institutional structures; experiences are affected by and affect the way that people employ social categories; and experiences play a role in the formation of bodily habits that have political implications. In discussing these configurations of power and experience, I draw from the classical social theorists, from contemporary anthropologists, and from social theorists like Bourdieu.

In the conclusion, I synthesize the various claims and arguments about experience, meaning, and power this book makes into an account of religion as a social practice. I then discuss the way that this theory relates to various subfields in religious studies, including history of religion, ethnography, textual studies, philosophy of religion, religious ethics, and religious thought.

CONCLUDING REMARKS

A couple final things bear mention. The first concerns the meaning of the problematic term "religion." It would be too much to try to give as full an account of religion as the topic warrants. However, a few words are in order to indicate what I mean by the word and why I think that it is viable, even though many find it suspect nowadays. The category of religion has recently received two principal complaints, and the complaints are severe enough that some have recommended doing away with it altogether. The first complaint is that the concept derives from the Christian tradition, and so it evidences a marked bias toward Christianity; the second is that the category is too vague: it is too difficult to proffer a precise definition of the term and to settle borderline cases, such as, for instance, deciding whether a shrine to Elvis is religion or not. I recognize the problems associated with any attempt to define religion. But I do not think religion is any worse off than other analytical categories, such as history, economics, politics, art, and so on. Each of these forestalls precise definition, but none is thereby rendered inoperative. I assume that the term "religion" does have very many sufficiently clear instances of application, however vague and muddled the borderline cases are. I also assume that there are multiple ways to classify nature and society, so there is nothing inherent in nature or society that demands that we classify it as religious or that demands that there is only one right way to differentiate the religious from that which is not religious. Our ways of classifying are context-specific and affected by our interests and aims. We must recognize that religion bears a distinctly Western and Christian history. We must also acknowledge that the fact that the term "religion" came to mean, in early modernity, "Christianity and that which is sufficiently like it" resulted in implicit biases in the category that privileged Christianity over the other "world religions" even as it included them.[20] Nevertheless, concepts are not static. The use of the term "cc:" in our emails does not perpetuate a veiled bias for carbon paper over personal computers. One of the principal erroneous assumptions that attached to the concept of religion was that religion is primarily a matter of belief and doctrine (privileging Christianity's existence as a creedal religion) as opposed to a matter of institution or ritual. Another has been to assume that religion is an inherently beneficial, humanizing force, thus overlooking the destructive and dehumanizing elements in Christianity and other religions. Another erroneous assumption, which owes its existence to the experiential vision of religion, is the notion that religion in general is primarily a matter of subjective experience, a tacit privileging of a Romantic, Pietistic form of Christianity. If we forego these and related assumptions, it is not as clear how retaining the concept religion to encompass a range of traditions that have a family resemblance perpetuates Euro-Christian domination. At any rate, it is up to the critic to show specifically how it does this. I also would like to note at this point that the most stringent critics of the term "religion" invariably, after a thorough interrogation of the term, introduce some substitute or replacement term: so Wilfred Cantwell Smith suggests "faith," Denys Turner suggests "faith tradition," and Timothy Fitzgerald suggests "culture."[21] In no case do the critics of religion subject their suggested replacement to the rigors through which they put the term "religion," and if they were to do so, should we really expect the substitute term to fare any better?

As for the vagueness of the term and the difficult border cases, the failure of twentieth-century analytic philosophy to provide necessary and sufficient criteria for so many concepts, and not for want of effort, does not indicate that vague concepts are unusable. Rather, it shows that many of our concepts are vague, involving paradigm cases where the concept clearly applies, cases in which the concept clearly does not apply, and marginal cases where it is not all clear, perhaps even in principle, whether or not the concept applies. I will be content to focus on paradigmatic cases, not marginal ones.

So what are the defining features of religion, in the paradigmatic cases? I find it helpful to start with Bruce Lincoln's recent statement on the topic, in the first chapter of *Holy Terrors*.[22] Lincoln says that religions involve four things: (i) discourse about transcendent concerns that claims a transcendent status for itself; (ii) practices oriented toward producing a proper world and/or self; (iii) a community that identifies with the discourse and practices; and (iv) institutions that perpetuate the discourse, practices, and communities. The definition is not perfect. For one thing, it excludes religious individualists like Ralph Waldo Emerson.[23] For another thing, it leaves the problematic term "transcendent" underspecified. In respect to this latter point, my own approach is to understand that which is transcendent (or divine or sacred) within the context of specific religious traditions, instead of searching for some common denominator of transcendence that is supposedly located in all religious traditions. I start with the observation that "religion" in both popular and scholarly uses of the term frequently refers to a set of traditions, especially the so-called world religions, a list that varies according to who is doing the tallying, but standardly involves a selection drawn from these: Buddhism, Christianity, Confucianism, Hinduism, Islam, Jainism, Judaism, Sikhism, Shinto, Daoism, and Zoroastrianism. Native American, African, and other indigenous groups also have practices in respect to divine figures and get counted as religious. Ancient, nonliving traditions involving rituals and the worship of divine beings, like the Aztecs, Mayans, Egyptians, Greeks, and Romans, also typically get referred to as religious. For all these traditions and others besides, we can locate the criteria that Lincoln specifies: communities, practices, institutions, and discourses oriented toward transcendence, although of course we need to bear in mind that none of these traditions is homogeneous. Each is better thought of as a set of smaller, related traditions that differ significantly and are oftentimes antagonistic toward one another. There are Judaisms, not any single, uniform Judaism. We can identify things that we would count as transcendent in each tradition, without assuming that it is the same thing across the board: some traditions revere God, gods, or spirits, and we can count these as transcendent; for others what we should think of as transcendent is a metaphysical principle like the Dao or a state of existence like nirvana. It is possible that there is some single underlying property to all these transcendent things that they all share. Or perhaps there is a family resemblance. I will not try to settle those questions here, and, to a degree, the issue of what is or is not a religion is in principle indeterminate, since some scholars might count one thing as a religion, given their particular aims of inquiry, that other scholars would not.

Finally, it is important to point out that this book falls far short of exhaustiveness. Each of the three approaches to religion that I treat deserves a book-length treatment or more in its own right. I have eschewed comprehensiveness and instead strived to deal with the most important figures of each approach at a detailed level. Moreover, while I have tried to draw the historical examples that I employ from a variety of traditions and historical contexts, I have selected examples disproportionately from my areas of expertise and familiarity. I think that my insights in respect to these literatures can be extended to other examples, but that work will have to come in the future. Furthermore, I have by necessity neglected much of importance in the theory and methodology of religious studies that has gone under other banners than experience, power, and meaning. I mention functionalist and psychoanalytic methodologies in passing, but I have not given them the treatment that they deserve. I have not had the opportunity to address important approaches such as Mary Douglas's symbolic approach, the religion-as-market perspective of Rodney Stark, and others as well. These exclusions do not signify that the unexamined approaches lack importance, but, for this study, as for all, constraints are necessary. As for the rationale for the three approaches I have included, even if I am wrong that these are the three most important and influential theories of religion in the last hundred years, certainly they are among the most important and most deserving of attention. All this is to say that while meaning, power, and religion do not exhaust the study of religion, whatever else we do when we study religion and reflect theoretically about it, we must attend carefully to these three.

PART ONE

1

From Experience to Meaning

AN OVERVIEW OF THE EXPERIENTIAL APPROACH

Nowadays scholars of religion emphasize institutions and social practices when they study religion, but a hundred years ago, the individual reigned supreme. Alfred North Whitehead spoke of religion in 1926 as "what the individual does with his solitariness," and William James famously defined religion in 1901 as the "feelings, acts, and experiences of individual men in their solitude" in relation to the divine.[1] In doing so, they reflected and propagated a widespread sensibility, one that is still with us today in popular culture, as we see in the commonly heard designation, "spiritual, but not religious." For James and likeminded people, experiences, or a special type of experience, is at the core of what religions most properly are. The experience is what is most authentically and essentially religious, whereas things like doctrines, creeds, institutions, sacred texts, and rituals are externalities. They are secondary and derivative.

The assumption that religion is primarily experience gave rise to an extremely influential approach to the academic study of religion that flourished from the nineteenth century through the middle of the twentieth century. Since that time, the experiential approach to religion has received stringent criticism and wide-scale rejection, to such an extent that many scholars now regard the category of experience itself (whether or not conjoined to a vision of religion as experience) with skepticism. It is an oversimplification but still instructive to say that the criticism of experience occurred in two phases. The first phase came about as the paradigm of meaning replaced the paradigm of experience in the humanities, and the second came when the paradigm of power came on the scene. My task in this chapter is to provide a brief account of the history of the category of experience in the study of religion and then chart the shift from experience to meaning. In the next chapter, I will discuss how power displaced meaning and, as it did so, took the criticism of experience to greater lengths. The story that I tell about these major trends in religion scholarship is a selective one. I necessarily leave much of importance out, and I focus on aspects of the history of religious studies that are most pertinent to the contributions I intend to make in Part 2 of this book. I try to write about experience, meaning, and power in this chapter and the next in a way that nonspecialists can follow the narrative and gain an introduction to these themes. Specialists, who will be familiar with the topics and figures that I address in these two chapters, will gain a sense of the developments in religious studies with which I am most keen to engage in Part 2.

First, I'll say a few words about what I have in mind when I use that slippery and elusive term "experience." Experience has three primary meanings that can be distinguished. First, there is experience in the sense of acquired expertise, as in "I am an experienced chef." Next, there is experience in the sense of an event (or series of events) of significance that an individual undergoes and can report undergoing ("I experienced Disney World last summer").[2] If a group goes through a common set of events or if a tradition is shaped by a common set of experiences, we can also speak of a group or tradition as having experience in this sense, as when people speak of the African American religious experience in America as synonymous with the religious history of African Americans.[3] Finally, there is experience in its most subjective, phenomenological sense, which refers to an episode or state of conscious awareness. This is the sense that is primarily at stake in discussions of religious experience and related things like mysticism. Obviously, conscious awareness is involved in the first two meanings of experience, too, but in this third sense, the state of consciousness is especially in focus.

For the study of religion, two types of conscious awareness are especially relevant. First, there is a state or episode of consciousness in which the practitioners take themselves to be aware of some religious object, usually supernatural (like a deity, spirit, saint, angel, ancestor, or something along those lines), or a state or episode of consciousness that is extraordinary and religiously significant. Examples of the latter would be a vision of nirvana or a meditative state, obtained in a religious context, in which the subject–object distinction is not present. Religious experiences in this sense are what people usually designate as mystical, and philosophers often treat these sorts of experiences as analogous to sensory perception or even as a special type of nonsensory perception.[4] The second type of religious experience that deserves our attention refers more broadly to any emotional state that is religious in nature, even if the subjects do not take themselves to be directly conscious of a deity, spirit, or transcendent condition. So, for example, a feeling of reverence or contrition that accompanies the performance of a ritual or the reading of a sacred text would count as a religious experience even if the subjects do not take themselves to be directly aware of God at the time.

The experiential approach to religion has a distinguished place in the academic study of religion. Its most prominent proponents, in addition to James (1842–1910), are Friedrich Schleiermacher (1768–1834), Rudolf Otto (1869–1937), and Mircea Eliade (1907–1986). I will discuss all four of these, not attempting to do justice to the full range of their thought, but merely aiming to demonstrate that all of them share two ideas that would become integral to the experiential approach to religion, in large part because of their efforts: religion is most especially a matter of a special type of experience and the experiential aspect of religion is cross-culturally universal. I recognize that pinning down views on these figures is complicated because, at a number of points, there is controversy among interpreters as to what their precise understanding of the nature of religion is, and my aim here is not to survey exhaustively the various things they say across their corpus about religion and experience. Though I do think I am right to attribute the views to these thinkers that I do, I am as interested in their legacy, in terms of what many students of religion have thought these thinkers thought, as much as I am in what they actually thought.

Schleiermacher has as much claim as anyone to be considered the originator of the two ideas in question. In two texts, *On Religion: Speeches to its Cultured Despisers* and *The Christian Faith*, the Christian theologian embarks on a bold reinterpretation of traditional Christian doctrines, presenting a theological system that reflects many of the intellectual values of early nineteenth-century Germany: Kantian philosophy, respect for the natural sciences, and Romantic ideals of interiority, self-expression, and emotion, to name a few.[5] Schleiermacher's theology had a substantial impact on the study of religion in two regards.[6] First, he located the essence of religion in subjective feelings, as opposed to doctrines, creeds, and institutions. Although the terms "experience" and "religious experience" are not themselves a central component of Schleiermacher's investigations, a number of related terms are, such as "consciousness," "intuition," and "feeling." In fact, Schleiermacher saw a special type of intuition (*Anschauung*) or feeling (*Gefühl*) as the central aspect of religion. In his systematic theology, *Christian Faith*, he identifies a particular type of feeling, the feeling of absolute dependence, as the primary factor in religion. Second, Schleiermacher conceives of the feeling that is the root of religion as something universal, existing across time, culture, and religious tradition. He tells us that in "its inner essence," religion is "a product of human nature," whereas it is only in religion's "extremities" that it is "a product of time and of history."[7] In *Christian Faith*, he says that the feeling of absolute dependence is common to all the monotheistic faiths and that it is present in an inchoate and confused manner too among the practitioners of what for Schleiermacher are lesser forms of religiosity, polytheism and idolatry.[8] We should not think that for Schleiermacher, religion is nothing but interior. It is necessarily social, too, and the social and historical context affects the nature of religious consciousness, as Andrew Dole helpfully points out in an important recent book.[9] But religion is a matter of interiority, and it is so in its essence. These two features of Schleiermacher's understanding of religion, a particular subjective state of consciousness as the central feature of religion and the commonality of this state of consciousness across religious traditions, would lay the groundwork for much of the ensuing study of religion. Following Schleiermacher, many would think of religion as consisting most especially in a particular state of awareness, the religious consciousness, and they would think of all religions, despite their diversity in doctrine, creed, practice, and organization, as having an underlying unity in sharing this special form of consciousness.

Around a hundred years after Schleiermacher first published *On Religion*, William James delivered a two-part lecture series (in the Gifford Lectures of 1901 and 1902) that would be published as *Varieties of Religious Experience*. It is safe to say that no single text has exercised more influence in giving religious experience the visibility that it has and in shaping how we think about experience than this still-loved classic. As many have noted, James's views on religious experience are similar to Schleiermacher's theology. We do not have evidence that James was directly influenced by Schleiermacher, but we can be sure that he was exposed to Schleiermacher's ideas to some degree, since James grew up in Transcendentalist Boston, and Transcendentalists were reading Schleiermacher from the 1820s on. Although Schleiermacher would not achieve his contemporary prominence in American theology until after the first complete English translations of *On Religion* (1893) and *Christian Faith* (1928), his ideas were steadily infused into the American religious intelligentsia throughout the nineteenth century.[10] The precise extent of this type of influence on James is difficult to determine, since James also imbibed the Romantic perspectives on interiority and subjectivity that so influenced Schleiermacher from other sources. Samuel Taylor Coleridge, for example, was far more of an influential figure in nineteenth-century American liberal theology than Schleiermacher. James was also steeped in proponents of individuality and subjective experience like Ralph Waldo Emerson, Henry David Thoreau, and Walt Whitman, all of whom he explicitly refers to in *Varieties*. It is safe to say that James's notion of religious experience owes something to Schleiermacher, even if only indirectly, and it is certain that it owes much to the Romantic milieu in which both worked. On that basis, we can fairly classify James as belonging to the same tradition as Schleiermacher, and we can speak of them as both promoting a vision, similar in important respects, of religion as experience.[11]

James shares the two significant elements of Schleiermacher's thought that proved to be so influential for the modern study of religion. First, like Schleiermacher, he sees subjective experience as the most important, defining aspect of religion. James distinguishes between the personal aspect of religion and the institutional, and he says that his concern in *Varieties* is wholly with the former.[12] Second, James's theory has a universalistic element. He thinks that one important type of religious experiences, mystical experiences, are the same across time, culture, and religious tradition. "The mystical classics have, as has been said, neither birthday nor native land," he writes.[13]

We should not overstate the similarities between Schleiermacher and James. Whereas for Schleiermacher there is a universal religious feeling, the feeling of absolute dependence, for James there is no such single universal religious feeling, rather, a "common storehouse of emotions upon which religious objects may draw."[14] James's view that mysticism, a particular form of religious experience, is universal need not imply that all religious experiences have a common core. Further, for James, experiences are typically episodic and pronounced, whereas for Schleiermacher, the feeling of absolute dependence is, in Dole's words, something that is "phenomenologically extremely 'thin'" and "'accompanies our whole existence' as a sort of background component of ordinary experience."[15] Nevertheless, Schleiermacher and James fundamentally agree that the most valuable aspect of religion is found in the subjective consciousness of the individual and that religious experience or some special subtype of it is universal. This would be a lasting legacy that both would bequeath to their intellectual heirs and to countless readers.

One of the most important heirs of Schleiermacher is Otto. In Otto's landmark text, *The Idea of the Holy* (first published in German in 1917), he introduces what for him is the fundamental state of consciousness underlying all religion: the feeling of the numinous, or as he also calls it, the feeling of *mysterium tremendum*. He presents the *mysterium tremendum* as a development of Schleiermacher's feeling of absolute dependence. Otto, a Christian theologian, admits that our idea of God owes much to the rational system of Christian doctrine. However, he insists that we must also take account of a nonrational, nonconceptual sort of feeling that the encounter with God evokes. This feeling involves a sense of wonder, awe, fear, and adoration directed toward an object that is "wholly other," unlike everything else that we encounter in our daily lives. Otto refers to the feeling of *mysterium tremendum* as a "'numinous' state of mind," which is a "mental state [that is] perfectly *sui generis* and irreducible to any other." It is an "absolutely primary and elementary datum" that "admits of being discussed" but "cannot be strictly defined."[16] Otto thinks that the *mysterium tremendum* and the idea of divinity to which this feeling contributes achieve their highest expression in Christianity, but he says the sense of the *mysterium tremendum* is present to some degree, however imperfect, in all religious practices. Further, it is the "real innermost core" of all religions.[17] So here again we have the two elements that we found in James and Schleiermacher: a view of subjective states of consciousness as the most important aspect of religion and a notion of a particular religious state of consciousness as universally present in all religious traditions.

The fourth of the major proponents of religion-as-experience is Eliade. Eliade's project is not only to catalog the historical and cultural contexts of various religious practices but also to discover the "common elements of the different religions."[18] Eliade was a prolific author, and he displayed an impressive breadth of knowledge about religions, drawing from materials that spanned enormous distances in both geography and history. His academic fame coincided with an extremely significant phase in the institutionalization of religious studies. A large number of religious studies departments in American colleges and universities were founded in the decades following World War II, in part because of a sense among educators and administrators that the higher education curriculum needed a renewed focus on moral education. The idea was that studying religion would be a major contribution toward this end.[19] Eliade had just what American academia thought it needed: a humanistic vision of religion that saw religion as a necessary element of decent human society. Eliade's theory of religion would be a foundational influence for many of the new religion departments that were proliferating all across the country. And he would prove to be a central figure in the development of two of the twentieth century's most important schools in religious studies: history of religion (or comparative religion) and phenomenology of religion. Both of these fields were developed as alternatives to the then-prevalent model of teaching religion in universities, a model based on the curriculum of a Christian seminary or divinity school. History of religion and phenomenology of religion sought to bring increased legitimacy to the study of non-Christian religion and to enable a nonconfessional way to study religion.

Phenomenology of religion—developed by Eliade, Dutch theologian Gerardus van der Leeuw (1890–1950), Eliade's contemporaries Ninian Smart and Charles Long, and many others—undergirded the history and comparative study of religion.[20] Phenomenology of religion should not be confused with the approach in philosophy known as phenomenology. Philosophical phenomenology owes its origin most especially to Edmund Husserl (1859–1938), according to whom philosophical investigation is attending to how things appear to the inquirer. One is supposed to investigate the phenomena of consciousness without the influence of preexisting assumptions. Husserl calls this *epoché* or bracketing: one should suspend one's judgment as to whether or not the objects that one experiences actually exist. The phenomenologists of religion borrow loosely from Husserl on certain points. For example, they too advocate for bracketing. In their case, they want to bracket the question of the existence of gods, spirits, and other objects of religious consciousness. And they too advocate a methodology of attending to the contents of consciousness, specifically of religious consciousness. But, in general, they are not trying to implement Husserl's overall research program. As Eliade presents it, the phenomenology of religion holds to the view that there is a cross-culturally universal experience, a consciousness of the sacred, which is present in all religions and is what the religions most fundamentally are. This understanding of religion gives rise to a scholarly methodology of inquiring as to what it is like to practice religion, from the practitioners' point of view. For example, phenomenologists of religion aim to describe what a particular religious ceremony or ritual is like for the practitioners, without passing judgment on whether the deities purportedly involved exist or not. A key element of this methodology is to practice empathy, that is, to imagine what it is like for the practitioners to practice their religion. This methodology facilitated the establishment of religious studies departments in the United States at a moment when the discipline was rapidly expanding but when considerable anxiety existed about whether or not the study of religion was appropriate in secular and publicly funded schools, given the principle of separation of church and state. The significance of phenomenology of religion was that it offered a sympathetic study of religion without endorsing the perspective of the believer.

Eliade's understanding of religion starts with a crucial distinction between the sacred and the profane. The profane is the mode of existence in which one interacts with ordinary space and ordinary objects, things as we encounter them when we are working, when we are conducting our practical affairs, or when we are bored. The sacred, on the other hand, pertains to transcendent objects, realities, and values. Sacrality appears to the religious person, the *homo religiosus*, in what Eliade calls hierophanies: manifestations of the sacred. The sacred can manifest itself in any number of objects, rites, and symbols; what is important is that the sacred elicits a particular type of response from the individual: "For those to whom a stone reveals itself as sacred, its immediate reality is transmuted into a supernatural reality."[21] If then the distinction between the sacred and the profane is not determined by the object—any object can be sacred or profane—what does distinguish the sacred from the profane? Here is where religious experience comes into the picture in a fundamental way. "For those who have a religious experience," Eliade continues, "all nature is capable of revealing itself as cosmic sacrality." Eliade calls this sort of religious experience "the experience of the sacred," and he refers to this as an "element in the structure of consciousness" that is universal to all humanity (although modern people have done their best to alienate themselves from the sacred in Eliade's view).[22] What is of greatest significance for my purposes is that Eliade agrees with the two principal views that I have sought to highlight in Schleiermacher, James, and Otto: that religion is principally a matter of a special sort of conscious state and that this special sort of experience is universal to all religions. Eliade writes, "'Religion' may still be a useful term provided we keep in mind that it does not necessarily imply belief in God, gods, or ghosts, but refers to the experience of the sacred."[23]

So whereas the bulk of Eliade's work concerns the various expressions of sacredness—myths, gods, rites, religious objects, religious buildings, and the like—underlying all of these is a conviction that what invests these with religious significance is the state of consciousness that they evoke in the practitioners, which is a matter of a special type of religious experience: the experience of the sacred.

These four thinkers—Schleiermacher, James, Otto, and Eliade—have been among the most influential figures in the modern study of religion, and they have set the parameters by which we understand the term "experience" and related terms. They installed the category of experience to a place of primacy in the study of religion, since they direct our attention to states of consciousness, psychological episodes, feelings, intuitions, and the like as the supreme element of religion. For these four, religious experience, however each of them understands it, is the most basic thing, and we are to understand religion in general as an outgrowth and expression of special states of consciousness. For them, then, of all the categories a scholar employs in studying religion, none is more important than experience, whether that be a feeling of absolute dependence, a variety of religious sentiment, the *mysterium tremendum*, or the experience of the sacred.

By the time of Eliade, the experiential approach to religion existed primarily in the form of phenomenology of religion. Subsequent to Eliade, both phenomenology of religion and the category of experience have come upon hard times, with the result that most scholars do not see the experiential approach to religion as viable. A number of factors are responsible for the demise of the approach. The two factors that I will discuss in this book, one in this chapter and one in the next, are the turn to language and the turn to power that occurred in the humanities generally and in the study of religion in particular.

The turn to language speaks of a broad paradigm shift that saw language emerge as a central site for inquiry in place of consciousness. "The focus," as Seyla Benhabib puts it, "is no longer on the epistemic subject or on the private contents of its consciousness but on the public, signifying activities of a collection of subjects."[24] At the beginning of the twentieth century, "consciousness" was a prime term in philosophy, whether in the phenomenology of Edmund Husserl or in the sense data of the Anglo-American empiricists. But in the wake of Ludwig Wittgenstein, the turn to language occurred, drawing philosophers' attention away from introspection to the analysis of language. The turn to language took another shape in Continental thought, as Heidegger replaced Husserl in the phenomenological tradition and phenomenology moved from a method purporting to give the subject direct awareness of reality to a method that frankly acknowledged the ineliminable aspect of interpretation involved in perception. Then in French thought, Ferdinand de Saussure put the sign, the pair of signifier and signified, at the center of cultural analysis. Structuralist anthropologist Claude Lévi-Strauss followed Saussure, and then structuralism gave way to the post-structuralism of Jacques Derrida. In one way or another, these trends in the academy all construed society on the metaphor of a text. The task of the social theorist, historian, and anthropologist is to "read" and interpret the meanings of the utterances, actions, and objects of a social group. Phenomenology of religion is deeply rooted in the paradigm of consciousness, and so as that paradigm waned, phenomenology of religion lost appeal.

The story is more complicated than it might first appear, however, because phenomenology of religion itself thoroughly took part in the turn to language, and, for a time, the paradigm of consciousness and the paradigm of language merged. So to understand how phenomenology of religion met its demise, we need to understand the way in which phenomenology of religion incorporated the turn to language.

A BRIEF HISTORY OF THE INTERPRETIVE APPROACH

Interpretation is a pervasive human activity. As people conduct their ordinary affairs in daily life, they are constantly engaged, usually without much conscious awareness, in attempts to understand and properly respond to the utterances of others and to the various other signs and symbols that they encounter. Interpretation is also a characteristic activity of scholarship. Scholars of religion, for example, strive to understand and to translate words, events, and actions from cultures other than their own. In another sense, interpretation identifies a specific intellectual tradition, an approach to humanistic and social scientific research that includes among its members such notables as Martin Heidegger, Hans-Georg Gadamer, Paul Ricoeur, Charles Taylor, and Clifford Geertz. This approach, at times referred to as philosophical hermeneutics, views the task of the humanist or social scientist as above all one of interpretation. The interpretive scholar considers the communities under investigation as producers of symbols, whether these symbols take the form of language, artifacts, or actions, and the scholar's job is to interpret these symbols as one interprets a written text. In fact, those in the interpretive approach regard human groups as analogous to written texts.

Just as Schleiermacher played a key role in developing the modern preoccupation with religious experience, discussed above, he is an essential figure with interpretation as well. Intellectuals in the Western tradition prior to Schleiermacher had long been concerned with interpretation in specific contexts, like the methodology by which one comes to understand a biblical passage, but Schleiermacher presents interpretation as a universal feature of human understanding.[25] A reader and biographer of Schleiermacher, Wilhelm Dilthey, develops this idea into the claim that what differentiates the academic study of human activities from the study of the behavior of the nonhuman world is that interpretation is distinctively an aim of the study of the human sciences. Max Weber, in turn, distinguishes a type of analysis distinctive of the social sciences, the study of the subjective meaning of action, from the analysis of the physical sciences, which deals strictly with causal uniformities.[26] The idea here is that the causal regularities that characterize the behavior of inanimate objects do not characterize human behavior because humans evaluate things that confront them and behave according to the way in which they understand their situation. So social scientists must acknowledge that the subjects of their studies are interpreting and that they too must interpret as they study.

It was Heidegger, however, who paved the way for the single most influential figure in the hermeneutic tradition, Gadamer. Heidegger's *Being and Time* draws our attention to the way in which humans are situated in a particular linguistic and practical context, a context that is the necessary precondition of achieving understanding about anything. Moreover, according to Heidegger, the particular practical-linguistic background in which the subject is situated affects the nature of the understanding that the subject achieves.[27] These are insights that Gadamer inherits from Heidegger and makes into a coherent program, above all in his magisterial *Truth and Method*. In that work, Gadamer takes aim at the Enlightenment "prejudice against prejudice." By prejudice, Gadamer means, "a judgment that is rendered before all the elements that determine a situation have been finally examined."[28] The Enlightenment philosophers, Gadamer tells us, wanted to privilege the intellectual autonomy of the subject and counseled that the subject should "accept no authority and . . . decide everything before the judgment seat of reason."[29] In other words, the individual subjects are themselves responsible to conduct the examination of their situation and proffer judgments on their own authority. Gadamer, in contrast, thinks that we constantly defer to epistemic authorities and that it is appropriate to do so, indeed impossible not to. For one thing, it would be extraordinarily inefficient to refuse to accept any proposition on someone else's say so. For another thing, on many matters, it is simply the case that others know more about the topic than we do, and so it is proper to defer to their judgment. It would be impossible, for example, for undergraduates in an introductory physics course to withhold assent to the tenets of physics that their instructor teaches without first verifying the experimental evidence first-hand themselves. So in many matters, we are inclined to think one way or another about a matter not because we have thoroughly investigated it ourselves but on the basis of someone else's testimony. This is not just in respect to the propositions that we believe; it is also a matter of how we conceptualize certain terms and how we assign meanings to symbols. We have fore-conceptions and fore-meanings that we inherit from particular authorities and from the tradition in which we are situated, and when we encounter some symbol or text, those fore-conceptions, fore-meanings, and prejudices lead us to understand the symbol or text in particular ways. In the encounter with the symbol or text, we may find that our fore-meanings and prejudgments are inadequate, and we may very well revise them. So our situatedness does not exercise such absolute control over the encounter with a symbol or text that our preexisting orientation is incorrigible. But one's situatedness, one's preexisting particular perspective that is a product of one's linguistic and cultural background and one's specific personal history, does affect one's encounter with a text or symbol and what one takes the text or symbol to mean.

Ricoeur works from a perspective quite similar to Gadamer's. To be sure, he makes his own contributions. He elaborates and extends the hermeneutic approach in important ways. For example, he explains how we can treat human actions, even nonverbal ones, as symbolic and as analogous to a text and thus a fit object for interpretation.[30] Further, he compares and contrasts the hermeneutic way of interpreting things with Sigmund Freud's understanding of interpretation in psychoanalysis, and he takes on particular topics, like evil and guilt, and applies the hermeneutic and phenomenological approach to them.[31] But in many important respects, Ricoeur keeps theoretical and methodological company with Gadamer.

Both Gadamer and Ricoeur, as is also the case for Heidegger, practice a form of hermeneutics that is phenomenological in nature. That is, meaning and understanding are treated from the point of view of the subject, how things seem to the particular individual. But despite their focus on the individual, their phenomenology is not acultural. It makes no appeal, as Husserl does, to the transcendental ego, a center of the knowing self that escapes history and culture. Gadamer and Ricoeur follow Heidegger in breaking from this sort of decontextualized knowledge. Rather, for Gadamer and Ricoeur, the knowing self is thoroughly immersed in a particular context or situation, one that is social, linguistic, and historical. That is the vantage point from which the subject encounters the object of knowledge. Gadamer's term for the context in which the epistemic subject encounters objects of knowledge is "horizon." The subject of knowledge occupies a particular perspective that both makes knowledge possible and limits it (the horizon is not boundless). The object of knowledge, say, a written text, also has its own horizon. The text originated in its own context—historical, social, and linguistic—and that context is not identical to the context of the subject who is reading the text. So for the subject to understand the text, a "fusion of horizons," in Gadamer's famous term, must occur. The subject encounters the text with fore-conceptions and fore-meanings that give some initial grasp of the meaning of the text, but this initial grasp is hardly adequate. An adequate understanding requires that subjects revise and adjust their own sense of the meaning of the text's concepts and terms to incorporate the context of the text into their own context.

The interpretive approach that Gadamer and Ricoeur represent enjoyed widespread influence throughout the humanities and social sciences and made its way into the academic study of religion through several routes. One avenue is phenomenology of religion, which drew from Gadamerian and Ricoeurian interpretive philosophy.[32] But perhaps Gadamer and Ricoeur's greatest and most lasting impact on the discipline of religious studies was indirect. Both served as key influences on one of the twentieth century's greatest anthropologists and theorists of religion: Geertz. Geertz (1926–2006) was a Harvard-educated anthropologist who did fieldwork in Indonesia and Morocco and spent much of his career at the Institute of Advanced Study in Princeton, New Jersey. Geertz did as much as anyone to put the interpretation of cultures, as the title of his popular book puts it, into the center of methodological discussions in religious studies and anthropology.

As Geertz interacted with communities in Bali, Java, and Morocco, he frequently gave particular attention to the religious aspects of the communities that he was studying. He evidenced interests in theoretical matters throughout his career but achieved full recognition as a theorist of religion with the publication of *The Interpretation of Cultures* in 1973, a collection of essays that he had written in the preceding decade or so.[33] In that work, he provides a theory of culture, a theory of religion, and a corresponding account of how one best goes about studying each. For Geertz, the study of religion starts when one encounters an unfamiliar society doing and saying unfamiliar things. Confronted with these strangers, one attempts to "find one's feet" among them, as Geertz puts it, and figure out what they're up to.[34] This is a process of interpretation, which is to say, a process of determining what the meanings of a society's words, actions, and objects are. Whether a gesture in a Buddhist's prayer, a configuration of objects on a Vodou altar, or the layout of a courtyard in a Sudanese village, the question to ask is, What does it mean? Religion, Geertz tells us, is a system of cultural symbols, and the student of religion is out to interpret those symbols. Symbols are things that carry a meaning. More precisely, according to Geertz, a symbol is "any object, act, event, quality, or relation which serves as a vehicle for a conception—the conception is the symbol's 'meaning.'"[35] Just as the members of the native culture deal with symbols by interpreting their meanings, so also the anthropologist who wants to study a culture does so by interpreting the symbols' meanings. One of the significances of Geertz's approach is the way in which it programmatically distinguishes human sciences from the natural sciences and confronts one prevalent attitude in the intellectual culture of Geertz's day and ours, what Fred Inglis calls the "absolute faith in the procedures of a data-collecting, numbers-grounded, formally modeled, confidently scientist social science."[36] Dilthey and Weber want to distinguish the study of human behavior from the methods of natural sciences, so also Geertz: the analysis of culture is "not an experimental science in search of law but an interpretive one in search of meaning."[37] Interpreting symbolic meaning is the proper methodology for the study of religion in particular just as it is for the study of culture generally, because religion is one type of culture, or, as Geertz more precisely puts it, religion is a "cultural system," a system of symbols whose identifying criterion is that they are involved in the "most comprehensive ideas of order."[38]

Geertz calls the methodology of interpretive ethnography "thick description." Discerning the meaning of a society's symbols is a complicated matter, because symbolic meaning is itself a messy affair. The data of the ethnographer are "other people's constructions of what they and their compatriots are up to," and so anthropological analysis is "sorting out the structures of signification . . . and determining their social ground and import." These structures are not simple or straightforward; they involve a "multiplicity of complex conceptual structures, many of them superimposed upon or knotted into one another, which are at once strange, irregular, and inexplicit." So, "doing ethnography is like trying to read (in the sense of 'construct a reading of') a manuscript—foreign, faded, full of ellipses, incoherencies, suspicious emendations, and tendentious commentaries, but written not in the conventionalized graphs of sound but in transient examples of shaped behavior."[39] We are to understand culture as a text, then, or rather an "ensemble of texts." The ethnographer, in a role similar to that of a "literary critic," "strains to read [the texts] over the shoulders of those to whom they properly belong."[40] The interpretative analysis happens through "microscopic" attention to detail, taking care to observe the particularities of actions, utterances, and symbolic actions in their multifarious relationships to other symbols that stand in a more or less coherent system. This whole enterprise of thick description is possible because symbolic meanings are not sequestered away in the private consciousness of individuals but are public, observable matters: "Cultural acts, the construction, apprehension, and utilization of symbolic forms, are social events like any other; they are as public as marriage and as observable as agriculture."[41]

All this has to do with the study of culture in general, a broad category for Geertz that includes religion as a subtype. But in addition to these general thoughts about how to study culture, Geertz has some specific views on the nature of religion. First, he famously defines religion as a cultural system that consists of: "*(1) a system of symbols which acts to (2) establish powerful, pervasive, and long-lasting moods and motivations in men by (3) formulating conceptions of a general order of existence and (4) clothing these conceptions with such an aura of factuality that (5) the moods and motivations seem uniquely realistic.*"[42] The "general order of existence" is what sets religions apart from other cultural systems. This order is a "cosmic framework" that concerns the "fundamental nature of reality" and "unconditioned ends," as opposed to the more particular and intermediate ends that characterize our ordinary economic, household, and political activities. People need such a cosmic framework to provide Meaning (in a capital-M sense of the term, which signifies the significance of life as a whole, as opposed to the lower-m sense of the meanings of particular words and symbols) for their lives. This is especially true in relation to the features of life that threaten to render life insignificant and meaningless for people, such as the existence of suffering and the presence of anomalous events, like "death, dreams, mental fugues, volcanic eruptions, or marital infidelity." [43] One of the important ways in which religion fulfills this meaning-giving function is by serving as a "model of" and a "model for." As a model of reality, religion provides a representation of how the world is, according to the religious practitioners. As a model for reality, religious symbols do not merely represent; they shape. They provide a template or pattern by which material, in this case psychological or sociological material, can be formed and fashioned.[44] Geertz also has a theory of religious rituals. Rituals, Geertz thinks, function to fuse two aspects of religions, the cognitive/theoretical aspect, which Geertz calls a "worldview," and the emotional/practical aspect, which Geertz calls an "ethos."[45] "In a ritual, the world as lived and the world as imagined, fused under the agency of a single set of symbolic forms, turn out to be the same world."[46] Undergoing a ritual instills in the participants a conviction and assurance that the world really is the way that their religion says it is and that their emotional and practical way of conducting themselves in relation to the world's fundamental nature is appropriate.

The influence of Clifford Geertz in the study of religion in the latter part of the twentieth century is monumental. Geertz was not only a foremost figure in the general shift toward the paradigm of language; he also played a direct role in bringing about the demise of phenomenology of religion. This did not so much occur because Geertz explicitly challenged the phenomenologists of religion. Indeed, at times he referred to his own approach as phenomenological, both early and late in his career.[47] However, his own approach had some key differences from the phenomenologists of religion, and thus the highly popular approach to the study of religion that he initiated would turn out to be a competitor to phenomenology of religion to the detriment of the latter.

But why is Geertz's account competitive with the phenomenologists? In many respects, Geertz's construal of religion as a system of symbols would seem complementary to theirs. The phenomenologists of religion, even those who think there is something universal to the sense of the sacred, do not think that humankind's experiences of the sacred occur in some acultural space devoid of social or cultural influence, and many of them practice phenomenology in a hermeneutical manner, following Gadamer and Ricoeur. Phenomenologists of religion are themselves concerned with meanings and symbols, and Eliade gives explicit attention to the meanings of myths, rituals, and words. Furthermore, both Geertz and the phenomenologists of religion have a methodological commitment to the priority of the actor's point of view. When phenomenologists investigate the nature of the experience of the sacred and when Geertz investigates the meaning of a symbol, both parties are treating the subject's own account of these things as the primary source of information and both are attempting to represent the subject's perspective on the matter faithfully.

However, Geertz's methodology involves two key differences from the phenomenologists, and these differences constitute a decisive break from phenomenology of religion as practiced by Eliade. The first difference is that a key element in the phenomenologists' method is the practice of empathy, which means that one is supposed to put oneself imaginatively in the position of the religious practitioner to ascertain what it feels like to undergo the practice. Otto insists that the only way to understand the numinous feeling is to undergo it yourself.[48] Smart has a similar view: "For in order to understand what it is like to be, say, a Winnebago one must really make-believe that one is a Winnebago, rehearsing the thoughts and attitudes of a Winnebago."[49] The problem here though is how does one know whether one has succeeded at such a task? How does one know that one is really feeling what it is like to be a Winnebago? Smart is assured that "with sufficient imagination I can gain some understanding of what it is like" to know how another feels.[50] No doubt there is some degree of truth to this, but when one applies this principal cross-culturally, dangers emerge, epistemological and ethical. The epistemological danger is that it is not easy to see what sort of clear and objective criteria exist to determine whether one has successfully accomplished this sort of empathic identification with another's inner world. The ethical danger is that one would illegitimately authorize oneself to speak on behalf of the other, to claim the ability to articulate the other's feelings, desires, and aspirations. It is not that all attempts to articulate the inner world of others are in principal illegitimate. If that were the case, we could not attribute beliefs and desires to other people, and doing so is a pervasive feature of social life. The problem for the phenomenologists is that the basis of the authority to represent someone's attitudes is one's own imagination, and, without clear criteria of success, imagination can serve as an introspectively achieved self-authorization in which solipsism easily masquerades as empathy. Geertz breaks from this approach. He rejects introspection as a method for achieving understanding of the other: "To undertake the study of cultural activity," he says, "is not to abandon social analysis for a Platonic cave of shadows, to enter into a mentalistic world of introspective psychology." This is because the objects of study are symbolic meanings and these are publicly available, not features of the interior recesses of the psyche; they are, as we have seen, public and observable like marriage and agriculture.[51] For the phenomenologists, empathetic imagination is the proper response to a view that sees experience as the fundamental aspect of religion, that which the scholar must access to understand someone else's religion. Geertz on the other hand is not looking to any special type of experience of the sacred or numinous in which to base the nature of religiosity. Religion for him involves experiences but is first and foremost a system of symbols, not a special type of experience.[52] Geertz is firmly within the paradigm of language whereas the phenomenologists, despite their attention to signifying activities, are still committed to the paradigm of consciousness. When Geertz says that his approach is a phenomenology of culture, he means that one must attend to the "native's point of view," that is, the way in which members of the culture understand the symbolic systems that they utilize. But he makes it clear that the phenomenology that he has in mind is not based in consciousness when he disavows Husserl, a founding figure of the paradigm of consciousness, for Wittgenstein, a founding figure of the social practices approach to the study of culture. Phenomenology for Geertz means simply "to describe the life world in which people live."[53] This is a key departure from the religion-as-experience model, as it appears in the Otto–Eliade–Smart trajectory.

The second key difference that differentiates Geertz from the phenomenologists' religion-as-experience perspective pertains to the fact that the phenomenologists, especially those committed to the comparative study of religion, have a tendency to look for commonalities across religious traditions, locations, and eras. This tendency leads them, critics accuse, to establish such commonalities on the basis of superficial similarities, all the while ignoring significant differences. A key element of Geertz's methodology, as we have seen, is "thick description." He wants us to describe other cultures with close attention to all the details of the society's life, considering every action, event, and word as it occurs in the context of and in relation to myriad other actions, events, and words. Ethnographic description, Geertz says, deals with the "complex specificness" of cultural symbols in all their "circumstantiality."[54] It stays "rather close to the ground" and avoids "imaginative abstraction."[55] When it does lend toward abstraction, it only does so "from the direction of exceedingly extended acquaintances with extremely small matters."[56] In contrast, in Eliade's classic *Patterns in Comparative Religion*, we find a chapter on sky gods, one on the worship of the sun, one on the worship of the moon, one on water, one on the earth, one on stones, and so on, and in each chapter, Eliade jumbles together numerous deities from cultures the world over within a few pages. This is not to detract from Eliade's voluminous knowledge of the world's religious practices, but in this book he most definitely does not articulate extended acquaintance with extremely small matters. As the academy has grown more specialized, the expectation has increasingly become that a scholar who writes on a particular group will have extensive knowledge of the language(s) and historical context of the community. Since linguistic expertise often takes years to master, cross-cultural comparison in religious studies holds less esteem than it once did. Geertz's notion of thick description supports caution against the boldness with which phenomenologists of religion studied different cultures side by side.

As phenomenology of religion transitioned from predominance to marginality, parallel developments were occurring in philosophy of religion in the study of religious experience and mysticism. One such important development was the constructivist criticism of the perennialist view of religious experience. The perennialist view, named after Aldous Huxley's 1945 work, *The Perennial Philosophy*, maintains (like Schleiermacher, James, Otto, and Eliade) that mystical and other religious experiences involve a common core that is the same across culture and history.[57] In the late 1970s and the 1980s an alternative perspective came on the scene, which insisted that the experiencer's cultural context determines the nature of experiences to such an extent that no cross-cultural common core could possibly exist. This constructivist perspective was established especially by the work of Steven Katz and Wayne Proudfoot.[58] Their central idea is that experiences necessarily involve the experiencer's concepts and these concepts are cultural artifacts, so experiences are culturally specific. Katz's criticism is both philosophical and historical. Philosophically, he claims that the human mind in general does not receive into consciousness "raw data," so to speak, from the senses but rather forms and organizes sensory data by means of its concepts. Since this is a general fact about human consciousness, it applies to the specific case of mystical experiences. Katz's historical argument consists of an examination of the way in which several key perennialists interpret the texts from various mystical traditions. Katz makes a convincing case that the perennialists take short snippets from different religious traditions and focus on superficial similarities to support their view that the mystical texts are speaking about one and the same mystical reality. Close attention to the texts, however, shows that the experiential descriptions that supposedly refer to identical realities are in fact not similar at all and only seem to be so when one ignores the historical, textual, and cultural context from which the perennialists extract the snippets. This is an illustrative example of the difference that "thick description" makes in the study of religion. Proudfoot's seminal contribution to the study of mysticism comes in his argument that the beliefs that mystics have about the object of their mystical experience are a constitutive element of the experience. Since these beliefs are cultural in nature and vary across religious tradition, there can be no universal, cross-cultural experience. In the wake of Katz's and Proudfoot's criticisms, the constructivist approach soon replaced the perennialist one as the preferred perspective in the philosophy of mysticism.

The shift from perennialism to constructivism in the study of mysticism transpired in conjunction with the shift from phenomenology of religion to Geertzian thick description, and both of these were part of broader shifts in the academy from universal consciousness to culturally specific meaning. As a result of these shifts, experience no longer secured what so many wanted from it—the cross-culturally universal essence of religion—and so its reputation suffered. After the turn to meaning, scholars regarded experience as important but no longer preeminent. Before long, however, the turn to power would overtake the paradigm of meaning, and influential scholars would express doubt that experience was a viable category at all. We can turn now, then, to the turn to power.

2

From Meaning to Power

Clifford Geertz's expertise as an ethnographer, the breadth and attractiveness of his theoretical vision, and the way that he conducted theory in constant conversation with ethnographic case studies propelled him to the forefront of theoretical influences on the study of religion in the latter part of the twentieth century. Geertz provided a way to think about the study of human culture other than the always-tempting model of the natural sciences, and he installed meaning, interpretation, and culture firmly at the top of the social-scientific agenda. Things have changed since the 1990s, however. Nowadays, Geertz, meaning, and interpretation are decidedly out of favor (even if they still have a devoted following). In reference to Geertz, it is not uncommon to find people asking, as Kevin Schilbrack does, whether we are "through with Geertz."[1] Bruce Lincoln says that Geertz's definition of religion "has fallen badly out of favor," and others speak of the "rise and fall of Clifford Geertz."[2]

How did this come about? The "fall of Clifford Geertz" was in part due to specific criticisms of his position, but it also owed much to broader shifts in the academy. The turn to language in the humanities and sciences propelled Geertz, Gadamer, and Ricoeur to prominence. But now another turn has occurred, a turn to power and practice. I have had the occasion already to refer to Seyla Benhabib's succinct summary of the turn to language: "*The paradigm of language has replaced the paradigm of consciousness.* This shift has meant that the focus is no longer on the epistemic

subject or on the private contents of its consciousness but on the public, signifying activities of a collection of subjects."[3] Twenty years later, we must update her
assessment in this way: The paradigm of practice and power has replaced or, more
accurately, subsumed the paradigm of language. This shift has meant that the focus
is no longer just on the public, signifying activities of a collection of subjects but on
the power-laden social practices, linguistic and nonlinguistic, that form people into
particular types of subjects and that establish, perpetuate, and resist differentiated,
hierarchical social structures.

In this chapter, I will present a brief overview of the key figures in the power approach and their contributions, discuss the impact of the turn to power on religious
studies, and then detail some of the implications, in religious studies, of the turn to
power for the meaning and experience approaches.

On many occasions, the dynamics of social power seem obvious enough. In the
paradigmatic case of domination, slavery, the slaveholder controls the slave, physically, economically, emotionally, and sexually. The slaveholder possesses weapons to
ensure that the slave does his bidding; the slave has none. The slaveholder has the
power of the state to enforce the relation should the slave escape.

On other occasions, however, things are not so clear. In a class-stratified society,
some social groups have access to a far greater proportion of the society's economic
goods than other groups. This seems like a recipe for violent insurrection and oftentimes is. But just as often, such societies persist in relative stability, with a small
group of people controlling the lion's share of productive resources while the masses
remain relatively impoverished. How does this asymmetry reproduce itself over the
generations? Or consider patriarchal societies. Men occupy positions of power in a
broad range of institutions, from government to business to families. In the modern
era, many such societies have seen feminist movements arise to contest these arrangements, but throughout history, women have often accepted patriarchy and
given it their active support. How do we account for such situations? Are these matters of false consciousness and ideology, wherein the subordinated embrace a value
system and set of beliefs that work to the economic interests of the powerful? Are
they matters of naturalization, wherein historically contingent institutional structures come to be viewed as natural, the way things are, should be, and always have
been? Even in regard to slavery, where the domination is physical and overt, things
are more complicated than they first appear. Slaves have "hidden transcripts," in
James C. Scott's terminology, social spaces in which they speak and act in ways that
criticize and oppose the slaveholders' control over their lives.[4]

Social theorists have taken as one of their principal tasks accounting for the way
in which societies reproduce persisting conditions of domination, exploitation,
and marginalization. Religion has long been central to these accounts. Two of the

classical social theorists, Karl Marx and Max Weber, examine the way in which religious practices involve power relations. For Marx, religion has a compensatory function, it provides psychological satisfaction that alleviates the suffering of the poor and thus renders them uninterested in contesting their subordination. Weber scrupulously details various means by which individuals obtain and exercise power in religious communities, whether such individuals possess charismatic, rational/legal, or traditional authority.[5] The third classical theorist, Durkheim, does not attend to power as much as Marx and Weber do, but his account makes religion highly relevant to social power. For Durkheim, religion binds social groups together as a group. Thus it creates in-group/out-group distinctions and all the potential for violence such distinctions engender. One other figure who is a major precursor to contemporary theories of power is Friedrich Nietzsche. Nietzsche's work exemplified two key methodological principles that would influence many twentieth-century theorists of power, especially Michel Foucault. These principles are, first, that our concepts are historical products of contingent processes and second, that these processes involve power relations. So, in Nietzsche's famous analysis of our moral terms "good" and "evil," he argues that at a certain point in history, the impoverished masses utilized religion to invent the concept of evil. Formerly the term "good" referred to the living conditions of the strong and healthy aristocrats and "bad" referred to misery and poverty, and the terms meant roughly desirable and undesirable. But with the help of religion, the masses invented the concept of evil to refer to the values of the noble elites, condemned by God. They transformed the concept of good to refer to the values inherent in their own deprived condition, which God approves ("Blessed are the poor. . . . Woe to you who are rich," as the Gospel of Luke proclaims). They had no other recourse to oppose the noble and powerful class, so they used religion. Social analysts who work in a Nietzschean mode, whether or not they buy into the specifics of Nietzsche's particular genealogy of moral terminology, set out to trace the origins of our contemporary concepts to understand the circumstances under which the concepts arose and the power-laden processes by which they mutated over time.

With the efforts of Marx, Durkheim, Weber, and Nietzsche, the nineteenth and early twentieth century saw plenty of attention to power. However, concerns with power would enter into the center of the academic study of religion in an unprecedented way in the latter quarter of the twentieth century, in the wake of a shift toward power in the humanities generally. This shift had numerous stimuli, but central to its occurrence is the influence of the work of Michel Foucault, Jacques Derrida, Pierre Bourdieu, and Judith Butler.

Derrida's most important contributions have to do with the nature of signification. Derrida was at the center of the post-structuralist approach to humanistic and social scientific inquiry, which sees signification as an inherently unstable matter.

The relations between signifiers, whether linguistic or not, and that which they sig-nify are not fixed and constant but rather in flux, and signifiers do not have their meaning from particular signifier–signified pairs in isolation but rather from the entire fluctuating structure of signifying relations. Meaning is deferred from sig-nifier to signified, and the signified is itself a signifier of some other signified, so meaning is deferred again, and so on. This account of signification generates anal-yses that treat the meaning of our terms as susceptible to manipulation by social power. Bourdieu did as much as anyone to bring bodily habits and the social prac-tices that involve them into social theory. Bourdieu proposes the "habitus" as an analytical concept, which refers to a collection of inherited bodily dispositions by which subjects unconsciously interact with their social environments. Habitus vary according to one's social identity and they dispose the subject to respond differently to members of different social groups (and differently as well to the various social goods that facilitate social group distinctions, such as status symbols). Since the in-stallation and employment of these bodily habits is largely unreflective, the result is that bodily habits perpetuate social differences and social structures in a way that puts the asymmetries of the societies beyond the pale of conscious attention and criticism. One unreflectively navigates one's differentiated social world as though the way things are is the way that they necessarily must be. Butler's signal contri-bution began in *Gender Trouble: Feminism and the Subversion of Identity*, where she advocates a performative theory of subjectivity and identity, according to which one's identity, sexual or otherwise, is not a stable, substantial thing but consists of a series of enactments. One implication of her theory is that sex, gender, and the sexual classifications that we make do not correspond to any natural divisions but are thoroughly social in their origins. Thus, these classifications are a matter of pol-itics, of social construction, negotiation, and contestation, not immutable features of our natural, biological constitution.

These three social theorists have had a substantial influence on the study of reli-gion. But in many ways, it is Michel Foucault who has set the agenda for how power is conceived and analyzed in religious studies. In particular, three of Foucault's ideas have had immense significance in the discipline. First is his genealogical approach to concepts and institutions. Foucault is a historicist, which means that when he studies a concept, practice, or institution, he seeks to find its historical origins, the processes that shaped it, and, importantly, the interests that it serves at each stage of its development. He is self-consciously a follower of Nietzsche in this regard. He conducts this sort of analysis for prisons in *Discipline and Punish*, for medical in-stitutions in *Birth of the Clinic*, for sexuality in *History of Sexuality*, and for mental illness in *Madness and Civilization*.[6] He treats none of these practices or the associ-ated classifications upon which they rest (like sane versus insane, in *Madness and*

Civilization), which many take for granted, as natural or inevitable or fitting responses to the "way things are." Rather, the practices and classifications arise under specific historical conditions and develop without intentional oversight in ways that result in the establishment of control over particular segments of society. This is closely related to a second key idea of Foucault's, which is that knowledge and power are intricately related: "Power and knowledge directly imply one another. . . . There is no power relation without the correlative constitution of a field of knowledge, nor any knowledge that does not presuppose and constitute at the same time power relations."[7] This is as true for supposedly objective and disinterested knowledge, such as that of the scientist and the academy, as it is for anything. "Each society has its regime of truth," he says, "its 'general politics' of truth: that is, the types of discourse which it accepts and makes function as true; the mechanisms and instances which enable one to distinguish true and false statements . . . the status of those who are charged with saying what counts as true."[8] Truth, then, for Foucault, is not a matter of the mind passively discovering the way that reality is; it is a matter of societies designating certain pieces of information (along with the accompanying vocabularies) as candidates for truth and designating certain parties as fit to determine which pieces of information are true. Foucault's third contribution that is of note for our purposes is his focus on bodily habits. He does not have as systematic of a theory as Bourdieu's, with its rather precise notion of the habitus, but he nevertheless manages to mark out the body as a significant site for the study of power. In Foucault's case, the body—its habits, dispositions, and postures—is especially relevant to an important modern form of power: discipline. Disciplinary power has to do with modern practices in schools, armies, prisons, and factories that train bodies to move in certain ways: to hold the pen just so, to salute just so, and to attach the bolt on the assembly line just so. This training is accompanied by normalizing judgments from supervisors who assess the performances and correct imperfect ones. Once trained, subjects' bodies are docile and useful; that is, they operate in ways that serve the overall pattern of economic production. People show up where they're supposed to show up and do what they're supposed to do because they have been habituated to do so; compulsion is unnecessary. Foucault calls this micropower and micropolitics. In this view, the habituated bodies, though docile, are not merely passive. It is not that elites possess the power and the rest of the society does not, rather every member of society exercises power and contributes to the overall patterns of power. Power occurs in the capillaries of the society, in people's bodies, in their bedrooms, and in their classrooms, not just in the halls of the presidential palaces or the boardrooms of multinational corporations.

Two other power-related approaches, which have existed in dynamic relationship with the ideas of Bourdieu, Butler, Derrida, and Foucault, deserve mention because of their prominence in the academy and in religious studies. The first of these is the feminist movement. At once a social and intellectual force, the version of feminism that emerged in the 1980s and 1990s pushed forward the project of predecessors, like Simone de Beauvoir and Elizabeth Cady Stanton, from previous waves of feminism. Feminism in the 1980s and 1990s took a variety of forms, from liberal versions to Marxist ones to the radical social constructivism of Butler and others to womanism, which focused specifically on the situation of African American women and other nonwhites. Feminism in the academy generated intellectual projects of an ethical and political character, which explicitly strove to advocate for the situation of women. But it also resulted in attention to gender in studies that did not explicitly have the character of advocacy. The focus on gender served as an important corrective to the tendency of scholars in various disciplines to overlook the situation of women, oftentimes devoting their inquiries exclusively to men's cultural productions. The formation of women's studies departments and programs in the university did much to institutionalize these concerns. One of the more recent trends in gender studies is that the focus has expanded to include men and the construction of masculinity. Another development is that there has been an increasing insistence that we analyze gender in relation to other social categories (race, culture, class, nationality) lest we treat gender as universally the same and suppress the variety of situations in which women and men exist.

Another intellectual movement that was integral to the turn to power and that has influenced religious studies is postcolonialism. Postcolonialism challenges the lasting effects of the intellectual and material domination that Europe exercised over much of the rest of the world during the colonial period. Frantz Fanon (1925–1961), who analyzed the psychology of the colonized and the need for a violent response to violent (psychological and physical) oppression, would prove to be an early figure in the movement.[9] Despite Fanon's lasting influence and insightfulness, we have to regard as the more immediate founding texts of postcolonialism Edward Said's *Orientalism* (1978) and Gayatri Chakravorty Spivak's essay "Can the Subaltern Speak?"[10] Said draws from Foucault to analyze the way that European scholars, artists, and administrators imagined and conceptualized the "Orient," conceiving the people of the East as psychologically different from the Europeans and inferior. Spivak declares at the end of her essay that the subaltern, the member of a subjugated class, "cannot speak."[11] What she means, drawing from Derrida, is that all the terms that a scholar might use to represent the attitudes of the subjugated person are so embedded in the scholar's social and economic context that we cannot take them as accurately reflecting the subaltern's perspective. It is evident from Said's and Spivak's work that postcolonialism is indebted to Foucault and Derrida. If Robert Young is right, though, that the Algerian War exercised a formative influence on post-structuralism, then the opposition to colonialism is as much an influence on post-structuralism as the latter is on the postcolonialist intellectual.[12] At any rate, critical attention to the way that the West represents colonized and formerly colonized groups, in its literature, philosophy, art, and scholarship is a defining characteristic of postcolonialism.

This quick introduction to some key moments in the turn to power necessarily simplifies complex matters and excludes a great deal of importance (for example, a longer account would have to discuss the confluence of the psychoanalytic tradition with power approaches, especially with reference to Sigmund Freud, Jacques Lacan, Luce Irigaray, and Slavoj Žižek). Nevertheless, I hope at least I have conveyed some sense of the broader intellectual background at work as religious studies has turned to power. We can now take a look at some of the ways in which the power approach transformed the academic study of religion.

THE TURN TO POWER IN RELIGIOUS STUDIES

Derrida, Foucault, Butler, Bourdieu, feminism, and postcolonialism have had an enormous impact on the study of religion. This impact has been multifarious, but we can distinguish two identifiable methodological tendencies. The first is a concern with how power operates in the religious communities that religious studies scholars study. The relevant questions are about how the practitioners' social identity (race, gender, class, ethnicity, etc.) affects the way that they practice their religion as well as the reverse: questions about how religion affects the social class structures that transverse it. The second methodological tendency has been toward reflexivity: attention to the power dynamics that exist between religious studies scholars and the communities that they study. Of special concern here is the fact that religious studies is situated in the European tradition, and so it is a beneficiary and heir, intellectually and materially, of Europe's domination of Asia, Africa, and Central, South, and North America. This reflexivity principally takes the form of critical attention to the key categories that religious studies scholars use, categories such as culture, experience, belief, myth, ritual, and, above all, religion. Critical studies on these categories aim to show how scholars' key concepts are not innocent of power but favor the scholar's social identity over that of the people the scholar studies. Many works in the contemporary study of religion combine both of these types of analyses, focusing on power in religious communities and in scholarship. For instance, in Grace Jantzen's discussion of mysticism in *Power, Gender, and Christian Mysticism*, she examines the history of the concept of the "mystical" in the Christian tradition and looks at how that concept has been deployed throughout the tradition to the advantage of men over women. Simultaneously, she provides a reflexive analysis of contemporary scholarly uses of terms like "mysticism" and "experience" to make the case that these terms have sexist biases inherent in them.[13]

One key moment that signaled the arrival of power in the study of religion is Talal Asad's criticism of Geertz in his essay, "The Construction of Religion as an Anthropological Category," included as the first chapter in his 1993 book, *Genealogies of Religion: Discipline and Reasons of Power in Christianity and Islam*.[14] Asad, like Geertz, is an anthropologist who has been widely read in religious studies. In this essay, Asad lays out a series of complaints against Geertz's definition of religion. Three in particular are worth our attention. First, Asad says that in principle there cannot be a universal definition of religion. As we saw in the last chapter, Geertz defines religion as a system of symbols that establishes moods and motivations concerning a general order of existence. Asad denies that any universal definition can be legitimate, "not only because [religion's] constituent elements and relationships are historically specific, but because that definition is itself the historical product of discursive processes." Asad thinks that the very attempt to define religion universally must posit a "transhistorical and transcultural" essence, an essence that is distinct and so insulated from power and politics. He is concerned that this ignores the way that what we refer to as religion is thoroughly permeated by power. Furthermore, it ignores the fact that the category of religion itself, a construction of the early modern Christian West, is not innocent of social power. According to Asad, contemporary attempts to theorize religion as a universal category either strategically confine religion, as secular intellectuals would have it (by removing religion from politics), or defend religion (by making it a universal human phenomenon), as liberal Christians would have it.[15] The second major criticism that Asad has against Geertz is that he says that Geertz defines religion as something that is principally cognitive and principally a matter of belief. This is because Geertz insists that religions must "affirm something" about the nature of reality. Asad interprets this to mean that these affirmations are beliefs, cognitive in nature. This implies, says Asad, that the theorist of religion, a "disembodied mind," can survey these beliefs and thus identify religion from "an Archimedean point."[16] Geertz's appeal to belief entangles him in "a modern, privatized Christian" conception of religion (though Geertz was himself not a Christian), according to which belief is a "state of mind rather than a constituting activity in the world."[17] So according to Asad, Geertz unwittingly imposes on all cultures and times a distinctly Christian conception of religion. The third criticism that Asad has for Geertz that is relevant for our purposes concerns what he has to say about Geertz's understanding of symbols. Symbols are at the heart of what religion is, for Geertz, since his definition construes religion as a system of symbols. Asad's charge against Geertz is that his conception of symbols ignores social power. This is first because Geertz analytically distinguishes between symbolic meaning and social practices. Asad counters with the historical example of Augustine's endorsement of the use of coercion against the Donatists, whom the theologian regarded as heretics. The lesson to be learned, Asad tells us, is that "it is not mere symbols that implant true Christian dispositions, but power—ranging all the way from laws (imperial and ecclesiastical) and other sanctions (hellfire, death, salvation, good repute, peace) to the disciplinary activities of social institutions (family, school, city, church) and of human bodies (fasting, prayer, obedience, penance)."[18] This gets to the heart of the problem. Geertz neglects, in his attention to symbolic meaning, the institutions and practices that discipline human bodies into particular types of subjects. That is to say, he neglects power. Asad's criticism of Geertz, with its focus on discipline, materiality, institutions, and the relation between power and knowledge, owes much to Foucault, as Asad acknowledges.

My intent here is not to pronounce judgment on whether Asad is interpreting Geertz correctly or criticizing him legitimately. What is important is that, whether Asad is right or wrong, his criticism of Geertz has proved extraordinarily influential, and it is now firmly established in the theory and methods of religious studies canon.

Subsequent to Asad's criticism of Geertz, a host of important studies emerged, each of which took some topic or concept of long-standing importance in religious studies and reinterpreted it or rejected it, with concerns about power in mind. These studies all involve one or both of the two features of power analyses that I mentioned above: attention to the way that power operates in religious practices and attention to the way that the categories contemporary scholars use are themselves implicated in a particular social and economic context. I will mention a few representative and influential examples from the wide swath of literature. Bruce Lincoln on myth is one such example. In contrast to Mircea Eliade's previously influential understandings of myths as paradigmatic models that informed practitioners how to participate in the sacred, Lincoln analyzes myth as ideology. According to Lincoln, myths serve to promote the interests of certain members of the social order over and against those of others.[19] Catherine Bell has a similar perspective about ritual. In contrast to Geertz's account of ritual, which holds that rituals serve to integrate the practitioners' worldview with their ethos, Bell argues that rituals serve to discipline practitioners' bodies to make them conform to their societies' power structure on the level of their bodily habits.[20] In *Throughout Your Generations Forever*, Nancy Jay presents a theory of sacrifice according to which religious sacrifice exists to enforce hierarchical social distinctions, particularly between women and men. (Only men are allowed to perform certain sacrifices in many religious traditions, for example, and certain sacrifices serve the purpose of establishing patrilineal descent by "expiat[ing] . . . the consequences of having been born of woman.")[21] Jay's focus is on the way that religious institutions oppress and exclude women, and a great number of other studies have amply documented these tendencies across religious traditions. Other studies, however, look at the way in which religions can empower women in various ways, even when they remain in an officially subordinate position. For example, R. Marie Griffith examines the way in which conservative Protestant women find strength and support in prayer and in relationships with each other, even while they endorse their churches' view that they should submit to their husbands.[22] Saba Mahmood details the way that wearing an Islamic veil bolsters women's agency in the Egyptian mosque movement, even though they understand submission as their proper role in relation to men and Allah.[23] Scholars, in their focus on gender, are looking at men and masculinity, and so today gender is not quite as much a code word for "women" as it was not long ago. For example, Mark C. Carnes examines the rituals of nineteenth-century secret societies, like freemasonry, to show how the rituals oriented young men toward adult male roles and responsibilities.[24] Related to the question of gender is that of sexuality. Mark Jordan's *The Invention of Sodomy* is an example of studies at the nexus of religion and sexuality. He traces the development of the term "sodomy" through the history of Christian theology, demonstrating that it has had since its inception an unstable meaning. Thus the concept sodomy has been well suited to serve as a "mask for violent exercises of power" as Christians used it to condemn same-sex pleasure and any sexual pleasure that is for its own sake.[25] Race has been a frequent topic of study as well. In *Exodus!*, for example, Eddie Glaude analyzes the role that the Exodus story from the Hebrew Bible played in eliciting and sustaining a political identity for African American slaves and the way that it focused their aspirations for emancipation.[26] One of the more important developments in the study of power and social classifications has been to examine the intersection of social identities, as when Evelyn Brooks Higginbotham examines race, gender, and class and their complicated interrelationships in her analysis of African American female Baptists. She concludes that religion fostered a "discourse of resistance" and supported "everyday forms of resistance to oppression and demoralization," as she attempts to "rescue women from invisibility as historical actors in the drama of black empowerment."[27] In connection to postcolonialism, scholars are attending to the way that European intellectuals constructed and represented non-European religions. Richard King, for example, critically examines the Western invention of the category of Hinduism and the way that mysticism has been conceived as the essence of the Hindu religion.[28] Also in a postcolonialist vein, David Chidester provides a study of how "the discipline of comparative religion emerged . . . out of a violent history of colonial conquest and domination."[29] Chidester traces the semantic instability and political nature of the concept of religion by showing how in southern Africa, Europeans would attribute a lack of religion to indigenous people when they were not under colonial control but then attribute religion to them after they had been contained. When Europeans encountered African populations and designated them without religion, this was in effect to class them as subhuman, incapable of industry and labor, and so without entitlement to their land.[30] After they had been colonized, the need to administrate the affairs of the native population required classifications of their beliefs and behavior, and, in these circumstances, the colonists determined that the Africans were religious after all. But either way, whether attributing religion or withholding the designation, the category of religion was biased toward Christianity, privileging it as the supreme and paradigmatic example of what a religion is. Tomoko Masuzawa fills out this story in a more global context, examining, among other things, the role of anti-Semitism in determining what got to count as a world religion in the nineteenth century.[31] Timothy Fitzgerald argues that the construction of the category religion by European scholars is thoroughly ideological, and the term is not sufficiently precise to have any legitimate analytical use.[32] Any effort to proffer a definition of religion, then, is an exercise in political power.[33]

These are just a few representative examples of the many studies in the past couple of decades that have focused on power. In conjunction with these concerns about power, materiality has come to the forefront in the study of religion. The attention to material artifacts, bodies, and the physical conditions in which people practice their religion is in significant part a reaction against the Western intellectual tradition's long-standing privileging of spiritual and mental qualities over and against physicality. In a review of the important book edited by Mark C. Taylor, *Critical Terms for Religious Studies*, Chidester refers to the emerging approach that analyzes power and materiality as "new materialism." Those subscribing to this approach, says Chidester, are materialists because they are centrally concerned with "material objects" and "material conditions, forces, and relations." They are *new* materialists, because, unlike the previous variants of materialism, whether "naturalist, empiricist, positivist, cultural, historical, dialectical, or otherwise," the new materialists want to retain the term "religion" as a valid category for analysis.[34]

The materialist focus is, as one would expect, hostile to mentalistic categories such as experience, belief, consciousness, and ideas. Two of these terms, "experience" (to be discussed below) and "belief" have their own entries in *Critical Terms*, in fact, and neither fares well. In "Belief," Donald S. Lopez Jr. takes aim at the popular idea that religion is preeminently about believing in something (nirvana, the Dao, God, etc.). This conception of religion has a universal scope, in that all religions are supposed to be identifiable on the basis of what their beliefs are.

But in fact the universality of the view that religion is primarily belief occludes its specifically Christian origins. It was Christians who constructed other traditions, like Buddhism, as religions by identifying them with a set of propositional statements to which the adherents assent. This was in direct opposition to how the Buddhists themselves understood their practices, and this way of conceiving religion authorized Europeans and Americans to determine which aspects of Asian religious practice were authentic and which were not: true Buddhism was in the ancient texts, not the lived religion of contemporary Asians. In fact, many of the Buddhists themselves were ignorant of the core beliefs of Buddhism, as Europeans and Americans had identified them.[35] The idea of religion as preeminently belief spread and became popular because of Christianity's political power in the nineteenth century, and it helped make the goal of Christian missions intelligible: converting people from one set of beliefs to another. For Lopez, the category of belief is an ideology, "an idea that arises from a specific set of material interests."[36] He says that he is not out to deny that there are such things as beliefs: "this is difficult to determine." But he clearly has no legitimate role for the category to play in the study of religion, as we see from his chiding remarks: "We continue to speak of the 'world view' of this or that religion, demonstrating that, even though we may no longer believe in God, we still believe in belief."[37] Whether or not it is his intent, the effect of Lopez's musings, if they are correct, is to make belief irrelevant to the academic study of religion; his arguments would effectively eliminate the category from the scholarly repertoire.

I am aware that by referring to this diverse and polyvocal group of scholars as belonging to a common school or approach, whether we designate said approach as the power approach or new materialism, I risk oversimplification. I would not want to convey the impression that the studies that I have mentioned agree with each other on all methodological matters or that all these figures focus on power to the exclusion of meaning, experience, or other analytical terms. Nevertheless, they do all focus on power in one way or another, and the sorts of studies that I am mentioning here all owe something to the key figures in the power approach—people like Derrida, Foucault, Butler, and Bourdieu. And even if it is wrong to think of this focus on power as expunging meaning altogether from the methodology of religious studies, there has been a definite shift of the center of gravity away from meaning and toward power, and a definite lack of theoretical attention to the relation between these two categories. Furthermore, now the experience approach is doubly removed from the contemporary scene: it has been displaced by meaning and meaning in turn by power. I will turn now more specifically to some implications for the meaning and experience approaches that the turn to power has effected.

THE IMPLICATIONS FOR MEANING

The waxing of power coincided with the waning of meaning in the study of religion. This has much to do with the specific criticisms that were lodged against Geertz. We have already seen what Asad has to say against Geertz's symbolic anthropology. Others have made influential criticisms as well. Many of these criticisms have to do with the need of the interpretive anthropologist to attribute meanings to a social group. Vincent Crapanzano says that Geertz treats the Balinese not as individuals but as a "generalized," "single subjectivity," an entity about which he can speak as a whole and, further, that he "offers no specifiable evidence for his attributions of intention." Therefore, his "constructions of constructions of constructions appear to be little more than projections . . . of his point of view."[38] Similarly, James Clifford says that Geertz treats the Balinese as a "cultural origin," an "absolute subject" or "whole subjects," to whom a collective intention can be attributed, a figure to whom the ethnographer can supply an "integrated portrait" instead of "ambiguities and diversities of meaning."[39] The idea here is to lay bare the power relations between the ethnographers and those they observe and to demonstrate that the ethnographers who claim to interpret a culture are authorizing themselves to occupy a certain vantage point, the center of a field of vision, from which they can supposedly perceive cultural patterns. Masuzawa calls this the "ideology of anthropological observation."[40]

The meaning approach owes much to Geertz, and no doubt the criticisms that undermined him significantly weakened it as well. However, the meaning approach is not reducible to Geertz, and, from one perspective it initially seems strange that meaning and power would wind up at odds, because of the shared regard for language that both approaches have. The theorists of power view language or discourse, as they often call language in use, as central to the processes of subject and social class formation, and so they share with people like Gadamer, Ricoeur, and Geertz attentiveness to language. However, language is a very different thing in their hands than it is for the hermeneutic tradition. For one thing, they do not see language's meaningfulness as the issue but rather its effects, in particular the way in which discourse produces and is produced by power relations. For another thing, two of the most influential advocates of the meaning approach, Gadamer and Ricoeur, are firmly wedded to the phenomenological tradition and so to the paradigm of consciousness, even with their attention to language. The power approach, as we have seen, tends to be dismissive of consciousness. Another strike against the meaning approach is that Gadamer, Ricoeur, and their tradition do not have an adequate account of the social conditions under which meanings are produced or of the way in which social power determines various meanings and interpretive processes to the benefit of certain social groups and the marginalization of others. So the shared interest in language among power theorists and meaning-oriented approaches does not typically bring about anything in the way of rapprochement between the two approaches. That this is typically so does not mean that it is always so. Some theorists of power are comfortable appealing to the idea of meaning in their analyses. A handful does so with explicit attention to theoretical matters, while the greater number use meaning without attending to it theoretically.

A number of key figures in religious studies associated with power approaches, however, have articulated a principled rejection or at least devaluation of meaning. We have already seen Asad's criticism of Geertz's account of religion as symbolic. In Asad's terms, what is at stake in the turn to power is the shift "from reading symbols to analyzing practices."[41] He insists in a study of medieval Christian rituals that he is not concerned with "symbolic meanings" but with the ways ritual practices "enabled discipline to take effect in different ways," quipping, "Searching for symbolic meanings is not the name of *my* game."[42] Other important scholars concur. Mahmood, for example, explicitly distinguishes her own approach from a hermeneutical approach, saying her focus is not on the meaning of discourse but rather "the *work* that discursive practices perform in making possible particular kinds of subjects."[43] Robert Sharf distances the study of ritual from questions of meaning and interpretation: "There is simply no a priori reason to believe that rituals stand in need of interpretation."[44] Masuzawa notes that scholars' approach to texts these days attends to the material properties of texts and their circumstances of production and circulation, "as opposed to the more ideational meaning supposedly hidden or contained in the text."[45] These sorts of remarks, especially from such a distinguished group, convey the impression that we must choose between two exclusive methodological options.

Such is the fate of meaning in religious studies after the turn to power. For those committed to the power approach, the predominant tendency is to shun the idea of meaning, whether through neglect or outright opposition.

THE IMPLICATIONS FOR EXPERIENCE

"Simply put, some now understand experience as a thoroughly sociopolitical construct," Russell McCutcheon summarizes.[46] If meaning is a troubled category in the "posthermeneutical" era of practice and power, then experience is much more so.[47] The paradigm of consciousness and the focus on experience in the study of religion are so removed that scholars can speak of mysticism as the "beleaguered" subject of a "precipitous" fall from "theoretical grace."[48] Religious experience, too, is for many "passé in an era that has abandoned experience for discourse *about* experience," as one proponent of the category admits.[49] There are worries about experience in general, not just of the religious sort, in the academy more broadly. Gadamer admits that experience is a concept that is "one of the most obscure we have."[50] Foucault is explicit about his break from phenomenological philosophy: "If there is one approach that I do reject, however, it is that (one might call it, broadly speaking, the phenomenological approach) which gives absolute priority to the observing subject." "Historical analysis," he tells us, does not need a theory of the "knowing subject," like we find in Gadamer and Ricoeur, but rather "a theory of discursive practice."[51] Joan W. Scott acknowledges the temptation in regard to experience to "abandon it altogether." Scott ultimately counsels against the elimination of the category, but she insists that we focus on "the discursive nature of 'experience' and on the politics of its construction," because, "what counts as experience is neither self-evident nor straightforward; it is always contested, and always therefore political."[52]

In the academic study of religion, the shift to power brought about a new phase in the study of mysticism and religious experience, and the key representatives of this phase are Jantzen and Sharf.[53] We can think of the philosophy of mysticism and experience as involving three phases. The first phase was the era of Friedrich Schleiermacher, William James, Rudolf Otto, and Mircea Eliade, all of whom hold that religious experience is a universal, transcultural reality. Scholars eagerly collected and collated reports of experiences from the sacred texts of the world's religions and from the devout among their contemporaries, intent on discovering commonalities across time and culture. At a more basic level, though, experience was a linchpin concept for theorizing the very nature of religiosity, as we saw in the previous chapter. The perennialists, the proponents of the first phase in the study of religious experience, view experience as the defining and most important aspect of religion in general. In their hands, the study of religious experience became an established and flourishing enterprise. The second phase occurred in the social constructivist arguments of Steven Katz and Wayne Proudfoot, which deny any universal, transcultural common core to religious experiences throughout time and place and which emphasize the degree to which the experiencer's linguistic and cultural heritage determines the nature of the experience. Despite their differences about the nature of the episode, representatives of both the perennialist position and the constructivist position agree that religious experiences are discrete, psychological episodes. Jantzen and Sharf, however, challenge this assumption. They help bring about a third phase in the study of mysticism, defined by its concern with power. Both Jantzen and Sharf subject the categories experience and mysticism to historicist analysis, examining the conditions under which the categories originated and the ideological purposes they served and continue to serve. Jantzen, a poststructuralist, is interested in the way in which the mystical has consistently been put to uses that served male interests against female ones, as the concept shifted in meaning throughout the centuries. Sharf is interested in the role that the idea of experience plays in serving the interests of Christianity, of nationalism, and of particular meditational schools vis-à-vis other ones.

As the principal examples of how the power approach critically handles experience, Jantzen and Sharf warrant closer attention. Jantzen, in *Power, Gender, and Christian Mysticism*, traces the history of the concept mysticism, registering the numerous changes the concept underwent through the centuries. Jantzen's aim is to show how each transformation privileged men and excluded women from positions of power and authority. In ancient Greece, the term the mystical ones (*hoi mustikoi*, from *muein*, to close one's eyes or lips) referred not to those who underwent intense experiences in an altered state of consciousness but rather to the participants in the secret rituals of the mystery religions. Then, in ancient and medieval Christianity, mystical referred to the hidden sense of scripture. Patristic and medieval exegetes saw all of scripture as referring to Jesus Christ, even those portions, the majority, that do not explicitly mention him. So in addition to the literal meaning of a passage, the medievals posited a mystical or spiritual meaning related specifically to Christ. The implication for gender relations of this conceptualization of the mystical was that women were effectively excluded from the mystical in two regards. First, since access to scripture was the preserve of men, women's ability to engage in the explication of the hidden sense of scripture was limited. Second, interpretations of scripture, including the mystical ones, were subject to ecclesiastical control, and here authority rested exclusively in the hands of men. Also in the medieval era, we find the development of mystical theology. Mystical theology emphasizes the inability of our finite, linguistic concepts to grasp the nature of an infinite God and teaches a spirituality of union between the devout and God that is often described in erotic terms. In this development, the term "mystical" expanded to include subjective experience. The union that mystical theologians promoted took two forms, an intellectual form (Pseudo-Dionysius and Meister Eckhart) and an affective form (Bernard of Clairvaux). Both of these strands denigrated the body, the former because medieval Christianity viewed the intellect as superior to the body and the latter because even though the mystical theologians employed the language of sexuality, they viewed physical sexuality as a dire threat to union with God. Since the intellectual tradition at the time associated men with the spirit and intellect and women with the body, both versions of mystical theology slighted women. Also, both versions came to agree that visionary experiences were suspect. Visions were a threat to church authority because they enabled the individual to claim to possess divine authority by direct means. This opened a potential avenue for female subversion of male ecclesiastical hierarchy, so the regulation of visionaries was one more instance of the subordination of women. Next Jantzen explores the manner in which authorities in the late Middle Ages and early modern period employed the distinction between true mystics and false mystics. They applied the categories heretic and witch to those deemed false mystics and used these categories to silence, punish, and kill women. Authorities also tortured and imprisoned as heretics members of religious movements, such as the Cathars and Waldensians, that accorded women a higher status than society did. Finally Jantzen turns to the modern conceptions of religious experience and mysticism. In the modern era, through such giants as Schleiermacher and James, mysticism becomes identified as a subjective experience, a private psychological state. Mysticism is now available to women, but only because it and religion in general are marginal. That which is mystical has been consigned to the ineffectual realm of private feelings, sequestered away from the public, masculine realm of commerce and politics. Another feature of the modern conception of mysticism is that ineffability is predicated of mystical experiences. Indeed, for James, ineffability is one of the defining features of mysticism.[54] Jantzen has two concerns here. First, this notion of mysticism is historically inaccurate, since the authors of the classic works of mystical theology view ineffability not as a quality of a subjective experience but rather as a corollary to their doctrine of God: God is infinite and transcendent, whereas language and concepts are finite, and so concepts are incapable of adequately corresponding to God. Jantzen's second concern is that the modern conception of mystical experiences as ineffable has the effect, once again, of silencing women. Now that women are permitted into the ranks of the mystics at last, they cannot speak of that which they experience. Jantzen concludes her study with a warning that, to the degree that contemporary philosophers of religion fail to recognize the historicity of the concept mysticism and the political purposes that the concept has served and continues to serve, they themselves are participating in a sexist endeavor as they study and analyze mysticism.

One of the primary lessons to be learned from *Power, Gender, and Christian Mysticism* is that the modern definition of mysticism is a "depoliticized" one.[55] The Jamesian legacy, according to Jantzen, views mysticism as intense, subjective states of consciousness, thus conceptualizing the mystical as removed from concerns of power. Jantzen writes, "Feminists have every reason, both historical and current, to be suspicious of an understanding of mysticism which . . . makes of mysticism a private and ineffable psychological occurrence and which detaches it from considerations of social justice."[56] Thus, philosophers of religion who use the terms "experience" and "mysticism" uncritically are perpetuating a potentially sexist practice.

We can turn now to consider Sharf's contributions. In a series of three related essays, "Buddhist Modernism and the Rhetoric of Meditative Experience," "The Zen of Japanese Nationalism," and "Experience," Sharf has challenged two of the crucial assumptions that formerly presided over the study of religious experience: that experience is a legitimate cross-cultural category and that reports of experiences refer to psychological episodes.[57]

One of Sharf's principal aims is to expose a widely popular notion of Buddhism as faulty. In the popular notion, Buddhism at heart is a religion of subjective experience. This is because the achievement through meditation of particular states of consciousness, such as *vipassanā* (insight), *samatha* (concentration), *kenshō* (seeing one's true nature), and *satori* (understanding), is what Buddhism most properly is, and any rituals or institutional features are, at best, secondary and incidental and, at worst, detractions from Buddhism's real essence. The meditational achievements are supposed to involve "pure experience," a state in which all conceptual activity is suspended and the distinction between the subject and the object of knowledge collapses.[58] The problem, according to Sharf, is that the historical record and ethnographic evidence stand in flat contradiction to this conception of Buddhism. Premodern Buddhists placed little emphasis on the achievement of altered states of consciousness. Buddhist monks used scriptural narratives of experiences ritually—memorizing them, reciting them, and revering them as talismans—rather than treating them as a guide for the achievement of extraordinary mental episodes. Evidence from actual monastic practices suggests that the performance of liturgical rituals, the cultivation of virtue, and the study of scripture were focal, not the attainment of pure experience.[59] In Zen practices, *satori* and *kenshō* referred not to a nonconceptual, immediate experience of subject–object unity but instead to "the full comprehension and appreciation of central Buddhist tenets."[60]

So whence originated the popular misconception of Buddhism? Sharf traces its genesis to the Meiji period (1868–1912) in Japan. At that time, Japan was grappling with modernization, and Japanese intellectuals were struggling to articulate Japanese identity in relation and opposition to Europe. The Japanese government embarked on a policy of criticism and persecution of Buddhism, construing it as a foreign, anti-modern influence. Buddhist apologists responded with what came to be known as New Buddhism, a version of Buddhism that downplayed the ritual, institutional, and "superstitious" elements of traditional practices and presented true Buddhism as a humanistic, universal religion rooted in subjective experience. This dematerialized version of Buddhism was, it seemed, far more amenable to modernity than the traditional one, not only in shedding the particular for the universal, but also in fashioning religiosity as a matter of nonrational experience. This shielded Buddhism from conflict with the modern scientific outlook by situating it in a domain of private interiority, outside the reach of scientific investigation. But even as the New Buddhists dismissed the particularities of rite and belief, they smuggled another particularity, Japanese nationalism, into the supposed universality. The proponents of New Buddhism argued that Japanese culture was inherently and uniquely suited to express and convey the true Buddhism, thus portraying Japan as superior to China, where Buddhism had degenerated, and to the West, where debased cultural values precluded an understanding of true spirituality. New Buddhists also promoted nationalism by connecting Zen to martial pursuits, historical and contemporary. They presented the virtues of Zen as identical to those of the samurai warrior, and then they enlisted Zen, the "religion of the samurai," to underwrite Japanese imperialist projects against China and Russia, and then, in World War II, the West. The individual who more than anyone brought this version of Buddhism to the United States and Europe is D. T. Suzuki (1870–1966). Western intellectuals happily overlooked Suzuki's nationalism, immersed as they were in their own post-Enlightenment religious crisis. Weary of Christianity in its institutional forms, they eagerly welcomed a Buddhism of subjective experience as an apt counterpart to the Christianity that liberal theologians were fashioning. The pluralist, ecumenical sensibilities prevalent in the late-nineteenth and early-twentieth centuries fostered receptiveness to an Asian religion that downplayed the external matters of belief, institution, and ritual for an emphasis on a universal spiritual experience. The irony is the extent to which New Buddhism itself was a product of this very Western religiosity. Nishida Kitarō (1870–1945), a personal friend of Suzuki, developed the notion of pure experience after reading William James. Suzuki studied for a time under Paul Carus in Illinois. The Japanese terms for experience, *kaiken* and *taiken,* were coined in the Meiji period by translators of Western philosophical texts.[61] So in Sharf's story, the rhetoric of experience in Japanese Buddhism was ideological through and through: the invention of the notion that Buddhism is centrally a matter of episodes of subjective consciousness served to legitimate Buddhism in the modern era and advance Japanese imperialism. As it turns out, the legitimating function of meditation experience is not confined to bygone generations. In contemporary Buddhist practices, particular meditational schools use the rhetoric of experience to validate their own approach and teacher vis-à-vis alternative ones, disputing the others' claims to have achieved the highest meditational states.[62]

The concept of religious experience in the West is, according to Sharf, no less ideological. Here he cites Proudfoot, who locates the origin of the concept in the work of the founder of modern Christian theology, Schleiermacher. According to Proudfoot, Schleiermacher makes religion a matter of feeling, an "experiential moment irreducible to either science or morality, belief or conduct," with the desired effect being to "preclude the possibility of conflict between religious doctrine and any new knowledge that might emerge in the course of secular inquiry."[63] Schleiermacher and his peers design the concept to serve apologetic and protective purposes for religiosity in the face of the challenges posed by Enlightenment philosophy and science.[64] New Buddhism inherited this function, and, just as Suzuki's Zen legitimated imperialism, so also the liberal Protestant redefinition of religion undergirded European colonial projects by covertly installing liberal Christianity as the prototypical instance of the newly universal category, religion. As the prototype of religion, Christianity had, for Europeans, an air of inherent superiority to non-Christian religions. In this manner, the theologians did their part to facilitate the European endeavor to dominate every continent.

In the simplest terms, Sharf's philosophical position regarding experience is this: according to the way that scholars of religion have conceived religious experiences, such experiences (if they occur) are absolutely private, whereas a term can only be meaningful if it pertains to publicly accessible realities. The meaning of a term is a product of the publicly available items or states of affair to which the term refers, and since experiences are not publicly accessible, the term "experience" does not have semantic content. Sharf says, "The category experience is, in essence, a mere placeholder that entails a substantive if indeterminate terminus for the relentless deferral of meaning," and, "all attempts to signify 'inner experience' are destined to remain 'well-meaning squirms that get us nowhere.'"[65] Sharf's criticism of experience is thorough: experience lacks "any possible discursive meaning or signification" whatsoever, and its main appeal is that it is "so amenable to ideological appropriation," precisely because it does not admit determinate meaning.[66] Sharf specifies that the "proper domain in which to situate the Buddhist rhetoric of experience" is ritualistic performances, "public enactments of enlightenment—ceremonial affirmations of the reality of nirvana in the here and now," as opposed to "whatever ineffable experiences might transpire in the minds of Buddhist meditators." [67] The upshot of these and similar remarks is that scholars can and should attend to experience reports but not as things that refer to mental episodes. Instead the object of scholarly inquiry is the ideological uses to which such experience reports are put. "Terms such as *samatha, vipassanā, sotāpatti,* and *satori* are not rendered sensible by virtue of the fact that they refer to clearly delimited 'experiences' shared by Buddhist practitioners. Rather, the meaning of such terminology must be sought in the polemic and ideological context in which Buddhist meditation is carried out."[68] So in effect Sharf preserves a place for experience by rendering the term as equivalent to "experience report." The latter term does refer to something publicly accessible, whether a text, scriptural or otherwise; an oral testimony; or a ritual recitation. In particular, Sharf wants us to attend to the way that experience reports are used to authorize particular individuals and social groups, a concern that he shares with Jantzen.

Sharf and Jantzen both claim that the understanding of experience and mysticism that the perennialists and constructivists assume is not self-evident or necessary but rather the product of specific discursive contexts designed to promote the social and political ends of specific social groups.[69] Although Sharf employs social constructivist assumptions at points in his arguments, we should not view him as a member of the constructivist approach to religious experience. He is initiating a different approach, and he makes it clear that he is at odds with crucial assumptions of the constructivists, especially that experience reports refer to some sort of event of consciousness. He writes, "It should now be apparent that the question is not merely whether or not mystical experiences are constructed, unmediated, pure, or philosophically significant. The more fundamental question is whether we can continue to treat the texts and reports upon which such theories are based as referring, however obliquely, to any determinate phenomenal events at all."[70] Sharf is skeptical that we can, and he seemingly abandons the study of experience for the study of discourse about experience: "Scholars of religion are not presented with experiences that stand in need of interpretation but rather with texts, narratives, performances, and so forth."[71] Sharf and Jantzen offer the most immediate challenge to the study of religious experience, and their arguments have proved particularly influential. These two scholars express the current sensibility in regard to experience and help to establish it to an even greater degree.

In addition to Jantzen and Sharf, others have contributed to effort to bring power criticisms to the study of experience. A group of feminist scholars has focused attention on certain aspects of Eliade's approach that are gendered in problematic ways. To highlight what he thinks is an irreducibly religious aspect to human existence, Eliade speaks of the *homo religiosus*, but it turns out, as it so often does, that lurking in the supposed universality implied by the term is a disguised particularity: *homo religiosus* is the religious *male*. In Valerie Saiving's treatment of Eliade's *Rites and Symbols of Initiations*, she shows how Eliade conflates the universally human meaning of initiation rites with the meanings of male initiation rites, rendering the distinctive meanings of female initiation rites less than fully human.[72] Similarly, Carol Christ faults the treatment of goddess religions in Eliade's *History of Religious Ideas* for privileging male symbols over female ones, universalizing male experience. Further, says Christ, Eliade exhibits a Platonism that distinguishes the sacred from the "flux of life."[73] Such a dualism supplies an analysis of religious symbols that assumes that such symbols "are not significantly affected by power politics." [74] Rosalind Shaw builds on Saiving's and Christ's work, agreeing with Christ that Eliade has conceptualized religion and the sense of the sacred in a way that excludes social and political power from the sacred. A *sui generis* conception of religion, "in which religion is treated as a discrete and irreducible phenomenon which exists 'in and for itself,'" according to Shaw, "entails the decontextualization of religion."[75] The problem extends beyond Eliade to the schools that he helped found, phenomenology of religion and the comparative study of religion. She counsels, "By reconceptualizing power as integral to—as opposed to a detachable 'dimension' of—religion, feminist religious studies has the potential to generate conceptual change and renewal."[76]

Despite all the critical attention and curt dismissals that the category of experience has received, it would be wrong to think that it is altogether defunct. Indeed, prominent scholars Ann Taves and Courtney Bender have given explicit attention to the term recently, and, far from dismissing it, they position it as centrally important to the study of religion.[77] Their aim is not to rehabilitate the experiential approach but rather to promote experience as a legitimate topic for religion scholarship. In chapter 5, I will give attention to Taves's important book, *Religious Experience Reconsidered*.

THE DETRACTORS

The power and practice approach is the newest of the three visions of religion that this book discusses: indeed it is *au courant*, and it has not yet received the same sort of explicit criticism that the meaning approach and the experience approach have. Nevertheless, not everyone has jumped onto the bandwagon, and there are a number of detractors who have challenged the focus on the political. Some of the criticisms focus on particular arguments. Schilbrack challenges Asad's reading of Geertz's theory of religion as cognitive and interior, for example, and makes a convincing argument that Fitzgerald overstates the case against the viability of the concept of religion, even while agreeing with them that our concepts are socially constructed.[78] Lincoln takes aim at Asad's claim that the fact that any definition of religion is "the historical product of discursive processes" invalidates the very idea that there could be a universal definition of religion.[79] Lincoln points out that all of our terms are "the historical product of discursive processes," but this does not prevent definitional enterprises in principle. So the historicity of language is not a particular mark against the attempt to define religion.[80] Terry Godlove appeals to the philosophy of Donald Davidson to defend the necessity of the concept of belief against Lopez's dismissal of it.[81] In Davidson's view, attributing beliefs to other people is a necessary element of our pervasive practice of communicating with one another, so belief is essential not just to religion, but to social interaction generally and to any study of human behavior, religious or not.

More indicative of opposition to the power approach, however, are a handful of comments that call into question the approach in general. When an interviewer questioned Geertz about his estimation of Asad's criticism of his work, Geertz responded, "I think [Asad] is a power-reductionist. He thinks that it is power that really matters and not belief. . . . I suspect Asad is a Marxist who cannot be material-reductionist anymore, so instead he is a power-reductionist."[82] The idea here is that, according to Geertz, Asad makes power the most fundamental term of social analysis and treats other things, like meaning, as having a social role that is, at bottom, determined strictly by its role in political contestation. G. Scott Davis has strong words for members of the power approach. He says of the theory of the postmodernists (who are critical of truth and rationality, but devoted to power), "There's not enough to bother" and it "should probably be uprooted altogether."[83] Davis is not entirely opposed to power analyses, since he speaks favorably of Foucault, Said, and Sharf, three people whose work is preeminently concerned with power, but it is clear that he is unimpressed by the relativism of those whom he calls postmodernists. He is worried about the way that postcolonialists warn "against making any critical judgments with regard to our subject matter," and he thinks that they hold that scholarship requires "postmodern therapy" or it will inevitably reproduce colonizing attitudes. Finally, he states that an exclusive focus on the power relations between ethnographers and those whom they observe will lead us to miss other sources of error and misinterpretation in ethnography.[84] Robert Orsi in *Between Heaven and Earth* takes aim at both postcolonialists and confessional Christian approaches to religious studies for "othering." There is some irony to Orsi's charge, because postcolonialists take as one of their principal objects of criticism the way that Europeans "other" non-Europeans, that is, imagine them as essentially different from Europeans. Orsi charges postcolonialists with "rely[ing] on the constitutions of others in doing their work," in this case, the "Christian other." He faults them for valuing non-Western religions "in part as expressions of not-Christianity, a perspective that often informs how these religions are described and interpreted." Orsi says that the challenge of religious studies today is "not to find new others, as both the evangelical and postcolonial approaches do, but to get beyond 'otherizing' as its basic move."[85] Another concern that Orsi expresses and that I share is a worry that the phalanx of critical treatments of belief, meaning, and subjectivity leaves us with a badly truncated conception of the person. "The necessary concern with the social production of religious experience and with religion's political contexts," Orsi writes, "has brought with it the construction of religious actors as mindless practitioners whose interiorities and imaginations do not matter, or matter only as a function of the social. Religious materiality and embodiment have been recovered as subjects of theory, in other words, at the cost of emptying ordinary religious people's minds."[86] We can be sure that the sorts of worries that Geertz, Davis, and Orsi verbalize are far more widespread than just these three scholars.

My aim in this chapter and the previous one has been to present an (abbreviated) intellectual lineage of each of the three major approaches to the study of religion and to discuss the factors that lent them appeal as well as the criticisms of them. In the next chapter, I will make a case that each of the three approaches is indispensable to the study of religion, in some form, but that each approach has distinctive shortcomings that require modifications if we are to preserve it.

3

Three Indispensable Concepts

⌒—————————————————————————————————————

THREE PERVASIVE FEATURES OF RELIGIOUS COMMUNITIES

Power, meaning, and experience are present in all religious communities, without exception. Individuals occupy different positions of authority and power, formally and informally, and their social identities class them into different groups with different relations of deference and status vis-à-vis others. Religious people make utterances and significant gestures, and they write and read texts and inscriptions. Their religious practices are not dispassionate; they are emotional and there are particular emotional responses that are appropriate in different ritual settings: awe, contrition, reverence, ecstasy, remorse, love, bliss, and so on. Frequently practitioners report experiences of sacred and divine things. Power, meaning, and experience are not the only three aspects of religious practices, of course, but they all matter and matter greatly. If scholars systematically ignored any of these while they studied religious groups, their representations of the groups in question would be distorted.

Given that this is so, it would seem to follow straightforwardly that scholars should employ, with sophistication, the categories power, meaning, and experience. It would make sense, too, to think that each of the three approaches associated with these respective categories would have something valuable, even essential, for the study of religion. However, things are not at all as simple as one might expect. The categories themselves and the approaches associated with them have a long and complicated history, which the last two chapters have explored, and the proponents of each of these approaches have oftentimes not thought highly of the other ones. If we were to take stock of where things stand after the successive waves of theoretical approaches to the study of religion detailed in the past two chapters, we could say the following.

Many religious studies scholars today would agree that attending to power is important. There is a broad consensus that race and gender, for example, matter when it comes to studying religion. Having said that, some do think that the contemporary focus on power is too exclusive, as Geertz indicates when he says, "The view, which seems to underlie so many analyses in these neo-Nietzschean, will-to-power days, that our driving passions are purely and simply political, or politico-economic, and that religion is but mask and mystification, an ideological cover-up for thoroughly secular, more or less selfish ambitions, is just not plausible."[1] Further, some influential scholars, including Geertz and phenomenologists like Mircea Eliade and Charles Long, have presented religion as something essentially separate from political power, which could imply that the fundamental task of the scholar of religion does not involve the study of political power. As for meaning, this category does not at all enjoy a consensus in support of it. Rather, many, including Asad, Masuzawa, and Mahmood, speak explicitly against its relevance. Those power theorists who discount meaning tend to hold the view that the relevant items worthy of scholarly attention come not from the semantic content of the practitioners' symbols but rather from the way power works, including the power effects of discourse. What matters is not what words *mean* but what they *do*, what they *produce*, in terms of the formation of subjectivity and social structure. As for experience, here the consensus, if there is one, is against the category. Religious experience has "lost at least some of its luster," as Martin Jay understatedly puts it.[2] Some scholars think of experiences as inaccessibly private and so fit to function ideologically (since they cannot be verified publicly). Others think of experiences as epiphenomenal—they are the by-product of material and often economic forces, and it is those forces to which scholars should attend.

I will argue in the next chapter that in his most influential theoretical work, *The Interpretation of Cultures*, Geertz separates religion from power in problematic ways. In his later work, however, he gets it right. In *Available Light*, he says, "In what we are pleased to call the real world, 'meaning,' 'identity,' 'power,' and 'experience' are hopelessly entangled, mutually implicative."[3] In this chapter I will make an initial case, drawing heavily from anthropological and historical studies, that meaning, power, and experience are all essential categories for religious studies and that they are, as Geertz puts it, mutually implicative: a commitment to any one of these terms entails the other two. It follows that we need robust theoretical concepts of all three. Unfortunately, the existing state of the discipline does not provide conceptions of meaning, experience, and power that are sufficiently robust, especially when it comes to the first two concepts. So at the end of this chapter I will highlight the principal unresolved challenges facing each concept. That will set us up for Part 2 of this book, in which I will provide a constructive response to these challenges, by presenting a social practical theory of religion that integrates all three categories.

In making a case for the indispensability of each category, I do not intend to imply that every book or essay in religious studies has to give equal consideration to all three categories or even make explicit reference to all three. Different studies have different ends, and no single study aspires to exhaustiveness. Nevertheless, scholars should frame their projects in awareness that all three factors are present in the religious community in question, exercising various effects and intertwined in complicated ways. They should make their decision to exclude one or more of the categories from explicit consideration reflectively, not out of neglect or a sense that the category is too outdated to warrant attention.

IN DEFENSE OF POWER

Unlike meaning and experience, no substantial and widely accepted criticism of the importance of power exists in the literature on theory and methodology in religious studies. Many scholars take it for granted that power is an important aspect of religious practices and that the power relations between scholars and the communities that they study require attention. The few criticisms of the power approach that have emerged thus far fault its advocates for too exclusive of a focus on power, that is, for analyzing power to the neglect of other significant aspects of religious practices. But they do not reject power altogether. G. Scott Davis, Geertz, and Robert Orsi all have criticisms of the power approach as it is currently practiced, which I presented in chapter 2, but they all admit the importance of power in the study of religion. Geertz says power is entangled with meaning and experience, Davis calls Edward Said's analysis of "orientalism" "brilliant" and identifies Robert Sharf's power theory essay on the relation between Zen Buddhism and Japanese nationalism as one of his favorite articles.[4] Orsi acknowledges that "holy figures get caught up and implicated in struggles on earth," and saints can empower the marginalized or just as easily be "dangerous enforcers of cultural structures, norms, and expectations."[5]

So scholars generally agree that power is important, but some of them complain about analyses that they feel focus on nothing but power. That means that what we need is not so much a defense of the category of power but a demonstration that we can analyze power in conjunction with meaning and experience, not to their exclusion. I will show that this is so in Part 2 of this book. However, there are two other things to say about the indispensability of power in religious studies. The first is that, despite the lack of criticism to the category of power, power still frequently fails to receive its proper due, simply out of neglect. Indeed, sometimes this happens in unexpected places, as when the important and in general theoretically sophisticated text, *Cambridge Companion to Religious Studies*, leaves gender off its roster of contemporary topics in religious studies.[6] My point is not that gender is reducible to power relations but that since gender and race have been ignored in much of the history of the academic study of religion, theorists of religion must remain vigilant and explicit in issuing reminders that power relations are ubiquitous within religious communities and between those communities and the modern academy.

Second, several influential theorists of religion have presented religion in ways that indicate that it is essentially separate from political matters. For example, Mircea Eliade, as we saw in chapter 2, distinguishes religion from politics in problematic ways. He admits, for example, that cargo cults are "obviously connected with sociopolitical circumstances" of colonialism, but that in addition to the political situation of the cargo cults, "These movements are equally creations of the human spirit, in the sense that they have become what they are—religious movements, and not merely gestures of protest and revolt—through a creative act of the spirit."[7] Passages like these lead to Rosalind Shaw's criticism of the way Eliade defines religion as sui generis, unlike any other feature of human life.[8] Long emphasizes the separation between religion and politics as well. We find in Long's treatments of religion, power, and oppression that he takes pains to compartmentalize religion from historical oppression. He thinks that religion exhibits its own distinctive sort of oppression that mirrors historical oppression. Long says that the distinctly religious power at work in religious experience is correlative to oppressive social power.[9] The operation of religious power in the psychology of religious experience mirrors the oppressive social situation, but it exists in its own sphere that is distinctly religious and not sociopolitical. The social and the religious are not altogether unrelated, since social oppression may elicit in the religious consciousness a peculiarly religious type of oppression. Oppression that is religious in nature occurs because the religious consciousness is concerned with that which is ultimate in existence, and ultimacy reveals itself, among other things, as oppressive. For Long, following Rudolf Otto, the religious consciousness is engaged with the sense of the holy, and the holy simultaneously presents itself as wonderful and terrifying. The overpowering reality of that which is over against us is experienced as oppressive, and this is, according to Long, the "oppressive element in the religions of the oppressed." The oppression that is "internal to religion" may be elicited from social oppression, but it is peculiarly religious in nature. Indeed, religious experiences involve "a mode of perception not under the judgment of the oppressors."[10] To be sure, Long views historical oppression as real enough, repugnant enough, and political enough. But Long carefully keeps religion and sociopolitical power in hermetic isolation.

When we examine records of the slaves themselves, we find that this interpretation of their religious experiences is hard to maintain. In several cases, God or Jesus appears in slaves' visions as white: "I saw the Lord in the east part of the world, and he looked like a white man," reports one ex-slave.[11] Another says, "I seen Christ with his hair parted in the center. He was white as snow. He had on a robe and girdle. I seen him in the spirit."[12] Another sees God dressed in white and then tours heaven and hell. In the latter place the slave encounters the devil, "his face black as it could be and his eyes red as fire."[13] It is clear that in these examples, against Long, the religious experiences are hardly "a mode of perception not under the judgment of the oppressors." The same terms that are used to divide races, "black" and "white," are applied to supernatural entities that are experienced. A more promising framework for assessing religious experiences of slaves is outlined in historian Albert Raboteau's text, *Slave Religion*.[14] Against those who see the slaves' appropriation of Christianity in polar terms, as either a corporate act of massive accommodation or a means for resistance to the white oppressors, Raboteau advises a more nuanced view of the matter. Unlike Long, Raboteau sees the slaves' religion as directly implicated in the social power structures, whether in the slave owners' active attempt to convert slaves to Christianity to foster docility or the slaves' use of prayer as "an effective symbol of resistance." At times both suppressive and emancipatory forces are at work in the same moment. Raboteau cites a slave's testimony that "my master would sometimes whip me *awful,* specially when he knew I was praying. He was determined to whip the Spirit out of me, but he could never do it, for de more he whip the more the Spirit make me *content* to be whipt." Raboteau remarks, "That contentment, it may be said, stifled outward political resistance, but it may also be argued that it represented a symbolic inward resistance, a testing of wills and a victory of the spirit over the force of brutality."[15] By placing religion firmly in contact with political power, Raboteau is able to uncover the complexities of slave religion in relation to white oppression in a way that the phenomenologist's determination to separate religion from politics altogether simply cannot.

Raboteau's treatment of slave religion also contests the account of meaning and power that Geertz provides in his most influential theoretical essays. It is difficult to pin Geertz down on the matter, and it is not clear whether he is entirely consistent, but at times he dissociates power from culture. This is one of Asad's criticisms of Geertz. Asad contests Geertz's account of religious symbols as things that instill religious dispositions (to act and feel in certain ways), saying, "It is not mere symbols that implant true Christian dispositions, but power . . . It was not the mind that moved spontaneously to religious truth, but power that created the conditions for experiencing that truth." [16] Further, Asad says, Geertz "insists on the primacy of meaning without regard to the processes by which meanings are constructed." [17] It seems like this criticism is justified, as when Geertz says that culture (and religion is a cultural system) is not a power: "As interworked systems of construable signs, culture is not a power, something to which social events, behaviors, institutions, or processes can be causally attributed; it is a context, something within which they can be intelligibly—that is, thickly—described." [18] In a discussion of ritual and social change, Geertz tells us that for any action, we can consider two different aspects of the action: the cultural aspect and the social-structural aspect. The cultural aspect is the meaning of the action, and the social-structural aspect is the effects the action has on the social system. [19] He says that the cultural aspect and the social-structural aspect are relatively independent. Neither is a mere epiphenomenon of the other.

At other times, though, Geertz speaks of culture as something that does bring about behavior, as when he says that religious (cultural) symbols "establish powerful, pervasive, long-lasting moods and motivations in men." And motivations are dispositions to act in certain ways, which would seem to imply that culture is in fact a power to which behavior can be attributed. [20] I won't try to settle the interpretive issues regarding Geertz's final position on the matter. My counsel is that we should reject those moments in Geertz's corpus when he speaks of culture as separate from power. Analyses like those of Raboteau show that it is just not plausible to compartmentalize, even by analytically distinguishing them, cultural symbols and socio-political power the way that Geertz does at times. Also, if slaves and slave-owners experience God as white in a society that is white supremacist and if people regard and experience God as male in a society that is patriarchal, it makes no sense to say that the symbols employed do not affect attitudes toward race or toward masculinity and femininity and so no sense to say that these symbols do not affect patterns of behavior in relation to race and gender. If slaves' religion was, as Raboteau says that it was, simultaneously a resource for empowerment and oppression, then cultural symbols very much are a power. Power relations are intrinsic to the symbols God, Jesus, black, and white, and it is problematic to keep the symbols and the social structures at bay from one another. I will treat these issues more philosophically in the next chapters, but if these thoughts about Geertz, Long, and Eliade make sense, then the student of religion who is a proponent of meaning or experience should also be a proponent of power.

IN DEFENSE OF MEANING

Despite the fact that the interpretive approach, especially as exemplified by Geertz, Gadamer, and Ricoeur, no longer has the luster that it once did, scholars of religion cannot avoid meaning, symbols, and interpretation as they conduct their work. Thus, what we need is not to articulate hasty dismissals of meaning and interpretation but to theorize meaning in a way that does not fall prey to the weaknesses of the hermeneutic approach. In this section, I will provide three reasons why meaning is essential to the study of religion and, thus, why a developed theory of meaning is essential to the study of religion.

The first reason why meaning is essential to the study of religion is that meaning is ubiquitous in human affairs, and anyone who wants to understand religion will have to deal with it. At the very least, one has to know what the important terms in the religion mean. One cannot properly understand Christianity without knowing what the word "Eucharist" means; Buddhism without knowing "sanga," or Islam without knowing "hadith." To know a religion one has to know the meaning of a whole host of terms that identify the religion's key personalities, deities, places, historical events, rituals, texts, and artifacts. Learning about a religion is, among other things, learning a set of facts, and facts are expressed with words, and words have meanings. So engaging with meaning is a pervasive feature of the study of religion, at least in this noncontroversial sense of what the religion's terminology signifies and refers to.

Dealing with meanings on this most basic level—what particular words and sentences mean—can be tricky enough in its own right, as anyone who has sat through an introductory class on an unfamiliar religion can attest. Coming to understand a foreign term is no simple affair. Terms are embedded in systems of other terms, and to get a grasp of any one you have to grasp a whole lot. You don't properly know what the word "Eucharist" means if you don't know what "Christ," "God," "church," "crucifixion," "resurrection," and "salvation" mean to a Christian, and many more terms besides. And even those approaches to religion that would seem to have as little to do with meaning as possible, scientific and quantitative ones, have to deal with meaning on at least this basic level. They don't always do it well. Consider quantitative studies that conduct surveys to gauge religious attitudes of a population and then statistically analyze the data to see whether such attitudes covary with other factors (such as denominational affiliation, sex, educational level, geographical location, etc.). For example, the Pew Forum on Religion and Public Life surveys religious people for their attitudes toward their scriptures. They ask whether people regard their texts as "to be taken literally, word for word," or not, and they treat the respondents' answer to this question as a gauge of how dogmatic they are in respect to their religion.[21] However, it's not clear what "literal" means in this context. If we mean literal as opposed to factually untrue, then such a question could well be a gauge of whether a person is "dogmatic" or not (although I wonder also what "dogmatic" means in this context: could not one subscribe to liberal theological or atheistic beliefs in a dogmatic manner?). But if literal refers to language that is not figurative or metaphorical, then a person who has a very conservative view of Scripture could well deny that everything in Scripture should be taken literally, since a great deal of, for example, the Hebrew Bible and Christian New Testament is metaphorical. Must someone who believes the Bible contains no errors believe that God has feathers because the psalmist prays for God to hide him in the shelter of God's wing? The Pew study gives no indication that the researchers took any efforts to ensure that the people who are being classed together as thinking that their scripture is to be taken literally have a shared understanding of what literality implies in relation to a text. Or, for another example, neuroscientific studies ask subjects to meditate on compassion and then conduct brain scans as they do so. They attempt to register the difference in brain activity between highly skilled meditational adepts and unskilled neophytes. These sorts of studies have an important place in the study of religion. However, they give little attention to issues of meaning, and, at times, this creates problems. As Wayne Proudfoot points out, we should expect that the term "compassion" would mean something quite different to someone who has meditated on it for decades as opposed to the person who had undergone just a week's worth of training for the experiment.[22] So getting at meaning in the basic sense of ascertaining the denotation and connotation of particular words and sentences can be quite an arduous task.

I assume that none of the scholars who say disparaging or dismissive things about meaning and interpretation mean to deny that meaning is an important part of scholarship in this relatively banal sense. When Asad says that searching for symbolic meanings is not the name of his game and when Mahmood says that she wants to ascertain the work that discourse does and not its meaning, I do not take them to be disputing the idea that words have meanings and must be translated and interpreted. Indeed, both Asad and Mahmood make reference to meaning as something that they acknowledge that terms have. It would be an extremely implausible view to deny that words have meanings that must be interpreted, and so it is inappropriate to attribute such a view to Asad, Mahmood, or anyone. My assumption, though Asad and Mahmood do not spell this out explicitly, is that when they make dismissive remarks about meaning, hermeneutics, or symbols they are contesting the particular approach to the study of religion that prioritizes those items and relegates other categories to a secondary and subordinate status. In effect, I am in agreement with them on this count, since I too do not want to see meaning and interpretation as having a place of primacy over and above other important terms, like power and experience. I suspect also that they are contesting a host of theoretical assumptions about meaning that interpretive approaches have held, and indeed Asad's project in his criticism of Geertz is to catalog a number of such assumptions and reject them. However, my worry is that in rejecting theories that prioritize meaning, Asad, Mahmood, and others leave us with no resources to develop a convincing account of meaning. The ubiquity of meaning in the banal, commonplace sense and the importance to scholarship of interpreting foreign utterances and symbols indicate that meaning and interpretation require some theoretical attention, even if we do not assign them the primary place in studying human behavior. How do we know whether or not we have understood the meaning of a phrase or term? How do we know if we have rendered a successful translation? Without a theory of meaning, we cannot outline the criteria by which we could answer such questions. Asad and Mahmood reject meaning in the theoretically laden sense of philosophical hermeneutics, and in doing so they neglect meaning in the banal, commonplace, but still extremely important sense.

This is especially problematic because—and here we come to the second reason meaning is essential to religious studies—power, Asad's preferred theoretical locus, implies meaning.[23] That is to say, Asad's project of analyzing power requires interpreting meaning. I'll look at a few examples from Asad's book, *Genealogies of Religion*. First, in the opening chapter of *Genealogies*, Asad discusses Augustine's willingness to coerce the Donatists into what Augustine regarded as true religious practices. Asad writes, "It is not mere symbols that implant true Christian dispositions, but power." This power, Asad tells us, operates in the laws of the Roman Empire and of the Christian church. It operates in sanctions like hellfire, death, and salvation. It also operates in disciplinary activities like fasting, prayer, and penance.[24] In response to this, I want to state the obvious, which is that laws, threats of hellfire, and fasting and such things all involve symbols, necessarily. Laws, in fact, since they are linguistically codified, just are symbols. And the person who bears a sword to enforce the law only does so through a capacity to receive and interpret orders. All this involves an exchange of symbols and meaning. Fasting, too, obviously is an activity fraught with symbolic meaning. Abstinence from food, in and of itself, has no inherent religious significance. One could abstain from food out of laziness, for lack of accessible fare, or for various nonreligious reasons. It is only when the person who is fasting understands the decision to forego eating as pertaining to her standing before God that fasting emerges as the sort of discipline that could shape people's dispositions toward religious truth.

I do not think that Asad would dispute any of this. But it is worth stating explicitly that the situation here is not that we have symbols, on the one hand, and social power, on the other. Rather the disciplinary and coercive practices through which power acts to shape subjects and hierarchies are themselves thoroughly symbolic. Power could not produce its effects without the symbolic context in which it operates. The question to ask, Asad tells us, is, "How does (religious) power create (religious) truth?"[25] But equally we have to ask questions about how truth and meaning create and facilitate power.

In the next chapter of *Genealogies*, Asad tells us that most social anthropologists look for "symbolic meanings or for social functions." In contrast, he says that he is not concerned with either of these but rather with the way rituals discipline their participants.[26] Specifically, Asad is discussing the discipline of ascetics inflicting pain and discomfort upon themselves. He admits that there is a symbolic aspect to self-mortification. Medieval Christian monks would inflict pain upon themselves to imitate Christ's Passion. However, he says, we must not "finally look" to the "traditional symbolism" associated with ascetic pain. Instead, we should look to "the place occupied by bodily pain in an economy of truth."[27]

Here is what I think that Asad means by all this. The interpretive anthropologist would attempt to discern the meaning of the ascetic practices. This meaning might relate to Christ's suffering or perhaps to the view that the body is to be despised. But Asad thinks that this is the wrong way to go. He acknowledges that we have to take the monastics' own meaning system into account, but what really matters, according to him, is how the discipline of self-inflicted pain created certain attitudes in the ascetic toward his own will, toward truth, and toward his community and its hierarchy. The ascetic comes to view his bodily desires as suspect and view pain as the tool that facilitates his attempt to determine the true state of his soul. Pain is a way to inspect the body and its desires. The discipline of pain, in the larger context of monastic practices, fosters the formation of the sort of person who is suspicious of his body and its desires and who is willing to submit to the authorities in his community.

Now Asad is quite right about all this. But it is puzzling to me that Asad would insist, as he makes this argument, that "searching for symbolic meanings is not the name of *my* game." This could only be true if he viewed symbolic meanings and disciplinary power as two separable items. But the exercise of power here occurs only because of meaning. Disciplinary power only creates the sort of ascetic subject that Asad says it does because the ascetic thinks that undergoing pain is a form of communing with the sufferings of Christ. It is not just any pain that the ascetic undergoes; it is pain undergone in a religious community and for religious purposes. The ascetic utilizes pain to inspect his soul because he is concerned about the state of his soul in relation to the moral and spiritual norms of his religious tradition. If he is suspicious of his will's capacity to make proper decisions, he is concerned because it is not properly oriented toward the standards of conduct that God commands. Were we to remove reference to these religious goals and the monastic understanding of pain and its effects, the discussion of power would be unintelligible. Symbolic meaning is a precondition for the operation of disciplinary power, so we need to analyze both symbols and power. Despite Asad's tendency on occasion to speak as though a conception of religion as meaning and as power are at odds with each other, in fact, the view that sees religion as power is committed to a view of religion as meaning. We should not have to choose disciplinary power over symbolic meaning or even to subordinate one to the other.

The third reason I want to mention for why we need an account of meaning in religious studies is that experience entails meaning. Just as a commitment to power in religious studies implies a commitment to meaning, so also a commitment to experience implies a commitment to meaning. This is the case for both senses of religious experience that I outlined in chapter 1: experience as an episode in which someone is aware of something that she takes to be a god, spirit, or some other religious object or state of consciousness and experience as an emotion undergone in a religious context. Constructivists think that the cultural and linguistic heritage of religious experiencers plays a dominant role in determining the nature of the religious experience. So it is obvious that for them the study of religious experiences implies the study of meaning. In their view, the experiencers' concepts, which are cultural artifacts, are present in and shape the experience. Thus if you want to understand an experience then you have to understand the concepts that determine the experience, which turn out to be the very concepts that the experiencer uses to report the experience. For perennialists, it might seem that things are different. Perennialists regard experiences as being entirely, or at least in some phenomenological "core," universal across religious traditions and cultural divides. For them, the experience in total or at least in some aspect is incommunicable, not influenced by or articulable in language. So it would seem that a robust account of meaning is unnecessary for the perennialists to do their work in relation to religious experiences. However, even the perennialists, to the extent that they are attributing mystical experiences to the authors of written texts, have to traffic in meanings. Even if you think the experience itself is nonlinguistic in nature, you have to sort through various reports, for example, "I saw a squirrel," "I went to the market," and "I felt one with all that exists," and decide which of these is a religious-experience report. The stakes are even higher in this regard since Steven Katz's 1978 essay, "Language, Epistemology, and Mysticism." Katz argues that noted perennialist W. T. Stace has not been sufficiently careful in handling mystical texts. In particular, Stace has taken Jewish mystical reports of experiencing God as "nothing" or "nothingness" and identified them with mystical reports from other traditions that seem to speak of experiences in which the normal distinctions among objects and between the self and the world are gone. Katz takes Stace to task for his ignorance of the texts and traditions in question. In the Kabbalistic context of the Hasidic text Stace cites, "Nothing" is "a translation of the term Ayin, which is used in Kabbalistic literature as a name of God relating to his first acts of self-revelation from his self-contained mysteriousness as Eyn Sof (God as He is in Himself)."[28] So Stace's attempt to have "nothing" designate "the absence of all multiplicity" disregards the textual and historical context in which the term appears.[29] Katz supplies comparable examples for Stace's treatments of Buddhist, Christian, and Muslim texts. The lesson to be learned here is that the perennialist position itself, the position that texts from divergent religious traditions all refer to the same type of religious experience, is dependent on complicated and highly controversial understandings of the specific terms involved in religious experience reports. So if one is committed to the study of religious experience, whether as a constructivist or a perennialist, one is committed to engaging with issues of meaning, and one should warmly welcome theoretical attention to the nature of meaning.

So we have at least three good reasons to regard meaning as a key term in the study of religion: signification is ubiquitous, a commitment to power as a key term for the study of religion entails a commitment to meaning as a key term as well, and a commitment to experience as a key term for the study of religion entails a commitment to meaning as well.

IN DEFENSE OF EXPERIENCE

Experience is the category most difficult to defend, in an "era that has abandoned experience for discourse *about* experience."[30] Whatever its faults, and it has significant ones, the experiential approach is correct to direct our attention to the fact that practitioners have religious experiences. From the outset, I want to state in no uncertain terms that in my effort to preserve the category of experience, I have no aim to defend phenomenology of religion or the two elements of the religion-as-experience vision that have received so much criticism: the theses that religions are primarily experiential in nature and that experiences have a cross-cultural common core. The criticisms against these tenets are compelling, and I welcome the turns to language and practice that served as the backdrop for the criticisms.

But as important as the critical study of discourse about experience is, I do wonder if it is suitable as a replacement for the study of experience. What do we mean when we speak of discourse about experience as opposed to the experiences themselves? Among other things we mean people's claims that they have had an experience. Or we mean their claim that someone else, some past or present religious figure, has had an experience. Discourse about experience also refers to descriptions of mystical experiences, such as a sacred text's delineation of a vision or audition. We can also speak of discussions of the nature of mystical experiences, for instance, claims that they are ineffable. In the past, scholars treated the value of such discourse as inhering in its relation to actual experiences. The scholar's estimation of the discourse centered on the issue of whether the discourse accurately reflected experiences. To treat discourse about experience as a matter of significance in its own right, then, approaches the discourse with a particular set of questions in mind, such as: In what ways does a claim that someone has had an experience authorize that person's opinions or legacy? In what ways do claims about experiences position the experiencers as worthy of deference from the other members of their community? In what ways do such claims delegitimate competing authorities? In what ways do claims about the nature of experiences, such as their ineffability, function to preclude criticism of the experiencer? How are texts that describe experiences used in religious rituals? How are such texts, as material artifacts, produced, preserved, and transmitted? All these questions have a purpose and a value independent of any consideration of whether or not the experiences described actually occurred.

The inquiries that result from a focus on discourse about experience are all worthwhile and essential scholarly pursuits. However, a focus on experiences themselves gives rise to a different set of questions. How and why do people seek religious experiences? What sorts of methods and disciplines do they implement to obtain experience? How are their experiences shaped by their cultural and religious context and by their personal histories? How do experiences affect experiencers and their religious practices? Do experiences bolster people's religious identities and increase the level of commitment they have toward their religious community? Can experiences lead people to discard a religious identity or undermine their commitment to their community? How are experiences implicated in the power structures of the experiencer's society? How do they shape the experiencer's attitudes toward such things as gender, sexuality, race, and class? How are they shaped by the experiencer's preexisting attitudes toward gender, sexuality, race, and class? What is it that religious experiencers experience? What are the causes of religious experiences? Even if religion is not especially or in its essence a matter of interior experience, religious practitioners do have experiences, and their experiences matter. In my view, one of the primary things of lasting importance in the religion-as-experience tradition to the study of religion is that we must attend to practitioners' experiences as we study religion, and that we should be ready to see such experiences as important factors in religious communities.

Even Sharf on occasion gives us an indication that these sorts of questions are legitimate and that the study of religion can concern itself with experiences, not just discourse about experience. In "Experience," he presents and dispenses with the view that the mystic's language "must refer to *something*," counseling, "It is a mistake to approach literary, artistic, or ritual representations as if they referred back to something other than themselves."[31] In contrast, he admits in "Buddhist Modernism":

> There would appear to be ample evidence that those involved in the *vipassanā* revival, or those training under Zen teachers in the Sanbōkyōdan lineage, do experience *something* that they are wont to call *sotāpatti, jhāna,* or *satori.* I readily concede this point; indeed, it would be surprising if those who subjected themselves to the rigors of a Buddhist meditation retreat . . . would *not* undergo some unusual and potentially transformative experiences.[32]

If this is so, then scholars can take representations of experiences as referring to something other than the representations themselves and ask the sorts of questions I have detailed about the causes, significance, and effects of these "unusual and potentially transformative experiences."

The most convincing case to be made for the necessity of a suitable category of experience is to present ethnographic studies that handle experience in a suitable way. A number of recent ethnographies of religious communities attend to the experiences that the practitioners report and treat the experiences as an important factor in the religious life of those communities. These ethnographies demonstrate that accurate descriptions of many religious communities require attention to experiences, not just to discourse about experiences. Theorists of religion should pay attention to these sorts of ethnographies if they are tempted to think that we can do without the category of experience or go without theorizing experience adequately. Other ethnographies, in contrast, downplay or neglect experiences in contexts in which they should not do so and indicate the degree to which religion scholarship would suffer without a viable notion of experience. I will deal with the philosophical challenges confronting the concept of experience later in the book, in chapters 5 and 6. In those chapters I confront the problem of privacy—how it is that we can study something that transpires in other people's consciousness—and the problem of power—how we can correct the tendencies in the study of experience to isolate experiences from social and political power. For the remainder of this chapter, I will survey relevant sectors of the ethnographic record to see what we can learn about the importance of the category of experience and how best to study it.

When Geertz makes a case in an essay later in his career that experience, meaning, and power are "hopelessly entangled," he cites Suzanne Brenner's ethnographic study of Javanese women to show the ongoing relevance of religious experience, in the broad sense of experience as emotions pertaining to religion.[33] The women whom Brenner interviews have all made a decision to begin wearing the veil as an expression of Islamic piety. This decision came, for many of them, at great personal cost. Members of their society, including family and employers, regarded the veil as foreign and extreme. Brenner acknowledges that the women's accounts of their decision to adopt Islamic dress reflect the political rhetoric and ideology of the transnational Islamic renewal movement of the last decades of the twentieth century. However, Brenner does not regard the decision to veil as strictly a political matter. What Brenner finds is that, in many cases, the women's decision to practice what they regarded as a more serious version of their religion was preceded by a personal moral and religious crisis. Brenner explains,

> For several women the decision to take up jilbab [Islamic dress] had been precipitated by a period of profound anxiety; that anxiety had then given way to a feeling of relative calm and a sense of renewal after they had begun to wear jilbab. The immediate cause of the anxiety for three of the women had been an overwhelming fear of dying and, in particular, what death might mean for them if they had failed to fulfill the requirements of Islam. The new awareness of sin they had acquired had led them to a deep distress about how they might suffer in the afterlife as a consequence of their own sinning . . . They experienced deep confusion, self-doubt, and a sense of being out of control. Donning jilbab . . . had alleviated their anxieties about death and given them a new feeling of control over their futures in this life and the next.[34]

The emotions here are distress about sin and calmness about obedient submission to God. But that does not mean that such religious emotions are the end of the story, the sole explanatory factor for the behavior. Brenner does not have the tendency that we find among phenomenologists of religion, to separate religious experience from social and political matters. Rather, she views the women's decision to veil as "simultaneously personal, religious, and political."[35] The "subjective transformation" that the women undergo is shaped by "larger processes of social change occurring in contemporary Indonesia." But the subjective transformation is not a mere epiphenomenon of such processes, an ineffective by-product. The women's subjective transformation is a matter of experience, not mere discourse about experience, and it plays a role in contributing to social changes.[36] It is important to note the importance of the emotional crisis and its resolution for any adequate account of the practice of wearing Islamic dress in this context. Any explanation that referred only to sociopolitical realities, or even nonexperiential religious realities, would omit important details about the Javanese women's religiosity.

Another informative source for our reflections on experience is the ethnographic literature on charismatic and Pentecostal Christianity. Few subjects in religious studies demand explanation as insistently as the spectacular growth of global Pentecostalism. In scarcely over a hundred years, this movement grew from a few individuals in Topeka, Kansas, to hundreds of millions of adherents worldwide. One of the fastest areas of Pentecostal growth has been Latin America, and explanations of the burgeoning movement there tend to focus on anomie, class, or modernization.[37] For example, in regard to anomie, explanations claim that Pentecostalism flourishes because it offers clearly defined social norms for those who are suffering the loss of shared norms brought about by mass migration to urban areas. In regard to class, explanations feature the economic uplift that Pentecostalism offers or the compensations it confers on those excluded from the capitalist class. In regard to modernization, Pentecostalism is successful because its structure mirrors the structure and functioning of the emerging, or at least sought, industrialized economy-state relationship.

Elizabeth E. Brusco's *The Reformation of Machismo* approaches evangelicalism and Pentecostalism in Colombia with dissatisfaction with Marxist and Weberian attempts to explain the rapid growth of evangelicalism in Latin America. She applies a gender analysis, claiming that evangelicalism is a tactic for women to transform male values and behaviors, specifically those associated with the prevalent culture of machismo. Machismo is a pattern of male behavior that involves drinking, aggression, promiscuity, and general neglect of family and household. In response to machismo, women participate in a religion that stridently forbids these very activities and that enjoins men to care for the well-being of their household. The men, for their part, have motivation to convert out of a violent lifestyle in a country with alarmingly high homicide rates.[38] Evangelicalism in Colombia by no means preaches gender egalitarianism, but nevertheless it has achieved success in reforming some of the male habits most detrimental to women's welfare. In short, Brusco theorizes, "Colombian women's involvement in evangelicalism emerges from a . . . disappointment of expectations" regarding male participation in the welfare of the household, and she explains conversion to evangelicalism in Colombia as a "form of female collective action." [39]

Brusco acknowledges that there is more to the Colombians' religion than just a means to redress domestic grievances.[40] However, she doesn't say much about what that more is, and she accords it no role whatsoever in explaining the growth of evangelicalism and Pentecostalism. In other words, religion is a nonentity as far as social explanation is concerned, an epiphenomenon, compared to the real movers like economics and the politics of gender. Rather than treating religion as an aspect of culture in its own right, capable of generating and sustaining motives, aspirations, desires, aversions, loves, and hates that pertain to specifically religious goods, whether real or imagined, Brusco effectively treats religion as a mere means to an end.

I want to be clear that I am not here just wheeling out the standard accusation of reductionism. I do think reductionism is wrongheaded, but we have to be clear what we mean by the term, since oftentimes people treat reductionism and naturalism as equivalent. A naturalist denies that the spirits and gods worshiped and feared by religious communities exist. For many, this denial itself is altogether too chauvinistic, but setting that issue aside for now, I want to note that one can be a naturalist and also an antireductionist. An antireductionist, in the sense I think important, does not want interpreters of religion, naturalist or not, to eliminate distinctively religious vocabulary.[41] One can watch a baseball game or a couple falling in love, believing full well that all that transpires is constituted exhaustively by microparticles and physical forces, but still regarding it a mistake to restrict oneself to the vocabulary of physics, foregoing terms such as ball, strike, and the like, furtive glance, coy smile, and the like, in describing and explaining what one is witnessing. So reductionism should not be equated with naturalism. (And further, we should not assume that the standard charge against antireductionists, that they think religion has an ahistorical, apolitical essence, is necessarily correct. To say that some terms pertain to religion does not mean that they do not also have economic and political ramifications.)

If religion is an aspect of culture, as are art, economics, gender, sexuality, and politics, why cannot religion too be a principle for personal and social action? Once religious rituals, beliefs, and institutions are up and running, why can't particular actions, events, and objects in religious practices be desirable themselves, and not merely instrumentally so? If this is plausible, then it is problematic to assume that the specifically religious goods on offer, whether experiences, values, or beliefs, and whether real or imagined, are not themselves an essential part of any viable explanation as to why a religious movement is gaining and retaining adherents.

At one point in her argument, Brusco notes that phrases such as "the Lord spoke to my heart" are common in male conversion testimonies. She says this phrase "refers to a deep emotional experience of contrition and a longing for personal change."[42] For Brusco, the contrition and desire for change indicate that the illness that usually precedes male conversion has worn down the *machista* attitude of independence, leaving the man receptive to a value system opposed to machismo. But why does not Brusco take the phrase "the Lord spoke to my heart" at face value, as referring not to contrition or longing for change, but to an event in which the convert believes God is communicating a message to him? If the convert did believe God was communicating directly to him, would not that itself, in addition to accompanying attitudes of contrition, play a role in explaining his conversion and subsequent involvement in a church? It is impossible to determine the answer to this question from Brusco's study, because she does not air the voices of the converts sufficiently. Her book includes only two brief male conversion testimonies and about as many female ones.[43] This is not to say that, at the end of the day, the interpreter is obligated to privilege the converts' interpretation as authoritative and inviolable. In many cases, given the divergence in the commitments of scholars and practitioners, this is not possible if the scholars are to take responsibility for their own perspective. Brusco is under no obligation to agree with the Colombians' own interpretations of their conversions. Perhaps it is the case after all that the best explanation for the growth of Colombian Pentecostalism is the social benefits women gain from the religion. But before reaching such a conclusion, should not the scholar at least consult, grapple with, and account for the converts' own take on their motives, desires, aversions, and beliefs? Shouldn't scholars permit the practitioners' self-interpretation to have critical traction on the scholarly assessment, giving the practitioners the right to place the scholars' assumptions under question?

Daniel Míguez, after surveying a number of theories of Pentecostal growth in Latin America, chastises them for failing to attend to specifically religious motives in conversion.[44] According to Míguez, "People also evaluate each religious group in terms of the proposal it makes of who sacred beings are, how they act in the world, how should believers relate to them and so on." In Míguez's account, the process to conversion frequently starts with an initial dissatisfaction with Catholicism. The converts-to-be do not attend mass and may doubt that God exists or is involved their lives. Míguez says, "What initially attracted these (partially) incredulous individuals to the Pentecostal church was exactly that, due to the experiences that its ritual, doctrine, and community life provided, it helped them establish more fulfilling relationships with sacred beings and forces." [45] Míguez emphasizes the role of religious experiences in conversion to and participation in Pentecostal communities. He says that the reports of most of the Pentecostals whom he interviewed show, "by referring to strong emotional experiences in ritual contexts, that the ritual and doctrinal assertions of sacred intervention in daily life are particularly significant in framing the [Pentecostal] identity." [46] The experiences Míguez's interviewees report include dreams, visions, healings, and episodes that they describe as the Lord touching their heart. R. Andrew Chesnut, too, places religious experience squarely at the center of his explanation of Pentecostal growth, this time in Brazil. Specifically Chesnut sees experiences of faith healing as the principal explanatory factor.[47] Were experience to drop out of the scholarly lexicon, the sorts of studies and explanations that Míguez and Chesnut conduct would be impossible. Of course, to posit experiences as an explanatory factor in the growth of a religious movement just pushes the question one step further: if experiences cause conversions to Pentecostalism, what causes the experiences? A variety of types of explanations are available, depending on the methodological orientation of the inquirer, from Feuerbachian projection to psychoanalytic dynamics, to supernatural causes. But however scholars address this question, the answer will have to make reference to experiences and employ, whether implicitly or explicitly, an account of what brings experiences about and what in turn effects they have.

R. Marie Griffith does not take explanation as her objective in *God's Daughters,* her study of North American charismatic women. But her treatment of subjectivity, religious experience, and power serves as another useful source for reflection on some important roles religious experience plays in religious communities. Like Brusco, Griffith brings feminist commitments to a religious community that is illiberal in nature in that it explicitly advocates patriarchal structures of power in congregational and domestic life. Also like Brusco, Griffith searches for the tendencies toward female empowerment within that structure.

Griffith's study concerns the charismatic women's organization Women's Aglow. She gives special treatment to the manner in which the doctrine that women are to submit to male authority functions in the lives of the women. She finds that within the overall context of subordination, which is disempowering, the women employ a number of strategies and tactics to elevate their own status, to care for other women and receive care from them, to bolster their self-esteem, and to criticize and reform behavior of men, especially husbands. Religious experience is an essential element in the empowerment their religion offers them; in particular, experiences of the persons of the Christian Trinity, God the Father, Jesus, and the Holy Spirit, in prayer. Griffith writes, "Women like those in Aglow claim to have found the true path to liberation and this-worldly fulfillment in a committed relationship with a Jesus who is at once father figure and lover, a relationship sustained and nurtured by communicative prayer." [48] The women's prayer purportedly involves, in Griffith's words, a "direct and immediate experience of God." [49] At times the experience is subtle, and at times it is more pronounced, involving visions or sensations of "liquid love" or "extreme heat surging through" one's body. [50] Oftentimes the experiences involve, according to the Aglow members, emotional and/or physical healing. The women's religious experiences are at times psychological in nature, but they may also be bodily, as in weeping, speaking in tongues, verbally relaying messages ostensibly received from God, and undergoing events that the charismatics term being "slain in the spirit," which consist in falling to the ground and lying motionless.

Such experiences have a tremendous impact on the women. Prayer, with its attendant experiences, is the "chief and most tangible practice wherein participants' social and religious identities are constituted," Griffith says. She explains, "A person's sense that God listens to her, cares about her sufferings, and delivers her from pain gives birth to a distinct sense of self-awareness, the feeling of discovering a self that was lost or receiving a new self in the place of one that was 'dead.'"[51] A woman's belief that she is in an intimate, personal relationship with God bolsters her own sense of efficacy and significance, transforms her interpretation of and orientation toward tragedies and difficulties in her life, and motivates her to actively care for and receive care from others, importantly, other women.

Griffith, Míguez, and Chesnut show the importance of giving experience a proper place in the study of religion. The religious practices that they describe are what they are in part because of the experiences the practitioners have had. None of these three is concerned to ask about the causal origins of the practitioners' experiences, and this is an important question for the study of religion.[52] However, whatever factors brought about the experiences, we have no reason to think that those factors themselves, if they existed without experiences, could bring about the same results that occur with the experiences. Also, we have no reason to think that mere discourse about experience and not the sorts of experiences to which the Pentecostals' discourse refers could bring about the effects that the experiences do. Experiences make a difference.

Griffith and Brenner are particularly significant for my purposes because they show us not just that it is important to study experiences when analyzing religious practices; they give us insights into how we need to study experiences. Specifically, Brenner and Griffith manage to attend to both meaning and power as they discuss experiences. Both Brenner and Griffith treat experiences as a matter thoroughly situated in the local religious and social context. For Griffith, the practitioners have experiences of the love of God the Father and Jesus. For Brenner, they experience anxiety about sin and then an emotional condition the Javanese call "awareness," which accompanies their acknowledgement of their responsibilities in respect to Islam. Unlike the phenomenologists of religion, Brenner and Griffith are not interpreting these experiences as any kind of universal event. Furthermore, in Brenner's and Griffith's accounts, the experiences that the women undergo are thoroughly implicated in various power relationships. The experiences themselves are shaped by the women's society's power structures and the experiences in turn shape those structures and the women's attitudes toward them. For Brenner, wearing the veil challenges the authority structures in the Muslim women's societies, including traditional Javanese norms, such as the norm that children defer to the authority of their parents. The women also view their action as oriented toward the transformation of their society, a step toward bringing about a greater degree of conformity to God's will in their society. Furthermore, veiling is an instance in which the women exercise power over their own body and life. It is a "gesture of autonomy," Brenner says, even if it involves constraints, such as greater scrutiny from others, as well.[53]

Griffith too attends to various operations of power as she studies Women's Aglow. She discusses the economic power that the leaders of Aglow have relative to the rank and file members, for example. But most of her discussion of power dynamics concerns gender. She spends considerable energy tracing the gender relationships among the women and their husbands, fathers, and pastors. Experiences are directly implicated in these gender relationships, since women experience God and Jesus as a father and/or lover. The God whom they experience and to whom they submit is male, just as they are enjoined by their religion to submit to the earthly men in their lives. However, Griffith wants us to see that things are more complex than this embrace of subordination would appear. The women's endorsement of a submissive relation to the divine and earthly males in their lives generates some forms of empowerment, Griffith argues. The women's experience of God as male and their belief that submission to earthly men is a form of submission to God does not just result in subordination. It also provides a model for ideal male behavior, and thus a paradigm to criticize men when they deviate from the ideal. "While [Aglow women] are preoccupied with pleasing an undeniably male God, the very contrast in their vision between God and most earthly men slides into an expedient critique of the gender ideals preserving the status quo."[54] The ideal love that they encounter in God provides a norm according to which they can judge the behavior of their earthly husbands and fathers. The doctrines and texts that the women regard as true support these gender norms, but experiences of God as a lover or father play a crucial role, too. Experiencing God as a powerful male, father or husband, legitimates the corresponding human male figures' power.

In these works by Griffith and Brenner, we have exemplary treatments of religious experience. They are exemplary because they achieve something that few others have been able to do: they successfully attend to experiences, meanings, and power. They show us what is at stake with the contemporary suspicions against the category of experience, since their studies would not be possible without a robust notion of experience. Griffith and Brenner view discourse about experience as important, but they are quite willing to view experiences themselves as an integral part of the religious practices of the people whom they are studying. They treat experiences as something that can have real effects in the lives and communities of the practitioners, not just an epiphenomenal by-product of nonexperiential factors. As a matter of ethnographic methodology, we have in Griffith and Brenner a clear example of the viability and fruitfulness of scholarly attention to religious experience.

UNRESOLVED THEORETICAL ISSUES

I have appealed to ethnography and historiography to point out the importance of attending to experience, meaning, and power. I have only mentioned a handful of cases, but I could cite numerous others, and hopefully I have said enough to motivate the desirability of retaining experience, meaning, and power as scholarly categories.

However, even if it is desirable and useful for scholars to attend to all three things, theoretical challenges face all three. Unless those challenges can be met, we might doubt that we can obtain sufficiently robust accounts of all three categories to assure ourselves that they warrant a central place in our methodology, no matter how much we would like them to do so. I will outline here what the principal theoretical challenges are and then in Part 2 set out to respond to them convincingly.

The principal theoretical challenge facing the idea of power is not so much a problem with the existing theories of power, such as that of Butler, Bourdieu, or Foucault. Of course we might quibble with this or that specific aspect of their theories, but there is broad support for these figures in religious studies. The real problem is how to integrate the analysis of power with attention to meaning and experience, especially experience. Power approaches tend to focus on bodily practices, not conscious experiences, and it will take some work to show that we can have both.

The principal theoretical challenges facing meaning are the problem of privacy and the problem of power. Meaning is a strange entity; it seems not to be strictly a product of the physical, nonmental world, nor is it merely in the subject's head. Ethnography's status as an "objective science" depends on cultural meaning being in the "things observed" and not the mind of the observer, Masuzawa points out, and, if culture is in part in the mind of the observer, the very notion of participant observation as the way to do ethnography is dependent on the "Archimedean point" of the ethnographer's subjective vantage point.[55] This is a view of subjectivity that that is contestable and so, if rejected, leads to skepticism about the possibility of anthropological knowledge. Perhaps ethnographic findings are really just the fictional imaginings of the ethnographer. To answer these worries, we need a thoroughly social account of meaning, one that does not depend on any mysterious, mentalistic entities, like intentions, beliefs, or consciousness, conceived of as sequestered away from the public world. Second, in relation to the problem of power, we need an account of meaning in which meaning and power are intertwined. Third, we need an account of how to construe the relationship between meaning and experience that advances us beyond the account of the phenomenologists of religion.

In regard to religious experience, we have once again a problem of privacy and of power, and these are more severe than the corresponding problems in relation to meaning, because experience is seemingly far more subjective and interior than meaning is. Sharf has raised a powerful challenge to the study of experience in his claim that experiences are too private for us to refer to them meaningfully. Even if we think that he is wrong about this, a full response has to answer the philosophical worries about the possibility of studying someone else's conscious states. Furthermore, the theories of religious experience that have been influential in the academy, whether of the phenomenologists of religion, of the perennialists, or of the constructivists, have all ignored issues of power in their theorizing.

I turn now to my attempts to reconceive experience, meaning, and power in ways that meet these theoretical challenges, a task that will occupy the remainder of the book.

PART TWO

4

Meaning and Power

∽——

Words have meanings. If you say, "Il pleut," and someone asks, "What does that mean?" I can answer straightforwardly, "It means that it's raining." That is all well and good. But some have thought that meaning should be a key notion for the study of religion, and when it comes to this proposal, things are not straightforward at all. A distinguished approach to the human sciences elevated meaning and the interpretation of meaning to a place of central importance, as we saw in Part 1 of this book. But that approach has faltered in the face of two significant challenges: the problems of privacy and power. The problem of privacy bespeaks the questionable location of meaning. Is it out there in the world? Is it in the mind of the interpreter? Or somewhere in between? If cultural meanings are not out there in the world, then the study of religion will not be suitably objective, and the meanings that scholars assign to a society will be fictions of their imagination, as James Clifford and Vincent Crapanzano charge against Clifford Geertz.[1] But meanings aren't part of the physical constitution of the objects and events that we observe, alongside their molecules. So are they subjective instead? The way that anthropologists have approached this problem, says Tomoko Masuzawa, is to appeal to the idea of participant observation, but she charges that this idea of cultural meaning supposes an "Archimedean point," a "seat of observation," from which the ethnographer surveys the "complex whole" of the culture in question. If we question the "ideology" of the "singular point participant of observation" and its "heightened rhetoric of empirical reality and self-evidence of data," then "the gossamer reality of the 'complex whole' will likely begin to appear no more substantial than the phrase itself."[2] Addressing these difficulties means showing that meaning is not problematically private and subjective but rather social in nature.

The problem of power has to do with the fact that the primary voices in constructing the category of meaning and the interpretive approach to the human sciences, Paul Ricoeur, Hans-Georg Gadamer, and Clifford Geertz, have not adequately accounted for the operations of social power in symbolic meaning and its interpretation. In this chapter, I will discuss the problems of privacy and power in relation to meaning by extracting some key Wittgensteinian insights from Clifford Geertz, developing them beyond the accounts that he gives of them in his writings, and then connecting them to social power in a number of ways.

If meaning is not something that we can casually dismiss and carry on without, as I have argued, we need to address the significant theoretical problems that confront hermeneutics and separate the unwieldy baggage that comes with philosophical hermeneutics from its legitimate resources. Obviously, it would take a book or more to do justice to any tradition involving such complex and enormous figures as Schleiermacher, Dilthey, Weber, Heidegger, Gadamer, Ricoeur, and many others besides. To make the task manageable, I will supply a focused treatment of a single figure, rather than attempt to grapple with the hermeneutic tradition as a whole. The figure whom I am selecting, however, is neither Ricoeur nor Gadamer, but Geertz.

I find Geertz the more promising person to evaluate in relation to the interpretive approach to the study of religion for two reasons. First, Geertz was an experienced ethnographer of religion, with theoretical and philosophical interests, so he exemplifies the aspiration to do theory of religion in close conversation with religion as it is lived and practiced, whereas Gadamer and Ricoeur argue in the abstract, and even when their work concerns religion, it does not have detailed and extensive reference to religion as practiced. One of the aims of this present study is to conduct theoretical inquiry in conversation with lived religion, to keep theory relevant to and constrained by concrete practices. Second, I find both Gadamer and Ricoeur problematically vague on key issues. For example, both of them construe the nature of texts and the process of coming to understand texts in terms that are quite imprecise. Gadamer likes to speak of the achievement of understanding as a fusion of horizons.[3] But what, specifically, is a horizon or a fusion of horizons? Such language has an intuitive appeal and a nice ring to it, but when it comes to the particulars, it is not entirely clear what we are talking about. Whatever Gadamer means by horizons are not observable entities. Do they exist in people's heads or in their linguistic practices? Gadamer wants to deny that fusing horizons is a "mysterious communion of souls," but he speaks of transposing oneself into the text (or other's) "situation" or "standpoint" in vague ways. We must "imagine the other situation" and "put ourselves in someone else's shoes."[4] But how do we know we have achieved this, and what specifically does it involve? How does one know that horizons have fused? Not only do we not receive answers on these questions, but we don't even get resources from Gadamer that could point in the right direction. Ricoeur uses the term "world" or "worlds" in similarly problematic ways. He speaks of interpretation as explicating the type of being-in-the-world unfolded in front of the text.[5] Another time, he speaks of the world as an "aura," and meaning too is something that has an aura in which we live.[6] A world is also an ensemble of references opened up by the texts, and to understand a text is to light up our situation or to expose oneself to the text.[7] The meaning of a text is a "direction of thought opened up by the text." All of these terms are analogies and/or problematically imprecise. What are an "aura" and its "light" specifically? By what criteria would one determine whether or not we are lit up or properly exposed? What is a "direction of thought"? How do the various worlds of particular texts and individuals relate to the common world that we all inhabit together, if there is such a thing? None of this can be satisfactorily addressed in the terms that Gadamer and Ricoeur provide. In fact, on many of these counts, the language (such as horizons, auras, and light) is influenced strongly by the phenomenological tradition, and for those who break from the phenomenological tradition, it is not clear what sense or use can be made of the terms.

Geertz has his own problems of this nature. He is eclectic in his theoretical influences, counting among them such figures as Weber, Ludwig Wittgenstein, Talcott Parsons, Kenneth Burke, Ricoeur, Gadamer, Gilbert Ryle, and many others besides. He does not write or think systematically. "I don't do systems," he shamelessly asserts.[8] As a result, it is often difficult to ascertain what the specific meanings of his key theoretical terms are. Further, he makes claims that seem incompatible with one another, as we shall see, and it is not always clear how to reconcile the tension between the claims. What's more, since he counts Ricoeur and Gadamer as primary influences, it seems he stands at risk to inherit the problems with their terminological apparatuses mentioned just above.

Nevertheless, despite these problems, Geertz has a great redeeming feature that makes him a more promising person to appropriate than Gadamer or Ricoeur, and that is his appeal to Wittgenstein.[9] The Wittgensteinian element to his work is the one I will highlight as I present a version of Geertz that I think is of ongoing relevance to the study of religion. Gadamer and Ricoeur speak of meaning in imprecise ways that are beholden to the phenomenological tradition, but Wittgenstein, in advocating meaning as use, tells us to look at how a term or sentence is used in a social practical context if we want to determine what its meaning is. These uses are publicly observable, and so by accounting for the circumstances in which a symbol is applied and the consequences of its application, we can give a detailed account of whether someone has successfully understood or interpreted the meaning of the symbol, and we don't have to worry about the "aura" or "light" of meaning, the "fusion of horizons," or even the "world."

However, Geertz has other tendencies besides Wittgensteinian ones, and my critical appropriation of Geertz will not evade the resulting tensions but point them out. Having identified the tensions in Geertz's work, I will not strive to harmonize these tensions or demonstrate that at the end of the day Geertz's theory of culture and religion is internally coherent. Nothing is at stake for my own project whether he is internally coherent, and I will remain officially agnostic as to whether or not his thought is unified. (Unofficially, I have my doubts.) What matters to me is take Geertz at his (Wittgensteinian) best, disregarding the conflicting tendencies in his work, to show that he has insights that merit our attention and that make him an essential resource for the contemporary study of religion.

For my purposes, what matters most in Geertz's corpus are his accounts of symbols, symbolic meaning, cultural systems, and interpretation as thick description. Those are the ideas of his that are most relevant for my attempt to show that meaning deserves an ongoing role in religious studies. In addition to these ideas, Geertz has numerous other influential views concerning the study of religion. I mentioned a number of these in chapter 1: his definition of religion as a system of symbols that establishes moods and motivations in people in respect to a general order of existence; his appeal to Meaning (with a capital M, as in the Meaning of life, death, and suffering) as something for which people have a need and that religion addresses; and his account of rituals as events that fuse the practitioner's worldview and ethos. I can, for the purposes of this book, remain agnostic on these ideas. For instance, Geertz's particular account of religion as that which pertains to a general or cosmic order of existence and the specifics of his definition of religion are not central to my own project.

I should say though that I think Asad makes a mistake in saying that "there cannot be a universal definition of religion, not only because its constituent elements and relationships are historically specific, but because that definition is itself the historical product of discursive processes."[10] Here Asad confuses the (historical and linguistic) circumstances under which a word originates and perpetuates and that to which a word refers.[11] The referent of a word, like "religion," is not limited to the provenance of the word's origin. (I can use the word "Mesozoic" to refer to an era in which no one was around to utter the word.) Furthermore, Asad mistakenly concludes that the specification of criteria by which one thing is distinguished from another, religion from politics, for example, entails that the things being distinguished have mutually exclusive essences, and so something cannot simultaneously pertain to both things; that is, something cannot be both religious and political.[12]

As for Geertz's views on the need that humans have for the "upmarket sense of 'the Meaning of Life,'" this is another item that I will leave aside.[13] I have no doubt that humans often do need cosmic frameworks of order and that they often do experience anxiety at the prospect of the absence of such an order, and I have no doubt that religion often does supply just the sort of cosmic framework that people need. But religion does plenty of other things besides this, and it is not important to me, as it is for Geertz, to construe the need for Meaning as a universal human trait. Finally, the clean distinction between ethos and worldview that Geertz wants to make and the role that rituals have in integrating the two are unimportant to me. The fusion of worldview and ethos in ritual is perhaps plausible for how rituals sometimes operate, but dubious as a universal account of how rituals always operate.

Setting these matters aside, we can turn to the things of most importance: does Geertz have a viable account of symbolic meaning and its interpretation? To try to sort out the answer to this question involves some complicated interpretive issues on how best to understand Geertz on some key matters. The unsystematic nature of his thought can lead to divergent interpretations of what his views are. At times, the reader might be tempted to think that Geertz's corpus is itself best described in the terms that he applies to cultures: a "multiplicity of complex conceptual structures, many of them superimposed upon or knotted into one another, which are at once strange, irregular, and inexplicit."[14] In fact, I find three key issues about which Geertz makes statements that are hard to reconcile with other things that he says. First, at times Geertz speaks as though he is committed to an understanding of symbols as public matters, and at other times he speaks as though he thinks of symbolic meaning as something that is private and interior. Second, Geertz oftentimes speaks of the symbols that anthropologists interpret as things that are transparent to the native users of the symbols. This has a problematic implication. If the task of the ethnographer is to interpret symbols and if symbols are transparent to informants, then the ethnographer's study is limited to those things that the informants could consciously avow. The problem is that surely in addition to those features of a group's social life about which they consciously know, the social scientist wants to attend to the features of a group's social life about which they are unaware. But if, as Geertz says, social science is the study of symbolic meaning and symbolic meaning is avowable by the informants, then there is no place for the study of behavior that has significance of which the practitioners are unaware. Since social theorists concerned with power are oftentimes keenly interested in unconscious motives and goals, this makes it hard to see how Geertzian anthropology could be compatible with power-oriented approaches. However, at times, Geertz seems to have a place for symbols as something of which the practitioners are not consciously aware. Third, Geertz on occasions speaks of culture as something that does not have social effects, and so we could conclude that it is disconnected from social power relationships, and at other times he speaks as though it does have social effects. All three of these issues get to the heart of the matters most pressing for my own project, and an appropriation of Geertz requires getting a handle on these problems. I will treat each in turn, pointing out that there are divergent tendencies in Geertz's work and counseling that we endorse some of those tendencies and ignore others. After all, what is important is not whether or not we side with Geertz in toto, but which of his ideas are live options.

So first, we have the matter of Geertz's views on whether meaning is mentalistic and private or social and public. Asad says that Geertz has a problematic commitment to belief, which Asad understands as a private, mental state and that Geertz wrongly thinks of the connection between religious theory and religious practice "as essentially cognitive, as a means by which a disembodied mind can identify religion from an Archimedean point."[15] He says that in Geertz's account of symbols, "cognitive questions are mixed up . . . with communicative ones."[16] Nancy Frankenberry and Hans Penner criticize Geertz for thinking of meanings as things that are "directly present to the inspecting mind."[17] In a response to Frankenberry and Penner and Asad, Kevin Schilbrack points out that it is strange for Asad to attribute to Geertz the view that religion is a private mental state, since Geertz so frequently affirms that meanings are public and social in nature, and he explicitly sides with Wittgenstein's rejection of meaning as private.[18] How are we to respond to such divergent interpretations of Geertz's views?

Geertz does repeatedly take pains to present his understanding of meaning as public, and he explicitly rejects the view that meaning is a private, interior state. Cultural patterns, he tells us, "lie outside the boundaries of the individual organism as such in that intersubjective world of common understandings."[19] Meaning is "as public as marriage and as observable as agriculture"; it is not "a psychological phenomenon, a characteristic of someone's mind, personality, cognitive structure, or whatever."[20] "Culture," Geertz tells us, is "public because meaning is." He appeals to Wittgenstein's and others' "generalized attack on privacy theories of meaning"[21] and says that "it is necessary to see to it that the news of it reaches anthropology."[22] He tells us, in a passage particularly important for my purposes, that social action, artifacts, and states of consciousness "draw their meaning from the role they play (Wittgenstein would say their 'use') in an ongoing pattern of life, not from any intrinsic relationships they bear to one another."[23]

So what could lead people like Asad, Frankenberry, and Penner to overlook all this? One problem is that Geertz also speaks of meanings as conceptions. It is hard to think of conceptions as anything but private, mentalistic things, in the absence of some explicit account of conceptions that clarifies the way in which conceptions are public and social. Geertz gives us no such account. A symbol, Geertz tells us, is "any object, act, event, quality, or relation which serves as a vehicle for a conception—the conception is the symbol's 'meaning.'"[24] Objects, acts, qualities, events, and relations are no doubt generally public. But where are we to find the conceptions for which these things are vehicles? It would be strange to think of the conceptions as inhering in the objects and events themselves, so they must be in people's minds. But if that is so, then it seems that Geertz is susceptible to just the sorts of charges that Asad presents, and Schilbrack has not sufficiently attended to Geertz's appeal to conceptions and the problematic associations with that term.

Perhaps Geertz has a way out of this dilemma, precisely in his statement that states of consciousness (and perhaps a conception is such a state) themselves "draw their meaning from the role they play (Wittgenstein would say their 'use') in an ongoing pattern of life." If mental states themselves are not private and interior but derive their significance from their role in a pattern of life, that is, shared practices oriented toward shared goods and shared ends, then it is to misread Geertz to think of conceptions or beliefs as private, interior mental states. Furthermore, Geertz's appeals to Gilbert Ryle, who rejects the "ghost in the machine" view of mind, and to pragmatists like John Dewey are important in this respect. It is not enough to label a certain item as mentalistic without asking the question if the mental, for Geertz, is private and subjective in the way that Asad seems to assume. When we pose this question to Geertz, we find that "'mind' is a term denoting a class of skills, propensities, capacities, tendencies, habits . . . it is neither an action nor a thing, but an organized system of dispositions which finds its manifestation in some actions and some things."[25] This does not seem problematically private.

This is in fact the way that I would prefer to read Geertz, but the problem is that he appeals to Susanne Langer's *Philosophy in a New Key* at the very moment that he introduces symbols as vehicles of conceptions. The influence of Langer on Geertz at this crucial point has not received sufficient attention. Although Langer presents interpretive difficulties of her own, at times she speaks in ways that sound not only mentalistic but that put her afoul of Donald Davidson's arguments against the possibility of a scheme/content distinction. To be clear, I am providing here a different rationale for attributing a scheme/content division to Geertz than Frankenberry and Penner do. They think that his use of "model of" and "model for" commits him to such a view. Geertz thinks that religion serves as a model of reality, that is, a representation of it, and a model for it, that is, a plan for how to modify and produce things. But Schilbrack convincingly refutes Frankenberry and Penner's concern by pointing out that it is perfectly consistent with Geertz's discussion of model of and model for to understand him as construing religious symbols as standing in relationship not to "prelinguistic or nonconceptualized noumena," but to "linguistically mediated, already conceptualized aspects of reality."[26] This sounds right to me, as far as Geertz's discussion of models of and models for goes. But his account of symbols as conceptions does not so clearly avoid the scheme/content dualism problem, insofar as his views coincide with Langer. For example, Langer says,

> Our merest sense-experience is a process of *formulation*. The world that actually meets our senses is not a world of "things," about which we are invited to discover facts as soon as we have codified the necessary logical language to do so; the world of pure sensation is so complex, so fluid and full, that sheer sensitivity to stimuli would only encounter what William James has called (in characteristic phrase) "a blooming, buzzing confusion." Out of this bedlam our sense-organs must select certain predominant forms, if they are to make report of *things* and not of mere dissolving sense. The eye and the ear must have their logic—their "categories of understanding," if you like the Kantian idiom, or their "primary imagination," in Coleridge's version of the same concept. An object is not a datum, but a form construed by the sensitive and intelligent organ, a form which is at once the experienced individual thing and a symbol for the concept of it, for *this sort of thing*.[27]

Similarly, "The symbolic materials given to our senses, the *Gestalten* or fundamental perceptual forms which invite us to construe the pandemonium of sheer impression into a world of things and occasions, belong to the 'presentational' order. They furnish the elementary abstractions in terms of which ordinary sense-experience is understood."[28] This sort of theory, according to which there is raw, unorganized sense data—the content—that the mind configures and organizes according to a symbolic and conceptual scheme is exactly the sort of thing that Davidson argues against. (His point is that concepts couldn't organize something undifferentiated; rather, the only thing that you can organize are items that have already been individuated.)[29] Of course, just because a person appeals to an idea from another person does not commit him or her to the entire project of the other person. So perhaps it is not fair to attribute to Geertz all the specific views that Langer has on symbols, conceptions, and sense experience. In *Islam Observed*, though, Geertz speaks in ways that resonate with the scheme/content division that Langer describes: "Religious patterns . . . are frames of perception, symbolic screens through which experience is interpreted."[30] So the tension in Geertz on this matter is that at times he sounds like he is thoroughly Wittgensteinian and has no privatistic account of meanings or symbols, and at other times it seems as though his notion of symbols is committed to a private, interior state of mind and to a scheme/content dualism besides.

The second interpretive difficulty with Geertz is the question of whether the Geertzian ethnographer is limited to the study of things of which the informants are aware and restricted from studying unconscious behavior, motives, habits, and goals. In Geertz's understanding of religion, as we have seen, there are three key terms: interpretation, meaning, and symbols. A symbol is some action, event, or relation to which a conception is associated. The conception is the meaning of the symbol. What I want to highlight here is that for Geertz the conception that is the meaning of the symbol is accessible to the religious practitioner. The meaning of the symbol is "the meaning particular social actions have *for* the actors whose actions they are," Geertz says.[31] The Geertzian anthropologist reads the culture "over the shoulders" of the people whose culture it is.[32] Scholarly descriptions "must be cast in terms of the constructions" the practitioners "place upon what they live through," that is, "the formulae they use to define what happens to them." The anthropologist's account "must be cast in terms of the interpretations to which persons of a particular denomination subject their experience."[33]

No doubt that in many cases this is just right. Some symbolic actions express a concept, and the concept is the meaning of the symbolic action. So in the Catholic mass, when the Eucharistic host is held high, the elevation expresses the concept of heavenly realities, in opposition to mundane ones.[34] When someone kneels during the ceremony, submission to both God and the church hierarchy is expressed. In many cases, these sorts of conceptions would be accessible to the practitioners. This is not to say that people are always consciously aware at the very moment of the meanings of the symbols with which they are dealing. Frequently we respond to familiar symbols tacitly, more or less automatically, without giving any attention to the meaning of the symbol. I don't have to recite to myself, "That means hello" when you wave to me. I just wave back. But I know that waving is a form of greeting, a way of nonverbally saying hello, and I could tell you so if you asked me. So in speaking of conscious awareness of the meaning of symbols in this context I do not mean to imply that we are always, at the instant, consciously aware of the meaning of the symbol. I mean that if asked we could say what the symbol means.

However, not every action or artifact that we would want to study is like this. For Michel Foucault and Pierre Bourdieu, there is a large class of actions whose point is not to express concepts but rather to shape the actor into a particular type of subject. In this view, people are socialized into particular habits that dispose them to feel, desire, perceive, and comport themselves in determinate ways. One result of that process is to reinforce the social stratifications of society. One acquires habits peculiar to one's social status, and thus one comes to regard one's social status as fixed and given, rather than historically contingent. So, for example, Iris Marion Young gives the example of "throwing like a girl," where she says that women are socialized to occupy their surrounding space timidly whereas men are socialized to occupy their surrounding space assertively.[35]For Young, this is one part of a larger pattern of different social behaviors between women and men that reinforces attitudes that take men as superior to women. The crucial thing here is that this shaping of bodily habits is not happening at a conscious, conceptual level. For the socialization to work in the way that Bourdieu and Young think that it does, the subject can't be consciously aware of the effects of her socialization. But if the cultural theorist is restricted to the study of symbols, and symbols are things that have meaning *for* the practitioners, then the sort of behavior that Young highlights seems off the table.

But there are times where Geertz says things that complicate any simple reading of him as rejecting the study of unconscious behavior.[36]For one thing, Geertz distinguishes between the ethnographer's use of "experience-near" concepts, which are the concepts that an informant would "naturally and effortlessly" use to describe the symbols in his environs and "experience-distant" concepts that are theoretically laden and are available to the ethnographer or cultural theorist but very likely not to the informant. "'Love' is an experience-near concept," Geertz explains. "'Object cathexis' is an experience-distant one."[37]This helps things somewhat, but I do not think that it gets us too far, because the notion of the hermeneutical circle implies that experience-distant concepts are, in some sense that Geertz does not fully specify, responsible to the experience-near concepts. But what people like Young give us is something quite different: an explicit willingness to apply scholarly interpretations to behavior for which no relevant corresponding experience-near concepts exist. Perhaps though this is too hasty of a dismissal of Geertz. Geertz initially characterizes the ethnographer's task as trying to "figure out what the devil [the informants] are up to," and he admits, "In one sense, of course, no one knows this better than they do themselves." However, he quickly qualifies that thought: "But in another sense, that simple truism is simply not true. People use experience-near concepts spontaneously, unself-consciously, as it were colloquially; they do not, except fleetingly and on occasion, recognize that there are any 'concepts' involved at all."[38]This does not come out and deny that people would be unable to express the meaning of the concepts that they are unself-consciously using, but it could be taken to imply such a denial. Similarly, in another context, Geertz says of the Javanese *wajang*, a shadow-puppet play with religious significance,

> The average man "enjoys" the *wajang* without explicitly interpreting its meaning. Yet, in the same way as the circle organizes Oglala experience, whether the individual Sioux is able to explicate its significance, or indeed has any interest

in doing so, so the sacred symbols of the *wajang*—the music, characters, the action itself—give form to the ordinary Javanese experience.[39]

Here Geertz seems to imply that the symbols have meaning whether or not the Sioux or Javanese individuals are able to say what the meaning is. I do not see how to reconcile this possibility with Geertz's claim elsewhere that scholarly descriptions are "our own constructions of other people's constructions of what they and their compatriots are up to,"[40] since in this case, the informants are unable to give a construction of what they are up to in relation to the circle or the *wajang*, or at least it does not matter to Geertz here whether or not they are able to. So in some parts of his corpus symbolic meanings are things practitioners know, and in other places they seem not necessarily to be.

The third and final interpretive difficulty in regard to Geertz's views on interpretation and symbolic meaning is that at times he dissociates power from culture, whereas at other times he seems to say that power and meaning are complexly intertwined. The former view is problematic because it presents culture as outside the contestations and struggles of social power relations, a viewpoint that would be anathema to gender theorists, postcolonialists, and race theorists, among others. Geertz says, for example, that culture is a context in which things can be described and interpreted, but it is not a power to which "social events, behaviors, institutions, or processes can be causally attributed."[41] In chapter 3, I challenged this notion of the relation between culture and behavior by pointing out, with Albert Raboteau's help, the example of slave religion as a practice in which culture and power are very much intertwined. Or consider a situation of ethnic conflict. In such a situation, members of one group symbolize the other group as subhuman, as vermin or cockroaches, for example. This symbolic activity licenses an attitude among the ingroup that the members of the outgroup are unfit to live, and horrific violence results. What sense does it make to say that the cultural activity of symbolizing is not a cause of the violence? Perhaps Geertz subscribes to maxims like that of the bumper-sticker: "Guns don't kill people; people kill people." In that case, Geertz's view would be that culture, as a system of symbolic meanings, doesn't kill people, but rather it is people appropriating symbols who kill people. This does indeed seem to be Geertz's take on the matter, when he speaks of the cultural aspect of an action as distinct from the social-structural aspect, relegating meaning to the former and social causality to the latter.[42]

I don't think, however, that the meaningfulness of an action can be abstracted from the causes and effects of the action. An intentional action, for example, is performed for a reason, and it is plausible to think of the reason as a cause of the action. So we can reconstruct the practical reasoning of someone who commits ethnic violence, say, between Hutus and Tutsis, in these terms: "This person is Tutsi. Tutsis do not deserve to live. Therefore, I will kill this person." The action that results from this chain of practical reasoning is an attempted murder. In many accounts of action, the belief, "Tutsis do not deserve to live," is a cause of the action. The belief is thoroughly cultural, in that it involves symbols, concepts, and meanings— everything of which Geertz says culture consists. It would seem entirely artificial to rend this belief from the action of the attempted murder and say that it was merely the *meaning* of the action and not a cause. Separating culture from the causes of actions conflicts with the nature of practical reasoning. Furthermore, in cases where violence is involved, separating culture from power insulates culture in ways that would prevent us from seeing the horrific power that cultural items, like racist and ethnocentric beliefs, can have. At times, though, Geertz seems to admit that culture can affect power. When he speaks of symbols as things that "establish powerful, pervasive, long-lasting moods and motivations," he seemingly admits that culture affects behavior, and thus, would affect behavior relevant to social power structures.[43]

I am now in a position to propose the aspects of Geertz's account of interpretation and meaning that are still indispensable for the study of religion and identify those that can be ignored or rejected, or at the very least that require supplementation with theoretical resources that Geertz does not himself have. We have looked at conflicting textual evidence on three key issues for Geertz's theory of culture, meaning, and interpretation: First, are symbolic meanings private and subjective in nature? Second, are we limited to the "native's point of view" when analyzing culture? Third, is culture a matter thoroughly infused with power?

What I want to suggest is that we take Geertz at his best (by my lights at least) on all three of these questions and discount the passages that conflict, at least apparently, with his more promising ideas. In other words, we should understand interpretation, symbolic meaning, and culture in the following terms. First, symbolic meanings are public and social, as Wittgenstein has it, and the meaning of a symbol is determined by its use or role in a set of social practices. Any appeal to conceptions in explicating the matter should regard conceptions themselves as things that are public and social in nature and have their meaningfulness by virtue of their use or role in social practices. Second, the "native's point of view," the practitioners' own account of their practices, is an essential resource in cultural studies and something to which social scientists should be responsible, but they are not restricted to it. Third, culture or, more specifically, symbolic meaning is indeed a matter that is thoroughly infused with power.

If we take these aspects of Geertz's thought as the promising ones, then we can preserve an account of meaning and interpretation in religious studies. What's more, Geertzian thick description is an appropriate methodological touchstone, as it is the fitting response to the complexities of human culture. It appropriately calls for close attention to myriads of details because cultural items have the significance that they do only in the larger cultural context and in relation to a whole host of other cultural items. This gives us the theoretical direction that we need to do justice to the ubiquity of meaning.

However, what Geertz gives us, while valuable as a theoretical direction, is not sufficient as it stands. Sorting through the relevant passages in Geertz's corpus, in all their complexity and messiness, indicates that we still have further work to do to achieve a theoretical understanding of meaning that not only avoids the problematic tendencies in Geertz's work but also gives us a way to integrate meaning with theoretical focuses on experience and power. So what do we need out of a theory of meaning and interpretation? First, a social (nonprivate) account of meaning and symbols, more developed than what Geertz gives us. Second, and in conjunction with this, an account of how a nonpractitioner (the outsider) can attain an understanding of the religious practitioner's (the insider) perspective. Such an account should be able to respond to concerns like those of Crapanzano and Clifford that ethnographers are projecting their own attitudes onto an imagined "whole [collective] subject," instead of describing social practices. Third, an account of meaning in which meaning and power are intertwined.

PRACTICAL SIGNIFICANCE AND SYMBOLIC SIGNIFICANCE

The account that I am about to give of meaning and interpretation will construe meaning as something that is determined by the role that utterances, events, and objects play in social practices. Before turning to the specifics of this account, I want to say a few words about what I generally have in mind when I speak of roles and the analysis of them. I will not say too much at a general level, because the ways that things play roles in social practices vary widely, and so the real account is in the specifics. One important thing, however, that we should address upfront is the distinction between things that we might want to interpret that are symbolic in nature and those that are not. Consider these remarks by Bourdieu, describing the interpretation of social practices:

> The typical hermeneutic paradigm of the exchange of words is perhaps less appropriate than the exchange of blows . . . In dog-fights, as in the fighting of children or boxers, each move triggers off a counter-move, every stance of the body becomes a sign (*un signe*) pregnant with a meaning (*une signification*) that the opponent has to grasp while it is still incipient, reading in the beginnings of a stroke or a sidestep the imminent future, i.e. the blow or the dummy.[44]

Here Bourdieu encourages us to think of the interpretation of social practices, not according to a model that treats society as a text, but on the model of physical interactions in which one evaluates another's bodily configuration and adjusts one's own accordingly. But are such bodily stances signs that require interpretation? Do they possess symbolic meaning? The standard account of symbolic meaning has it that a symbol is something that represents something else. Does a boxer's cocked fist represent the jab that will likely follow it? Certainly it indicates to the opponent that a jab will likely follow, but is such an indication symbolic representation? If not, should we still say it has meaning and allow that there are other types of meaning besides symbolic representation? The answer to these questions is not obvious. In certain cases, it is clear that a cocked fist is representational. A poster that displays a boxer with his fist cocked to advertise a fight can have representational content, for example, serving to symbolize the strength of the boxer or the powerful physicality that the fight will involve. But in the heat of the fight, things are not as easy to assess. Certainly we would not want to treat every event that indicates the imminency of some other event as symbolic. When a softball player assesses the trajectory of a ball in flight, takes that trajectory to indicate that the ball will land fifteen feet to her right, and responds by relocating in that direction, it is a strain to call the trajectory a symbolic representation of where the ball will land. Not every event that indicates to an observer the likelihood of a subsequent event is a representation of it.

For my purposes, it is not necessary to resolve decisively the question of whether we should call a boxer's cocked fist a meaningful symbol. But the example does show that it is important to distinguish objects and events that we would want to interpret because they have symbolic, representational content and objects and events that we would want to interpret because of the practical role that they play in a social practice, when such a role is not symbolic. I will call the role of events and objects in a social practice or activity their practical significance. I will refer to things that represent other things as symbolically significant. Significance is a helpful term here because, whatever its etymology, in contemporary parlance, it has a dual meaning of consequential or important, on the one hand, and symbolically meaningful, on the other. In my view, something that has symbolic, representational significance has that significance in virtue of its practical significance, since meaning is determined by use. But some things are practically significant that do not have symbolic significance in any relevant sense, and such things are still important objects of social analysis and interpretation.

Consider, as an example, a step in a recipe. I oftentimes cook chocolate-chip pancakes for my children on weekends. When I do so, I add four tablespoons of vegetable oil to the batter before mixing it. This action has practical significance in the context of the social activity of cooking. It ensures that the batter has the correct properties for producing pancakes. The action is not symbolic in any relevant sense. In certain cases, recipe steps can have symbolic significance; adding leaven to bread or not doing so has symbolic significance in the Jewish tradition and in the Christian New Testament. But this is not a case like those. Certainly it is true that adding cooking oil requires the use of symbolic meaning. I read the symbols that are words in a recipe for instruction as to how to prepare the pancakes. My action is an intentional one; it is done for a reason. My beliefs about what the recipe says and the propriety of following recipes are relevant to understanding the action. However, it is not helpful to think of the action itself as a symbol. If my child were to ask me what putting oil in the batter represents or means, I would think that is the wrong question to ask about adding oil. Interestingly, the exact practical significance of the action is unknown to me. I am not sure why it is important to add oil to the batter. Does the recipe instruct this because of the way oil affects the consistency of the batter or the resulting pancakes? Does it have to do with the heating process, improving the way the pancakes cook? Or the flavor? Or something else? I have no idea. I do not perform the action because I understand the practical significance; I do it because the recipe says so, and I know better than to go without recipes. People do not fully understand the practical significance of everything that they do.

When observers encounter unfamiliar religious rituals, they should not assume that every (or any) feature of the ritual has symbolic significance. The ritual could be merely practically significant. This is an important departure from conceiving the study of religion specifically as the interpretation of symbols, as Geertz would have it. When scholars encounter an arrangement of objects on an altar, the configuration could have symbolic significance. On Chinese domestic altars, for example, the tablets with the names of inferior ancestors are positioned to the right of the superior ancestors.[45] However, on another altar in another religion, the arrangement of items might be without symbolic significance, even if it is crucial that the objects be arranged just so, just as it is important to add four tablespoons of vegetable oil, but not symbolically significant to do so. Part of the scholar's task in interpreting rituals is to ascertain whether there is symbolic significance to the various features of the rituals or merely practical significance. For some rituals, it could be that what matters for the ritual is that things happen in a certain way to bring about the appropriate result, for example, the strengthening of ties between the participants and the god being worshiped. But the particular ritual action might not be symbolically significant, merely practically significant. The ritual's effectiveness depends on performing the action the right way, the practitioners think, but the action does not obviously represent anything. For ritual actions or objects that have symbolic significance as well as practical significance, the interpreter might want to focus on one or the other of these or both, depending on the goals of inquiry.

Should we reserve meaning as a term to refer only to symbolic significance or make it broad enough to designate practical significance as well? It seems a bit odd to me to think of adding oil to batter as having a meaning, so I will speak of meaning as pertaining to symbolic significance, but nothing is at stake for my theory of religion on the matter, so long as we are clear about it. However we think about meaning, I find it helpful to speak of interpretation as an activity that takes both symbolic and practical significance as its subject matter. So whether we regard Bourdieu's boxer's cocked fist as meaningful or not, we can speak of interpreting the posture, and the interpretation would be that the fighter is about to jab or feint.

To interpret the significance, practical or symbolic, of something is to understand the role the action or object plays in the social practice in which it is employed. What is it to understand the role something plays? First and foremost, it is to understand two things: the conditions in which the action or object properly occurs and the relevant consequences of the occurrence. To understand the significance of adding vegetable oil to batter is to understand the conditions under which one typically would do so (after adding milk and eggs, at breakfast time, in a kitchen, with a tablespoon, and so on) and the consequences of doing so, that is, the contribution the vegetable oil makes to the desired outcome of pancakes. To understand the role of an initiation ceremony is to understand the conditions under which the ceremony is performed (for example, when males reach a certain age) and the consequences of the ceremony (the male is now permitted to join in hunts and take a wife). With these preliminary thoughts in mind, we can now examine in turn verbal symbols and nonverbal ones.

THE NATURE OF VERBAL SYMBOLS

What is it to understand the meaning of a term or sentence? As I have shown, influential figures like Ricoeur and Gadamer speak of grasping meaning in problematically vague terms: such as fusing horizons or living in an aura. The account that I favor is far more specific.[46] It begins with the observation that to understand a term, one must be able to make proper inferences from and to sentences that contain the term. For example, to count as knowing what the term "dog" means, you must be able to infer from statements such as "Winston is a dog," statements like these: "Winston is a mammal," "Winston has a heart," "Winston has fur," and even the sorts of things that we so take for granted that we don't think about, such as, "Winston is not a number," "Winston does not fly," and "Winston does not dissolve in water." Someone who could not make those and other inferences, when asked to do so, does not know the meaning of the word "dog." A baby or a parrot who can exclaim "Dog!" at the sight of Winston can recognize dogs as opposed to other things but does not yet know the meaning of the word "dog." As the baby grows to a toddler and increases her linguistic skills, she will gradually learn more and more of the sorts of inferences that "x is a dog" licenses. As "light dawns gradually over the whole," in Wittgenstein's words, she comes to understand the meaning of "dog" as she comes to understand the meaning of a great number of other words besides.[47] If this makes sense, then we can think of the meaning of a term, most basically, as the role that it plays in facilitating inferences from and to any declarative sentence in which it occurs. "Winston is a cat" licenses different inferences from "Winston is a dog" (and many of the same ones, too), and the different inferences that the terms license when used in a sentence indicate the different meanings of the two terms.

To understand the meaning of a term or sentence as the inferential role the term or sentence plays in its language is a philosophy of language that owes much to Wittgenstein's celebrated idea that "the meaning of a word is its use in the language."[48] In the version of this Wittgensteinian philosophy of language that I am appropriating, developed by Robert Brandom, Wilfrid Sellars, and others, grasping meaning is understood as a practical skill. *Knowing that* is construed as a type of *knowing how*, that is, knowing that Winston is a dog is knowing how to use the sentence "Winston is a dog" (and other sentences with the words "Winston" and "dog" in them) in making inferences. Meaning, then, is not a mysterious mental entity but rather a matter of the norms involved in the practical skill of knowing how to make utterances appropriately and infer the proper things from and to the utterances. Perception and action are important too, in addition to inferring, in establishing the semantic content of a term. To know what "dog" means, one must not only be able to make inferences from and to sentences that contain the word, one must also be good at identifying certain items as dogs and others not. This ability to differentiate certain items from others is one that we share with nonlinguistic creatures like babies, cats, and parrots, and such a skill works in conjunction with our skill of inferring to make the word "dog" mean what it does. The case is similar for action: our ability to act properly in relation to dogs contributes to the meaning of the word. Petting an object when one has correctly identified it as a dog, instead of asking it whether it has read any good novels recently, is one way to show that one knows the meaning of the term. All of this presupposes that meaning is a normative matter. There are proper and improper inferences that we can make from any judgment and proper and improper ways to act. Knowing a meaning of a term is being familiar with the norms by which we assess the proper applications of a term and the proper (inferential and practical) consequences that follow from using the term. So to return to the language of understanding the significance of something by understanding the conditions in which it occurs and the consequences of its occurrence, for verbal meaning, understanding the meaning of a sentence is understanding the conditions in which it is appropriate to utter the sentence and understanding the consequences of the utterance. The conditions could be a certain perceptual event (it is appropriate to utter "It is snowing" when it is snowing) or some other sentence from which it is appropriate to infer the sentence. The consequences of an utterance could be an action or they could be some beliefs that can be inferred from the uttered sentence.

This account of linguistic meaning is not just practical; it is social practical. We acquire the ability to infer, to recognize dogs as dogs and to act appropriately in relation to them through a process of socialization that centrally features language learning. The norms inherent in language use are socially instituted, and we learn them when we learn language.

Furthermore, meanings are public in nature, not private. "Cut the pie any way you like," Hilary Putnam exclaims, "'meanings' just ain't in the *head*!"[49] For example, one might be mistaken about certain facts about dogs, believing, for example, that they reproduce by laying eggs instead of live births and still successfully use the word in conversation. One might not be mistaken, but merely ignorant, of a great many facts about dogs but still use the term successfully. One might not know that dogs are members of the Chordata phylum but still use the term successfully. One might not be able to infer, like biologists can, that "Winston is a chordate" from "Winston is a dog," but one can nevertheless converse intelligently about dogs, because the meaning of a term is not the product of any one person's mental state. Putnam even speaks of a division of linguistic labor, whereby certain parties are in a relatively authoritative position in determining the meaning of a term. Biologists or veterinarians would occupy such a position in relation to dogs and metallurgists would in relation to zinc. The meaning of terms also owes something to what they designate. It is possible that, not just one person, but the entire linguistic community could be ignorant of or mistaken about certain aspects of dogs' biological constitution. If it were one day discovered that dogs have two hearts, instead of one like we had erroneously been thinking all along, then we would still have been successfully talking about dogs even though we all previously would have agreed that "Winston has one heart" is a proper inference from "Winston is a dog." The meaning of our terms that refer to objects is in part responsible to the objects to which they refer. This is so not because of some mysterious metaphysical link between the idea dog and the class of objects that we designate thus but because of the way that we conduct our practices. Our practice of using the word "dog" is such that we continue to apply the term to the class of objects, even as we revise and correct the faulty inferences that had previously attached to the word, and even as we accumulate new knowledge and thus new patterns of inference around the word. (Of course, there are exceptions. In some cases, the errors associated with a term are so severe that we retire the word when we discover them, as with "phlogiston" and "aether.") The objects about which we speak are incorporated into our social practices, not external to them.

But one might wonder what sort of skill inferring is and whether it is private, subjective, and mentalistic in problematic ways. After all, even though one must be able to infer that "Winston is not a cabbage" from "Winston is a dog," probably no one besides the readers of this book has ever even considered this inference, much less made it. So it seems that whereas inferring is occasionally a public matter, as when you see someone reasoning out loud, or you read a philosophical essay, much of the inferential capacities that are essential to the determination of words' meanings are not publicly exhibited. There is truth to this, and there is a private dimension to inferring and thus to meaning. But this private dimension is not absolutely private, and it relies on socially acquired learning. What matters for meaning is that one could, should the need arise, make inferences like "Winston is not a cabbage" from statements like "Winston is a dog," not that one actually has or ever will. This means that the inferential skills in question are dispositions. If X is disposed to do Y in circumstances Z, that means that X won't necessarily do Y when Z is not occurring. If a glass is disposed to break when struck, you won't see it breaking in most other circumstances. So a particular disposition may not be observable in many circumstances. This does not give rise to any peculiar problems regarding meaning, however. After all, upon meeting someone, you cannot tell by mere observation if the person is disposed to make free throws reliably or not. Not until you see her on the basketball court can you observe that she is disposed to sink most of the shots. Does that mean that the sport of basketball is problematically private? Of course not. The case is similar with inferring. The skills in question with inference are in significant measure shared by the competent users of a language. Further, they are acquired through the process of learning the language, which is why these dispositions, even when they are private because they are not being activated, presuppose the social. Their privacy is not absolute.

So in all these ways, Geertz was quite correct to say that meaning is public, as "public as marriage and as observable as agriculture." This brings us to the next important question, which concerns the task of interpretation. The understanding of meaning that I am sketching facilitates far more of a precise delineation of the nature of interpretation than Ricoeur, Gadamer, or Geertz are able to provide. To interpret someone's statement is to attribute a belief to the person and to understand the inferential relationships in which the belief stands. By understand here I mean that one is able to make a wide range of inferences to and from the belief in question. Thus, there is a method in principle of verifying whether someone understands the meaning of a term or not. If you want to know whether a person, say, an ethnographer, understands the meaning of a term, you can ask questions to test the inferential roles that the ethnographer assigns to the term vis-à-vis those of the competent language users.

Appealing to beliefs at this point is somewhat problematic, because "belief" is a beleaguered term in contemporary religious studies every bit as much as "meaning" is. The most direct challenge to the concept comes in Donald Lopez Jr.'s essay, "Belief," in which he identifies belief with "inner assent to a cognitive proposition." Lopez expresses agnosticism regarding whether such a thing exists, but he seems to doubt that religion can be represented "as something that derives from belief."[50] Lopez and other contemporary critics of belief rightly note that it is problematic to think of religion as especially a matter of belief, that is, to think that what one believes is the most important, the most definitive aspect of one's religion. However, they oftentimes run together their criticism of belief-as-preeminent-aspect-of-religion with a criticism of belief-as-an-essential-aspect-of-religion. (By essential here I just mean that religions necessarily involve beliefs, not that beliefs are the most important thing about a religion.) Another tendency in the critics of belief is to conflate belief with belief-in-God and to speak as though by pointing out that belief-in-God is not essential to religion they have shown that belief is not.

Davidson has effectively argued that attributing beliefs is a necessary feature of linguistic communication. When we try to understand something that someone has said we do so by attributing beliefs to the person. If you and I are on the seashore, and you point and say, "That is a ketch," I attribute to you the beliefs that ketches are boats and that the object before us is a boat and, though I don't do so consciously, a whole host of other beliefs as well such as that boats float on water, that water is not solid, and so on. Furthermore, when we interpret people's actions, we attribute beliefs. If a friend asks why you rushed out of the room at 1:30, I can answer that you want to catch the bus that leaves at 1:45, and in doing so I am attributing to you the belief that the bus leaves at that time.[51] Terry Godlove effectively applies the lessons to be learned from Davidson to religious studies and to Lopez's criticism of belief.[52] One of Godlove's points is that if we did not attribute beliefs to people we would be unable to differentiate between religious actions and nonreligious ones. We identify certain actions and practices as religious because we attribute to the agents beliefs and motives surrounding their actions, beliefs and motives that concern things that we classify as religious in nature.

Brandom's view of beliefs has similarities to Davidson's, but Brandom emphasizes the normative and deontological dimension of beliefs more explicitly. Brandom challenges the notion that beliefs are inner states and presents a model instead in which they are social statuses, better thought of on the analogy of signing a mortgage than some interior "belief box" in one's cognitive architecture.[53] When one signs a mortgage, one obligates oneself to pay the bank a certain amount of money every month. The signatures that one inscribes on multiple pages of the mortgage contract put one under that obligation because the signer, bank, lawyers, judges, tax collectors, insurance company, and indeed society generally understand the contract and its signatures to involve the obligation to pay. These parties and society generally have instituted the activity of making and signing contracts in this way. The obligation to pay is not something that exists in the mind or body of the signer. Rather, it exists because of the status that the signer's society confers upon the signer. Something similar is going on with beliefs. A belief is a commitment. It is an obligation and responsibility to make certain inferences and to act in certain ways. If I believe that Winston is a dog, I am obligated to believe that Winston is not a cabbage. This obligation is a social status, not the property of my mind, brain, or even my body. Of course, bodily dispositions matter, in that I will likely be disposed to say, "Yes," when someone asks me if Winston is a dog. But the beliefs are not identified with the dispositions but rather with my normative obligations in respect to the inferential and practical role of the sentence "Winston is a dog." I have these obligations because my linguistic community recognizes me as a language user and thus as someone whose utterances are subject to norms. My linguistic community understands an utterance of "Winston is a dog" to involve these inferential and practical roles, and furthermore my linguistic community understands the utterer of the sentence "Winston is a dog" to be undertaking a commitment to what follows (inferentially and practically) from the belief that Winston is a dog.

Because the members of a linguistic community hold each other responsible for the normative status that is a belief, they can attribute more beliefs to people than the people themselves would or could explicitly articulate. For example, if Marie has been talking about Winston and Gus asks who he is, and she responds, "Winston is a dog," Gus will not only attribute the belief that Winston is a dog to her but also associated beliefs, such as, "Winston needs water and food." And when she says, after a few hours at the beach, that she has to return home to take care of Winston, he will attribute to her the belief not only that Winston needs water and food but also that Winston presently is hungry and thirsty. Gus will understand her action of leaving the beach as the result of those various beliefs about Winston's dietary schedule, even though she said nothing explicitly about it. This example shows that people not only attribute beliefs to speakers in addition to ones that they explicitly articulate, but they also explain actions in terms of beliefs, whether articulated or not. If Jesse turns to Gus and asks where Marie went, Gus will answer that she went home to feed her dog, though she said nothing so specific about her plans. We make these sorts of belief attributions and action explanations constantly in our daily lives, and any account of religious studies (or the human sciences) that would like to dispense with belief owes us an account of how it is that these everyday practices of speaking with and about people can transpire without attributing beliefs. I will venture to predict that no such account will soon be forthcoming, and so belief, as a category of great importance for the study of religion, is here to stay.

If the meaning of beliefs and concepts is a product of their inferential role, then one important thing to note is that different observers can and often do infer different things from any given utterance. Inferential roles of terms are not limited to the specific contexts in which they are uttered. Roles precede and succeed particular uses of a term. Interpretation, then, is relative to the ones doing the interpretation, to their social context and their aims. If when leaving the beach, Marie says to Gus that she has to feed her dog, then in response to Jesse's question about her departure, Gus might say that Marie is going to give her dog some tuna, chicken, and salmon. Marie actually does not know that her brand of dog food contains these things and so she could not herself have specified her action in these terms. But Gus, a veterinarian, knows the brand and, what's more, has intense interests in dog nutrition. Given his collateral beliefs and his interests, he specifies Marie's actions in a way no one else in their party would have. Jesse, more interested in the emotional dynamics of feeding animals than the nutritional ones, says, "Oh, she is going to give her dog love." From Marie's assertion, "I am going to feed my dog," Gus infers, "Marie is going to give her dog tuna, chicken, and salmon," whereas Jesse infers, "Marie is going to give her dog love." The meaning of the phrase "feed a dog" is determined by its role in licensing inferences about ingredients in dog food and about emotional attachment to pets and also its holistic role in countless other inferences. Gus's and Jesse's interpretations of Marie's action are relative to the context and interests of each of them, but they are still objectively true or false. If, unbeknownst to Gus, Marie has just bought a new vegetarian formula dog food, Gus's assertion about her action is wrong. If, unbeknownst to Jesse, Marie has grown to hate her dog, then Jesse is wrong.

What this means is that when the scholar of religion interprets the sayings and doings of religious practitioners, the interpretations are a product not just of the practitioners' activities but also of the scholars' context and interests. As social statuses, meanings derive from the attitudes of the person being interpreted and from the attitudes of those doing the interpretation. If the scholar is one of the interpreters, then what the scholar is disposed to infer from the actions and utterances of the practitioners is implicated in the meaning of the practitioners' beliefs and concepts. This does not detract from the possibility that the scholar's interpretation can be objectively right or wrong, better or worse. As we shall see, though, it does mean that the scholar is in a relation of power, not just interpretation, to the practitioner.

NONLINGUISTIC SYMBOLS

Much more could be said about linguistic meaning, and I will fill out a few more details to the story when we come to the topic of experience, but for now I will turn to the topic of nonlinguistic symbols. In the most general sense, a symbol is something that represents something else. Linguistic symbols are a special case of this more general phenomenon. Influential pragmatists like Richard Rorty have gone on record as being anti-representationalist, but Brandom is not.[54] Brandom is opposed to giving representations explanatory priority in accounting for the capacity of our utterances to refer and have meaning. Rather, the social practices of attributing beliefs to others and assigning normative significance to those beliefs accounts for representation. For linguistic meanings, the capacity of the sentence to represent a state of affairs is explained by the role that the sentence has in the social practice. People treat each other's utterances as talking about something. They regard the sentence as something that can be right or wrong; that is, it can be successful in representing a given state of affairs or not. If I think you are knowledgeable and sincere when you say that Winston is a dog, I will take that belief as one of my own, and I will think that it is a belief about a particular object, namely Winston. The sentence, "Winston is a dog," represents the state of affairs of Winston being a member of the dog species. Linguistic representation and the capacity of our language to refer to things and states of affairs, just as is the case for meaning, are products of our social practices.

This is also the case for nonlinguistic representation. Something stands for something else because we treat it as doing so. Our social practices institute and maintain the relation of representation. These social practices are practices because they have to do with what people do (or are disposed to do), and they are social because they have to do with shared patterns of behavior, shared attitudes, and shared norms about appropriate and inappropriate ways of offering and responding to symbols. What is typically relevant is an occasion in which a person encounters a symbol and responds to it as such. This encounter and response occur only because the person implicitly or explicitly takes the thing to represent something else. The response could be emotional, cognitive, practical (involving an action), or all three. More precisely, since emotion, cognition, and disposition to act typically come packaged together, the response will typically involve all three, though one or two of the three might be more prominent. A skull-and-crossbones on a vial of liquid represents life-threatening danger, and my proper response is not to drink the liquid and not to leave it accessible to others who might unwittingly do so. A picture in a store window with a cup and wavy lines above it is an occasion for a passerby who wants hot coffee or tea to enter. Even if I have no interest in a warm beverage, if I notice the symbol, I still acquire a belief: "This store serves coffee."

The relations between symbols and that which they represent are so varied and multifarious that it is hard to say much more about symbols that is generally true. Symbols can have as many uses as people can have ends and goals, and the same thing can serve to represent different things for different people. The same thing can represent more than one thing at a given time or represent different things at different times, even for the same person. A flag represents a country and its ideals, and the proper response to it, for nationalists, is respect and pride, but for radical dissenters, scorn and contempt. Furthermore, symbols have their status contingently. Nothing need serve as a symbol. Surveying the broken soup bowl that I just knocked off the table, I might set about cleaning it up without ado, or I might sigh and turn to my friend forlornly, remarking, "Doesn't that just sum up the state of my life?" In the former case, my response to the mess does not take it to represent anything whereas in the latter case it does. Symbols are remarkably flexible. The relation between the symbol and that which it represents can be clear and specific. Sailor (Nicholas Cage) in David Lynch's *Wild at Heart* explicitly designates, "about fifty thousand times" according to his girlfriend Lula (Laura Dern), his leather jacket as a symbol of his "individuality" and his "belief in personal freedom." A dot on a map represents a city and all competent users of the map will recognize and agree upon the city that the dot picks out. Such symbols have a precise referent that is widely agreed upon. In other cases, the symbol's meaning is not at all clear and may even be disputed. This is often the case in art. What does a storm cloud represent in an impressionistic landscape painting? It might be evil or suffering, it might be depression or sadness, it might be the mystery of existence, it might be the sublimity of nature, or it might be some combination of these. In many cases, the emotion the symbol elicits is as important or more important than anything extra-subjective to which it might refer, and the meaning of the symbol may come to be the emotion that it elicits. Indeed, eliciting emotions is one especially important role that symbols play in religion, as when a ritual's or ceremony's material environment is arranged to elicit religiously significant emotions like awe and reverence. But whatever the use to which it is put, the symbol can have the role that it does because people take it to be a symbol, and they regard the thing as being the occasion for certain appropriate responses.

Symbolic meaning, like linguistic meaning, is holistic. That is, a symbol derives its significance not just from the naked encounter of an individual and the symbol, considered apart from the larger context, but precisely from the larger context of the social practices in which the individual and the symbol both occur. A red light at an intersection does not convey meaning to drivers independently from everything else but precisely because of the role that it plays in the activity of driving and everything that comes along with it: automobiles, norms about what areas of a city are appropriate to drive in, the laws and penalties in respect to violating these norms, the physical constitution of vehicles and human bodies and the economic cost of repairing both, and so on. A blurry scene of hanging beads in an avant-garde film has its meaning in relation to the history of film and art in general, and it plays the social role that it does, serving as the occasion for proper and improper aesthetic responses, only because of the artistic traditions in which it stands and the familiarity of the viewer with those traditions. Here we see the importance of what we could call a "division of symbolic labor," following Putnam's discussion of a "division of linguistic labor." The art critic who is familiar with the relevant traditions is in a more authoritative position to pronounce on the role of the shot of beads and the attendant aesthetic norms than the casual filmgoer.

Because symbols are so varied in their uses, it is hard to say anything general about how people do or should go about interpreting them. Furthermore, interpreters of symbols may have different aims and agendas in interpreting them.[55] Someone who urgently needs to relieve himself looks at the symbols on the bathroom doors to determine which restroom he should enter. Someone familiar with queer theory may approach the same with an interest in understanding the exclusive gender categories presupposed by such symbols and the way in which the symbols reinforce those dichotomies and marginalize and exclude those who do not identify as female or male. Nevertheless, we can be confident that anyone who is out to interpret symbols does so by obtaining an implicit or explicit understanding of the role that the symbols play in the social practices. Understanding the meaning of a symbol is understanding what sorts of occasions are appropriate encounters with the symbol and what sorts of responses to the symbol are appropriate. What makes this a feasible undertaking, even for outsiders, is that symbols are instituted and maintained for certain purposes, and these purposes are publicly ascertainable. The practitioners learned the appropriate occasions for encountering their symbols and the appropriate responses through public processes of socialization. The outsider can observe the occasions in which the symbol plays a role and can observe and make inferences about the sorts of responses people have in encountering the symbol. The outsider can oftentimes even participate in the relevant processes of socialization, if she is present among the community in question for a sufficient duration of time.

Symbols are so frequently indeterminate in their meaning and reference that we might take this to be a reason to doubt that interpreting symbolic meaning can be a successful endeavor. Sometimes everyone agrees and could readily tell you what a symbol stands for, but oftentimes there is no such agreement. In those cases where the meaning of the symbol is indeterminate, an important part of interpreting the symbol is recognizing the indeterminacy. The existence of imprecise and underspecified symbols does not serve as a reason to doubt the feasibility of symbolic interpretation; rather it orients the analyst toward a specific set of questions about what roles the symbol can and does play precisely because it is indeterminate. The degree to which a symbol is determinate or imprecise and underspecified is itself socially instituted. Indeterminacy allows for symbols to play certain social roles that determinate symbols could not play, and vice versa. A highway sign representing the pattern of lanes at the intersection of two major interstates needs to be precise and specific in indicating that to which it refers. An arrangement of dots in an abstract painting should not be.

We also might doubt the feasibility of symbolic interpretation when we consider the fact that the employment of symbols is so frequently tacit. People interact with most of the symbols in their environment without consciously attending to the fact that they are symbols. I can stop at a stoplight, wholly preoccupied in thinking about the stressful meeting to which I am traveling without even consciously realizing that I have responded to the symbol. If you wave to me, I might wave back unthinkingly and automatically. In these cases, even though I am not consciously attending to the symbol and my response to it, I could do so, were someone to ask me what a red light or a back and forth hand motion means. In other cases, it seems possible that there are symbols, the referents of which I am unaware of altogether, or I may consciously understand one thing to which the symbol refers but not some other. Durkheim thinks that totems and gods are symbols whose referents are the community that reveres them as sacred, but he does not think that the members of the community are aware of this fact. If Durkheim is correct, then the analyst arrives at a conclusion about the meaning of the symbol by observing practitioners' attitudes toward the symbol and hypothesizing that in eliciting these attitudes the symbol is fostering or reinforcing attitudes toward something other than the symbol itself and other than what the community thinks the symbol represents. In sum, frequently one can ascertain the meaning of a symbol simply by asking the symbol's users what it means, but in other cases, one must proceed by carefully observing the responses to the symbol that occur and how those responses themselves relate to attitudes toward other things in the social practice, even when the community members themselves do not understand their responses as relating to the other things.

So whether we are dealing with linguistic or nonlinguistic symbolic meaning, we have reason, despite the complexities involved, to be optimistic about the interpretive endeavor, at least in principle. Symbols are socially instituted and have their meaning as a result of the role that they play in social practices. Symbols are instituted in such a way that properly socialized people will have a typical sort of response (cognitive, practical, and emotional) to the symbol. This response is such that there are indications, whether explicit or implicit, that the attitudes that arise in the encounter with the symbol are relevant not just as directed toward the object in question but also to some other thing(s). The task of the interpreter is to recognize that there are such attitudes and to determine what the other thing is. The interpreter does this by attending to the occasion in which the symbol is encountered and the consequences of the encounter (in terms of the attitudes elicited in the encounter) in the context of the larger social practice(s) in which the encounter occurs. These attitudes may be easy to observe directly, or they may have to be inferred from other things that the symbol-user does and says, but the attitudes are public and social in nature, in that they are socially acquired, socially expressed, and have a social normative status. Symbolic roles do have a dispositional and private component, as we saw above in relation to linguistic meaning. The private component originates in and is only possible because of the social process of learning the role of the symbol and it is what it is only because of the public and social expressions that it actually (or counterfactually) has. The private and the public are inextricably linked: there are no private, interior wheels that turn though nothing public moves with them.[56]

These reflections on symbolic meaning come nowhere near serving as an exhaustive treatment of such complicated matters, but I hope that I've said enough to indicate how further questions could be answered about symbolic meaning. At the very least, it should be evident that interpreting symbolic meaning is a pervasive and necessary element to our everyday navigation of our social world, and thus it is an ineliminable aspect of the human sciences generally and religious studies in particular. In emphasizing symbols as items that have social roles within a larger context of social practices and that are socially instituted so as to serve as elicitors of a set of appropriate responses, I have avoided the problematic mentalism that could be attached to Geertz's appeal to symbols as "vehicles of conceptions." I have also given a more specific account of what it is to interpret and understand a symbol than we find in Gadamer or Ricoeur. But I have done so in such a way that is consistent with the key insights of Gadamer, Ricoeur, and Geertz about the nature and importance of meaning and its interpretation.[57]

The account offered here can respond to the sorts of criticisms against interpretation that Clifford, Crapanzano, and Masuzawa have lodged. All three of these are worried that the process of interpretation necessarily presents divergent, contested, and fragmented realities as a homogenous whole. Clifford and Crapanzano are worried about the way Geertz attributes attitudes to a generic Balinese subject, instead of supposing that there is actually a conflicting diversity of perspectives among the individual Balinese. Masuzawa is worried about Geertz's appeal to culture as a "complex whole." By focusing on social practices as the context in which meaning transpires instead of culture, I can address these sorts of concerns. Social practices are shared, so whatever the diversity of individual perspectives, this diversity is not absolute. Language requires that people recognize their fellow communicants as committed to the same (or similar enough) norms of perception, inference, and action as they are. If these norms were not shared, conversations would not exist. However, I do not presuppose that norms, linguistic or otherwise, are shared to the same extent or in the same way by all the members of a given society, ethnic group, or nation. It is up to the anthropologist to discern the extent to which and the group among whom any particular social practice is shared. This is observable, since sharing norms results in similar patterns of response by the practitioners to similar sorts of situations. The "Archimedean point" of the participant observer is not an ideology, as Masuzawa worries, or at least it is not necessarily an ideology. Attributing shared norms to a group of people engaged together in a practice is not peculiar to anthropology; it is a pervasive feature of human social life in general, and though anthropologists might employ some methods peculiar to their undertaking, they are not doing anything categorically different than what language users and social actors in general do every day of their lives.

SOCIAL AND NORMATIVE PRACTICES OR POST-STRUCTURALISM?

That brings us to the second principal issue confronting a theory of meaning and interpretation: the problem of power. Gadamer, Ricoeur, Geertz, Brandom, Davidson, and Sellars all have extremely important things to say about meaning. However, none of them gives us anything approaching an adequate account of the interrelationships of meaning and power. Those working in the power approach take as a central premise to their analyses of religious practice that discourse, signification, and claims about truth are laden with power. They tend to agree with Foucault: "Power and knowledge directly imply one another . . . there is no power relation without the correlative constitution of a field of knowledge, nor any knowledge that does not presuppose and constitute at the same time power relations."[38] A theoretical approach to the study of religion will have to provide an account of the interrelationships between meaning and power.

Post-structuralists, following in the trajectory of Foucault and Derrida, emphasize the interplay of meaning (or discourse, in their preferred terminology) and power, but they do not have a satisfactory account of interpretation. They typically speak of language in use, that is, actual utterances, and so they do not have anything to say about the necessity of attributing beliefs to speakers when conversing with them. A satisfactory account of communication and interpretation must make a place for attributing beliefs, and so philosophers like Brandom and Davidson get something important right that post-structuralists do not address successfully. Furthermore, Derrida's account of the link between signifiers and that which they signify is well-nigh inscrutable. Derrida thinks of language as a structure of signifiers and signifieds that is inherently unstable. The significatory relation is not simply between the individual pairs of signifier and signifieds but has to do with the various differential interrelationships of signfiers and signifieds as a whole. The account is complicated by the fact than any signified is itself a signifier for some other signified. Meaning is deferred then and a product of the differential significatory relations. Thus, *différance*, a neologism that combines deferral and difference, is key to Derrida's semantics. But *différance* is mysterious indeed, as are the various similar terms that Derrida employs to explicate signification, "trace," "iteration," and "play": the trace that one signifier leaves on another, the iteration of applying signifiers over and again in time, and the play of meaning deferral throughout the structure. The trace of meaning deferral "can never be presented: that is, appear and manifest itself, as such, in its phenomenon." Further, Derrida says, "Always differing and deferring, the trace is never as it is in the presentation of itself. It erases itself in presenting itself."[59] The trace "retain[s] the other as other in the same," and "it does not exist," even though it is the condition of signification for Derrida.[60] As I argue in more detail elsewhere, the social practical account that I am advocating has an advantage of not appealing to such strange things, which are effectual but do not exist and cannot appear or manifest.[61] The normative statuses that constitute meaning are observable in that we can see people correct improper inferences and endorse proper ones.

Furthermore, the social practical account of meaning that I favor agrees with Derrida's and Foucault's post-structuralism that meaning is not fixed and stable. The meaning of our terms and sentences is a product of the social norms that we institute. We institute these norms in such a way that our utterances have objective import. There is a sufficient degree of stability in our norms that two people can take themselves to be talking about the same thing when they converse with each other. There is a sufficient degree of stability that we can correct our beliefs about the objects and states of affairs we are talking about when we discover that we have been in error. However, the meaning of our words is not fixed. Every time we use a term in a sentence, we are contributing to the ongoing institution of the norms associated with the term, and if our practices of applying terms changes over time, the meaning of the terms accordingly changes. Further, meaning is plural and relative both to the context in which an utterance or text is situated and to the aims of the interpreter. The meaning that a person assigns to an utterance or text in part has to do with the particular beliefs and aims that the interpreter holds. "Meaning is a product of the words on the page and other features of the context in which it is situated," Brandom writes. "For instance, a tradition in which it features, or the concerns and questions a reader brings to the text. . . . Texts can be assessed with respect to many different contexts and kind of context. Each provides a perspective on 'the' meaning. . . . Further, the set of possible readings, contextual perspectives, is open-ended."[62]

The pluralism and impermanence of meaning and other features that result from the fact that meaning is socially instituted entail that the semantic content of our language is susceptible to being manipulated by social power. For the remainder of the chapter I will detail a handful of key ways in which power and meaning are interrelated in the social practical theory that I favor, without intending to exhaust the interrelationships.

MEANING AND POWER

We need some initial idea of what we're talking about when we talk about power. Here I will follow the typology that Philip Petit presents in *Republicanism*:

1. Power is possessed by an agent (person/group/agency) OR by a system
2. so far as that entity exercises OR is able (actually or virtually) to exercise
3. intentional OR nonintentional influence,
4. negative OR positive,
5. in advancing any kind of result whatever OR, more specifically, in help-ing to construct certain forms of agency OR shape the choices of certain agents.[63]

I am content to embrace all the various conceptions of power generated by Pettit's schema, with the caveat that I am interested, not in "any kind of result whatever," but only in those results that grant certain individuals and groups access to social goods and restrict others.

With that in mind, I will present seven important ways in which power inter-twines with meaning—symbolic significance—and practical significance.

1. *Power can transpire through other means besides meaning but still be dependent on it.* Most of the ensuing discussion will concern symbolic meaning and power, but I want to make clear from the outset that symbolic meaning is not always the principal concern when it comes to operations of power. Guns and pepper spray in the hands of the police are symbols of state power, but, in addition to their symbolic significance (as designating the power of the state), they also have causal properties that allow the police to injure people with them. What matters for suppressing dissenters is not just the association of these objects with the state's power to dominate but the way

that the police officers' weapons can incapacitate, wound, and kill citizens. So Asad is quite right to challenge the notion that "mere symbols" implant religious disposition. The coercive power of the Roman Empire and the Christian church does so as well, he notes, as does judicial torture and ascetic pain.[64] I would not want to reduce power to meaning or confine its operations to something that only occurred by means of symbolic operations. A blow to the head smarts regardless of what its symbolic content is and shackles confine irrespective of what they represent.

Thinking about these sorts of examples, involving violence, makes clear one sort of way in which the practical significance of an action can overshadow whatever symbolic significance that it might have in its relevance to power and hierarchy. The practical significance of various activities of policing consists in the deployment of coercion and confinement. Practical significance can have other sorts of relationships with power, though. A difficult ritual or meditation technique, for example, may take years to master. Those who have mastered the requisite skills may occupy a position of status in a group for doing so and thus have power over other members. Furthermore, if training in the skills is restricted to certain social classes, like men, for example, then the skills readily serve to perpetuate asymmetrical power relations. Even in these cases, though, where a particular action's effects are relevant to the distribution of power because of its practical significance, not its symbolic significance, it transpires in a background of meaningfulness. As I mentioned above, the relevant significance of adding cooking oil to pancake batter is practical, not symbolic, but the action only occurs because of the symbolic background of beliefs and language involved in the activity of cooking. The recipient of a blow might not at the instant care much about the symbolic background of the police officer's bludgeon, but it matters nonetheless, and the authorization of the police to use coercive violence is a product of the legal and governmental symbol systems that institute police forces.

2. *Beliefs, which are meaningful, serve as reasons for actions, and actions are a primary means by which relations of power are established, perpetuated, and contested.* I mentioned this important way in which meaning and power are related in my discussion of Geertz above. There I pointed out that beliefs about members of another ethnic group can serve as a motive and reason for acting to harm them. Similarly, religious beliefs serve as motives and reasons for all manner of actions, including those actions that are relevant to power relations. For example, slave owners' belief that God appointed whites to be masters and Africans to be slaves resulted in particular patterns of behavior,

including physically and sexually abusing slaves, confining them, pursuing them when they ran away, and resisting emancipation. A married couple's belief that God has appointed husbands to be in authority over wives results in unilateral patterns of deference and subordination in decision-making. Civil rights activists' belief that God regarded segregation as unjust served as a motive and reason for performing acts of civil disobedience.

We should think of beliefs serving as reasons for action as a way in which meaning and power are related. The meaning of a sentence or term is not only a product of its inferential relations but also of the way that the sentence or term is related to actions. "Dog" has the meaning that it does because a sentence like "Winston is a dog" licenses not just inferences but also certain types of actions when Winston is present (such as scratching him behind the ears but not drizzling him in chocolate sauce). If religious words like "ordination" are only applicable to men and words like "marriage" only to heterosexual couples, then the actions that pertain to such terms are going to involve social exclusion and marginalization. Correspondingly, the very meaning of the terms does as well.

Acting for a reason (and acting in such a way that one's peers treat you as responsible to have reasons for your action) is acting intentionally. Not everything that people do is an intentional action. A white man might unconsciously tighten his grip on his briefcase when a man of color gets on the elevator with him. So we should not exclusively concern ourselves with intentional actions when we are thinking of the ways in which things people do affect power structures. Nor should we assume that intentional actions are always done for the reason that the agents themselves might give for the action. Clara might claim that she hired Jonah because Jonah is the best qualified for the job, but really (and unconsciously) it is because the other applicants were nonwhites. But neither can we afford to ignore intentional actions, actions that people perform for reasons. Intentional actions are one highly significant way in which the meaning of religious terms are implicated in structures of domination, exclusion, and resistance.

3. *The inferential role of a term can license power-relevant evaluative judgments of social identities.* The meaning of a term is determined by its inferential role and the way that it is applied in perceptual experiences and actions. In many cases, the inferential roles of a term are such that applying the term to someone or something licenses inferences that have sociopolitical consequences. This is clearly the case for derogatory terms like ethnic slurs. An ethnic slur is applied to the members of a particular ethnic group, and once they have been designated by the slur, negative evaluative judgments are inferentially

licensed for users of the slur.[65] Once the chauvinist has classified a person with an ethnic slur, inferences are licensed, such as, "She is stupid" or "She is lazy." Certain actions are then licensed, everything from minor snubs and mistreatments to physical, often lethal, violence. Slurs are a particularly heinous example of the way that terms' inferential roles are infused with power, but the same principle applies to words more generally, especially social classificatory terms and especially those that involve stereotypes. Even supposedly positive stereotypes ("Asian Americans are hard-working" and "Indians are spiritual") have harmful social consequences in the way that they universalize and generalize across a diverse population and buttress the essentializing and otherizing divisions among social groups. More perniciously, supposedly positive stereotypes can license forms of control, like how Victorian ideals of women as more ethically pure than men licensed efforts to contain women within the domestic context, supposedly protecting them from the rough and tumble world of commerce and politics outside the home.

David Chidester's *Savage Systems* details the way that Europeans applied the term religion to Africans or did not do so, according to whichever classification best served their strategies of control and domination. We could reconstruct the story Chidester tells in terms of inferential roles. In the sixteenth and seventeenth century, the judgment, "X has no religion" was taken by the Europeans to license a set of inferences, such as, "X's society has no system of law," "X's society has no institution of marriage," "X's society has no formal political organization," and "X is no better than a beast." These inferences in turn were taken to license the inference, "X has no entitlement to the land in which X lives." That in turn could license actions of violent land and resource appropriation.[66] This story involved a lot more than just the meaning of the relevant terms, of course. It involved guns and swords and their capacity to tear through human flesh. But the semantic content of terms like "religion," "natives," and "savages" played an integral role in the justification and administration of colonial domination.

Since contemporary religious studies is an heir of colonial inequalities, the lessons that we learn from Chidester's account and similar ones are not restricted to the past. Scholars apply concepts to what they study, and these concepts have attendant evaluative implications. Meanings are social matters, not psychological entities, and as we have seen they are a product not just of the people to whom the meaning is ascribed but also the one doing the ascribing. When a scholar calls premodern Japanese Buddhists religious because their practices reference supernatural powers, the application of the terms "religious" and "supernatural" reflects the scholar's context, since the Buddhists would not have had the equivalent concepts. Scholars are not limited to the conceptual repertoire of the people whom they study, but it is part of their job to keep track of the differences between their own conceptual repertoire and that of the communities that they study and, to the degree possible, to examine their own concepts for embedded evaluative implications that would distort their analysis and tacitly express European supremacy.

European difference, though, is not necessarily European supremacy. In some cases, scholars seem to assume that if they can merely show that a term like "religion" contributed to domination in the past, its current usage must still somehow carry that baggage with it. Oftentimes terms do carry baggage from their past, since all present uses of a term owe themselves to the norms that have been established over the course of its usage. However, these norms change over time, and, when we get specific about the nature of meaning, we can design specific tests to determine whether terms that had problematic power implications in the past still do. If the term "religion" is used in contemporary discourse in such a way that denying that someone has religion licenses inferences to the effect that the person is a savage beast, unfit to manage property, then the term retains its problematic heritage. For most relevant contemporary users of the term "religion," however, this is not the case, so pointing out that "religion" had these implications in the past does not damn it in the present. What the critic of the term has to do to convince us that the term is illegitimate for scholarly use is establish what the inferences are that the term presently licenses that involve dangerous evaluative judgments. Further, the critic has to show that these inferences are so central to the concept that we cannot correct them and retain the term.

4. *Certain groups can exercise more control over the norms that govern the use of terms than others.* In an analysis of Christian speech about God that employs a similar philosophy of language as the one I am presenting, Kevin Hector notes that not all social groups are in a position to exercise as much influence in instituting and maintaining linguistic norms.[67] As feminist theologian Elizabeth Johnson puts it, women "have been robbed of the power of naming, of naming themselves, the world, and ultimate holy mystery, having instead to receive the names given by those who rule over them."[68] This is not true in absolute terms. The philosophy of language to which I subscribe generates an insight similar to Foucault's notion of micropolitics, where there is no exclusive preserve of power that one group holds and exercises over and against another group who has none. Every use of a term contributes to the maintenance of the term's norms, whether in the mouth of the slave or the master, the subordinate wife or the patriarch. But even if no one lacks power altogether, this does not imply for Foucault or for my theory that there are no asymmetries. Indeed, the asymmetries are pronounced. In the Christian tradition, men wrote the canonical biblical texts that established the inferential relations of terms like "God," and men predominately and in many cases exclusively officiate the church rituals, preach

the sermons, and write the books that further develop the inferential norms of the Christian vocabulary. Further, men are the primary decision-makers in regard to official religious organizations.

So to put the point more generally, certain parties have the position within the community and tradition to exercise more influence in determining the linguistic norms than others. These parties might exercise this influence because they have been the ones in the position to write the texts, tell the stories, and issue the exhortations that the community regards as authoritative. They also might exercise influence because they have the means to punish and silence anyone who would attempt to revise the linguistic norms in ways that challenge their received form. Medieval Christian women who claimed to receive visions and auditions from God could be punished or killed for doing so or at the very least required to submit their message to a male authority for verification and validation. Regardless of the content of the message that they received, the mere fact that women professed to have a message from God for the church licensed inferences from "X is a woman who speaks on behalf of God" to "women can speak on behalf of God" or more generally, "people who are not priests can speak on behalf of God," and these served as challenges to the norms associated with the terms "woman," "God," and "priest."

It is helpful to consider in this regard Putnam's idea of the division of linguistic labor. Putnam does not present the idea as relevant to social power, but it is nonetheless. Putnam's lesson is that we can use terms like "elm" and "beech" meaningfully without being able to distinguish the two types of tree from each other or even from other trees. In using these terms, I and my society more generally are implicitly deferring to the authority of experts in our community, in this case, botanists, who have disproportionate influence in determining what inferences are proper from "That is a beech." In religious communities, too, there is oftentimes a division of linguistic labor, or more broadly, symbolic labor, where certain parties have a normative status within the community as possessing special authority in determining the proper inferential roles of the religious terms, the proper sorts of religious actions, and more broadly, the proper use of religious symbols in general, linguistic or not. The members of the community implicitly defer to these authorities in their use of the symbols, just as I implicitly and at times explicitly defer to botanists when using my terms to designate trees and to metallurgists when referring to metals (to determine whether I have successfully picked out a piece of aluminum depends on the judgment of the experts and the criteria that they designate). For religious communities, the relevant authorities might be rabbis, shamans, theologians, or anyone the community regards as especially competent to pronounce judgments and adjudicate disputes about the symbols.

The mere fact that certain individuals and classes of individuals have an authoritative status in a religious community is itself a matter of social power, since that group can be in a position to dominate others in the community. However, we have the added consideration that often the membership in the group that possesses the authoritative status is restricted along lines of gender, race, sexual orientation, or class, either through explicit and official rules or through unofficial patterns of bias in appointing people to positions of power.

Just as people might defer to some members of their community, so also they might disregard and discredit the pronouncements of others. Miranda Fricker explores this feature of social life systematically in her book, *Epistemic Injustice*.[69] She refers to the tendency to discount the assertions of others in unwarranted ways as a prejudice that results in a credibility deficit. She identifies this as an epistemic injustice, specifically, testimonial injustice. If the prejudice is linked to the social identity of the asserter, then we have an identity-prejudicial credibility deficit, the condition in which the assertions of the members of some social group are systematically accorded less credence than their assertions would be accorded were they to have some other, more highly regarded social identity. The presence of identity-prejudicial credibility deficits in a religious community is one important way in which certain groups exercise less influence in determining the inferential roles of religious terms. If women are subjected to a credibility deficit by men, then women's utterances about God will systematically receive less acceptance than those of men, and so they will play less of a role in instituting, maintaining, and revising the inferential roles. This is the case for linguistic symbols, which is what Fricker discusses, but we could say similar things about symbols in general. If women's conduct in relation to non-linguistic religious symbols is accorded less respect and recognition than men's (or outright prohibited), then the women will not exercise as much influence in determining the norms that govern the use of the symbols as men.

5. *Particular terms in a group's vocabulary can advantage some members of the group and disadvantage others.* Fricker develops this insight as well, drawing from feminist standpoint epistemology. Standpoint epistemology shares with Gadamer the idea that all knowing and interpretation take place in a particular situation. Knowers and interpreters are situated in a particular tradition and social status, and that situatedness affects what they know and how they interpret.[70] But feminist epistemologists, unlike Gadamer, emphasize that certain situated positions are more powerful than others. They argue that those at the top of the society pursue knowledge in ways that systematically render them incapable of understanding the perspective of those who are marginalized. Fricker develops these insights into an idea that she calls hermeneutical injustice. Testimonial injustice occurs when people discount the plausibility of an assertion because of the social identity of the

asserter. Hermeneutical injustice occurs when the very terms that people use to describe their conditions favor certain groups over others.[71] Fricker gives as examples the shift that occurred with the introduction into the collective vocabulary of the terms "post-partum depression" and "sexual harassment." Prior to the circulation of these terms, women who underwent depression and harassment had no language to label what they underwent, and so they felt isolated, as though the experience was uniquely theirs. They did not have proper resources to respond to the depression or contest the harassment. There is a "gap in the collective hermeneutical resource," Fricker says about such situations, and it is a gap that disadvantages women and advantages the sexual harasser or the husband who thinks his wife needs just to get over it. "Renaming things," Nancy Fraser says, "facilitates new moral assessment of them and mobilizes new social movements and collectivities."[72] So here again meaning and power are intricately related, and the lack of proper designations as well as their introduction can have significant effects on social relations.

6. *Unconscious symbols.* Oftentimes we are aware of what our symbols represent, even if we aren't thinking about it consciously when we employ a given symbol. In other cases, though, people go about their business without being aware that certain things are symbols and/or without being aware of what the symbols represent. This can be relevant for social power in a wide range of cases, because the symbols are shaping people's evaluative attitudes in ways that they cannot critically think about. Bourdieu is one of the keenest analysts of these sorts of symbolic functions. Bourdieu argues that in Kabyle society, the people's houses, their agriculture practices, the food that they eat, their rituals, and their habits of bodily comportment are all structured in such way to represent a distinction between female and male. The effect of this symbolic distinction is to contribute to the villagers' tendency to take gender role differences for granted, regarding them as natural and unquestionable rather than socially instituted. These gender role differences are hierarchical, so the unconscious symbols play a role in perpetuating social relations of masculine domination.

The status and prerogatives that one enjoys or is denied according to one's gender is something Bourdieu calls symbolic capital. One may possess symbolic capital for any number of statuses, abilities, or achievements. In our own society, academic degrees, familiarity with certain traditions of art, and particular styles of diction all are forms of symbolic capital. They are not themselves economic capital, although they require and give one access to it. The differential distribution of symbolic capital in a society plays an essential role in maintaining the relations of domination that occur across the social classes in a society. One of the ways that possessing symbolic capital facilitates a class's maintenance of its privileged position is that the society as a whole is socialized to regard the possessors of certain forms of symbolic capital as properly suited to enjoy a greater share of economic capital than lower classes. Those with a refined sense of taste in art and cuisine are regarded by themselves and by the lower classes as well suited to possess wealth and transfer it from generation to generation to similarly refined progeny.[73]

It is important to note that the sort of symbols that Bourdieu discusses primarily achieve their status as symbols through means other than conceptualization. Symbolic capital is "readily convertible back into economic capital," and thus serves to keep the rich rich and the poor poor, but only because the members of the society do not recognize symbolic capital as having that role and those effects.[74] Geertz defines symbols as vehicles for conceptions, but here we see how inadequate such a definition is. The representational role of the symbols that Bourdieu discusses is instituted through unconscious bodily habits (which Bourdieu calls the habitus), not any concept that people attach to the symbol. Or if there is a clear concept attached to the symbol, there is an additional unconscious role that the symbol plays, an additional thing that the symbol represents about which the people do not know, alongside the one that they do. What Bourdieu is theorizing is that the Kabyle villager's bodily attitudes toward the way his house is arranged, for example, are related to his bodily habits and evaluative attitudes toward gender role divisions. Socializing Kabyle youth into particular patterns of bodily behavior in respect to their house's configuration has some effect in forming habits of acting differentially toward women and men. Thus socialized, it is unlikely that they will question or deviate from the society's general attitudes that women are exclusively suited for some social roles and men for others. It is not necessary for the members of a society to recognize that certain bodily postures, certain shapes, certain flavors, certain areas of the house, and certain periods of time represent femininity and others masculinity. It is not even necessary that such representational relations remain consistent. The agent's "actions and works are the product of a *modus operandi* of which he is not the producer and has no conscious mastery."[75] Nevertheless, the similarities between attitudes among the Kabyle, for example, toward a meal that swells when boiled and toward femininity structure the world into feminine and masculine divisions that perpetuate hierarchical relations between the sexes.[76] The concept attached to the meal is not what is necessary for the meal to have its status as a symbol; rather, the status results from practical patterns of behavior in regard to the meal that are analogous to one's behavior toward women and toward other artifacts and actions that are associated with women.

Unconscious symbols present particular challenges to interpretation. Unlike conscious symbols, which a member of the community in question could report as having some referent, here there is no way to consult the symbol-users directly on the matter. A firm handshake with the right hand can represent masculinity, heterosexuality, and assertiveness whether the shakers know so or not. Since the meaning of symbols that acquire their representative role through unconscious bodily habits is not ascertainable by consulting the practitioners, the scholar will have to issue theoretical hypotheses that are perhaps more tentative than would be for the case when the practitioners can verify themselves the meaning of the symbol. One important cue for the scholar is to see how the community responds to violations of norms. If a girl adopts the posture that is appropriate for a boy and is met with correction or ridicule, there is in an important indication that the bodily comportment is playing a social role of representing gender distinctions. Bourdieu's attention to symbols that are unconscious and that acquire their role through nonlinguistic bodily habits indicates an important way in which Geertz's theory of symbolic meaning is as it stands inadequate for an approach to the study of religion concerned with sociopolitical power. Bourdieu supplements and corrects Geertz in essential ways on the point.

7. *Symbols do things in addition to mean things.* In Bourdieu's account, what matters about symbols is not just what they mean, but what they do. Specifically, they bring about various social effects, including a reinforcement of gender distinctions. Power theorists are particularly interested in the effects of social actions, artifacts, and discourse. Saba Mahmood is typical, for example, in saying that her analysis of the Egyptian women's Islamic movement "should not be confused with a hermeneutical approach, one that focuses on the meanings that particular utterances, discourses, and practices convey." Instead, she "analyzes the *work* that discursive practices perform in making possible particular kinds of subjects."[77] Analyzing the way that discourses and practices shape actors into different types of subjects, that is, subjects with various habits of feeling, desiring, perceiving, and comportment, is central to the work of Foucault, Butler, Bourdieu and many who have been informed by them. One result, though certainly not the only one, of subjectivation, the social practice of forming individuals into subjects, is to reinforce social stratifications. People acquire habits peculiar to their own social group and simultaneously acquire the habits to differentiate others into different social classifications and respond to them accordingly. Subjectivation brings about this result in ways such that the subjects regard their way of classifying their social environment as natural and fixed, instead of historically contingent and socially instituted.

Symbols bring about a number of effects, then, that many have attributed to ideology, in the sense of "a body of meanings and values encoding certain interests relevant to social power."[78] Terry Eagleton mentions several such effects of ideology: it is thought to be unifying, rationalizing, legitimating, universalizing, and naturalizing. That is, ideology theorists think ideology unifies by bringing about social boundaries and groups with which people identify, thereby excluding others; it rationalizes by supplying justifications of social arrangements that might otherwise be criticized; it legitimates by fostering attitudes of deference toward the individuals who occupy positions of institutional power; it universalizes by fostering attitudes that take one's societal arrangements and values as proper to humanity as such, instead of historically specific and contingent; it naturalizes by fostering attitudes that one's societal arrangements are so taken for granted that one cannot imagine things being different.[79] A flag, for example, can do all of these things for the nation that it represents. Or a Catholic shrine can establish a sense of unity among a diasporic group of Miami Cubans, even as it maintains their allegiance to and regard for their homeland and fosters criticism of the regime that led to their displacement.[80]

Theorists of power, whatever they think about the legitimacy of ideology as a contemporary notion, analyze the way that artifacts and discursive and nondiscursive practices bring about these kinds of effects in a society or community. Other effects are relevant too. Mahmood has criticized power theorists for focusing too exclusively on the tendencies of social practices to repress or emancipate, and she wants us to attend to other effects of practices, like the way that religious practices can shape people into particular ways of being pious and ethical that are not neatly repressive or emancipatory.

What is important for my purposes is to express my agreement with power theorists that symbols produce socially relevant effects that are not reducible to their meanings and that an essential task of the social analyst is to attend to these effects, the *work* that practices do, as Mahmood puts it. However, in response to the tendency to downplay the importance of meaning and its interpretation that we see in people like Mahmood and Asad, I want to insist that practices do their work, have their power-relevant consequences, only because they have meaning. The posture that Egyptian Muslims adopt in prayer and the headscarves that they wear produce certain types of religious and ethical subjects, as Mahmood says, but these aspects of their practice do so only because the women regard them as religiously significant, as representations of piety toward Allah. If a friend put a piece of fabric on a woman's head as a prank or if a woman came into the posture of prayer because someone shoved her, these religious behaviors would not play a role in shaping the woman into the sort of pious subject Mahmood describes. The person who wants to analyze the work that religious practices do has to examine the symbolic meanings embedded in those practices (and indeed Mahmood does this quite admirably, despite her disavowal of interpretation).

Janice Boddy provides a helpful model for how to think about these things. Asad and Mahmood express an orientation toward power and away from meaning. Geertz, on the other hand, oftentimes speaks of culture as something that does not *do* anything. "Culture is not a power," he says, but a medium for expression and interpretation. In respect to the Balinese cockfight about which he famously writes,

he says, "The cockfight . . . makes nothing happen. . . . It does not kill anyone, cas-
trate anyone, reduce anyone to animal status, alter the hierarchical relations among
people, or refashion the hierarchy."[81] Boddy, in studying Sudanese possession trance
rituals called *zār*, regards spirit possession as a text, a system of meanings, but one
that can do things. Once you have a system of meanings, it is available for all sorts
of things, and her task is to attend both to the meanings of the trance rituals and
what they produce in their social context. Trance rituals are a "metacultural, secondary text" that "speaks about the village in selective portrayals of what it is not"
(because spirit possession rituals reverse and subvert the hierarchical norms of the
village). Once such a text is available, it can be put to all sorts of uses, no one of
which should be thought of as the explanatory factor for the existence of the ritual,
according to Boddy. For example, the meaning system of the possession rituals can
challenge gender norms and reinforce them, even simultaneously. Possessed women,
for example, can chastise men in the voice of the spirit in ways they never could in
their own voice, but all the while presupposing hierarchical gender role differences.
"Expressions of cultural inversion in the *zār* embody an analysis both critical and
reinforcing, destructive and reproductive at the same time."[82] In this sort of account,
Boddy is attending simultaneously to the symbolic meanings of the spirit possession
rituals and to their power effects without downplaying or reducing either to the
other.

   We are not faced with a choice between power and meaning. Indeed, we must
attend to both. Power is intrinsic to meaning. The very social roles and normative
statuses in which symbolic meaning consists are themselves roles that privilege certain social groups and marginalize others. Power is not reducible to meaning. There
are certain power relations and power-relevant events that operate by means other
than symbolic meaning. However, even those operations take place in conjunction
with and in coordination with symbolic systems and could not do so independently
of them. Students of religion can and should attend to meaning without committing themselves to strange mentalistic entities or to a domain of social practices that
is separable from power. In doing so, however, they cannot ignore power since it is
always present and operative wherever meaning is. But what about our third concept, experience? I will turn now to detail the ways in which that category is itself
implicated in both meaning and power.

5

Experience and Meaning

⌒⟋

RELIGIOUS EXPERIENCE AND THE PROBLEM OF PRIVACY

Rudolf Otto is famous for privileging the insider over the outsider. The religious person, in his account, occupies an authoritative vantage point compared to the external observer. Otto thinks that a special sort of experiential state is the central, most important aspect of religion. He calls this state of consciousness the sense of the *numinous*, and he says that it is characterized by *mysterium tremendum*, a feeling of awe in the face of the divine; a feeling that one is in the presence of something both wholly other and fascinating. In the classic text in which he lays out his views on these matters, *Idea of the Holy*, he instructs his readers to call to mind a time when they have undergone this religious feeling and then states, "Whoever cannot do this, whoever knows no such moments in his experience, is requested to read no farther." He thinks the holy must be immediately experienced and cannot be conveyed by verbal description, so the uninitiated simply cannot profit from his book.[1] The sense of the numinous "is perfectly *sui generis* and irreducible to any other; and therefore, like every absolutely primary and elementary datum, while it admits of being discussed, it cannot be strictly defined" or "taught," merely "evoked."[2] Otto is not too worried about this; he seems to figure that his readers will have had the experience in question or, if not yet, ample opportunities to do so in the future. For contemporary scholars of religion, however, things are not so straightforward. Must one be an insider, a practitioner of the religion, to understand religion adequately? Scholars tend not to view their task in studying religions as becoming religious themselves. They are wary of claims that privilege the interpretive authority of the religious person, since such privileging can serve to protect the religion from criticism.

But Otto has his finger on something important about religious experiences, which is that people who have undergone an experience do seem to be in a different situation in relation to the experience from those who have not. Only the experiencers know what the occurrence felt like, and only the experiencers know whether or not they actually had an experience. For all the outsider knows, the one reporting an experience could be lying. It seems, then, that religious experiences are problematically private in nature and the scholar is in a position of relative ignorance in respect to the experience. Otto's insight that the insider has a sort of privilege made its way into phenomenology of religion, which methodologically prioritized the way that the religion is experienced by the practitioner as that which the scholar must seek to access. Geertz incorporates a version of this tenet into his approach as well, as my discussion of his relation to phenomenology of religion in the last chapter shows.

The asymmetry between the experiencer and the third party is one aspect of what I am calling the problem of privacy in relation to the study of experience.[3] The other aspect of the problem of privacy concerns the relation between experiences and the social, cultural, and historical context in which they occur. Are experiences so private that they are independent of the socio-cultural context of the experiencer? Many of the people who have written about religious experience have thought so, as we saw in chapter 1. Or at least they have thought this is the case for some special class of religious experiences, sometimes designated as mystical experiences. William James speaks of the classical mystical texts as perennial and universal, with "neither birthday nor native land."[4] Mircea Eliade speaks of the sense of the sacred as a universal "element in the structure of consciousness."[5] In this chapter, I will address both problems of privacy concerning religious experience. I will argue that experiences are not too private for scholars to study but that there are significant differences between the insider and the outsider. This is one of the insights from the experiential approach to religion, especially in its phenomenology of religion guise, that I want to preserve. As for the much-debated question of whether there are crossculturally universal experiences, my primary aim is to advance and reframe the discussion by situating experiences in social practices, but considering the issue in the light of social practices does lead to some specific considerations in favor of the constructivist position as well as a possible avenue of argumentation for perennialists to pursue.

PERENNIALISM VERSUS CONSTRUCTIVISM

The question of whether some experiences are universal and removed from the effects of cultural, religious, and historical context has been vigorously debated for decades, under the banners of two competing camps, the perennialists and the constructivists. Perennialists agree with people like James and Eliade that there are experiences of the same basic type that are universal across culture and religious tradition. Notable contemporary proponents include Robert K. C. Forman and G. William Barnard.[6] Constructivists think that experiences are culturally constructed to a degree that no such cross-cultural common experience is possible. The most influential people to advance this view are Wayne Proudfoot and Steven Katz.[7] Following the work of Katz and Proudfoot in the late 1970s and 1980s, the weight of scholarly opinion shifted decisively to the constructivist side of things, but a committed and sizable group of perennialists remains active and productive. Some have suggested that the debate has exhausted itself, but I will show that significant unresolved issues remain and require attention.[8]

The first unresolved issue is the fact that despite the widespread acceptance of Katz's and Proudfoot's important work on the topic, their arguments leave some important questions unresolved. Katz's contribution to the discussion is primarily found in his essay, "Language, Epistemology, and Mysticism." This essay tackles both philosophical issues and textual ones. In respect to his claims about textual interpretation, Katz is quite successful. I have already discussed, in chapter 3, his criticism of the noted perennialist W. T. Stace's attempt to construe references to "nothing" in a Hasidic text as universalistic experiences of "the absence of all multiplicity." Katz looks at a number of examples as well where perennialists have collated excerpts from mystical texts from different religious traditions, claiming that the texts are describing the same sort of experience. He demonstrates in detail that in doing so, perennialists extract textual fragments from their larger linguistic and historical context. This allows the perennialists to present apparent similarities in textual descriptions as though they referred to the same phenomenological experience, but Katz shows convincingly in the cases that he examines that these similarities are but superficial. Attending to the fuller linguistic and religious context makes it clear that there are significant disparities between the experience reports that the perennialists regard as identical. Subsequent to Katz's criticism of the sort of hastiness Stace and others display, the perennialist position has declined. Perennialists still at times employ the technique of collating snippets of religious texts to support their view, but it is much harder to take them seriously for doing so.

So Katz's negative arguments, concerning the perennialists' handling of mystical texts, are persuasive, but what about his positive arguments for the constructivist view? Well, here we find that Katz sees fit merely to posit the constructivist position as an assumption, apparently in need of no defense.[9] He tells us early in his essay that he subscribes to the "epistemological assumption" that "there are NO pure (i.e., unmediated) experiences." He continues, "The experience itself . . . is shaped by concepts which the mystic brings to . . . his experience."[10] Despite his professed agnosticism on metaphysical matters,[11] he in fact employs all manner of controversial beliefs regarding the relationship between mind and reality. The foremost such assumption is that "the mind is active in constructing [some experienced object] x as experienced," and "the object of experience . . . is regulated by structures of consciousness and experience."[12] In making these sorts of claims, Katz commits himself to all manner of metaphysical views, seemingly Kantian in inspiration, and he figures that his audience will be favorably disposed enough toward them that he need not defend them.

Proudfoot, to his credit, takes the involvement of culture in experiences as something that needs to be defended, not merely assumed. Proudfoot's work on religious experience is path breaking in a number of regards, not just for its treatment of experience, but also for its account of the nature of emotions and its discussion of interpretation and explanation in religious studies. It still rightly enjoys a sterling reputation in the field. Proudfoot's position is similar to Katz, in that both of them subscribe to the view that concepts are essential constituents of experience and that concepts are cultural in nature. That is, concepts are historically particular, and people obtain the concepts that they possess through processes of social learning. If that is so, then experiences themselves must be culturally specific. If religious people from different traditions use different concepts in recognizing their experiences as religious experiences and if those concepts are essential constituents of the experience, then the experiences themselves are culturally particular.

The focus on concepts in Proudfoot's analysis is distinctive, and it generates a number of the book's signal accomplishments. Proudfoot views the experiencers' concepts as what are necessary to identify an experience as a religious experience. When we identify something as a religious experience, we must do so in terms of the experiencers' own concepts pertaining to whatever they think that they have experienced. It is fair to disregard the experiencers' beliefs and concepts in our attempts to explain the experiences, that is, to account for their origin and nature. But to describe the experiences and identify them, we cannot disregard the experiencers' own testimony of what they have experienced. As important a role as concepts play in Proudfoot's account, the emphasis on the conceptual aspects of experience could lead us to overlook the possible importance of the nonconceptual aspects of experience. Proudfoot acknowledges that concepts and beliefs only constitute experiences "in part."[13] But then what are the nonconceptual features of experiences? Proudfoot speaks of a "felt quality" to experiences, and he also speaks of physiological states, though he says that these are not in themselves sufficient to identify the experience.[14] But this raises the question of whether felt qualities, physiological qualities, or some common causal origin might serve as a universal aspect of the experience, regardless of the culturally specific contribution of concepts and beliefs to the experience. It might be good enough for the perennialist to say that even if there are culturally specific aspects of mystical experiences, there are also universal aspects. In fact, this is just the view that Stace holds about sense experience. He says, "Although we may never be able to find sense experience completely free of interpretation, it can hardly be doubted that a sensation is one thing and its conceptual interpretation is another thing. That is to say, they are distinguishable though not completely separable."[15] So if there is a nonconceptual aspect of religious experiences, then that aspect could itself serve as the common core that is universal. An additional question concerns the fact that some perennialists have spoken of experiences that are devoid of concepts altogether, and this is not one of the topics that Proudfoot discusses extensively in *Religious Experience*.

A SOCIAL PRACTICAL THEORY OF PERCEPTUAL EXPERIENCES

To get further clarity on these matters, the first thing that we need is a more precise understanding of what a concept is. The term "concept" has been central to the debates surrounding the possibility of universal religious experiences, because the constructivists' key contention is that experiences involve concepts, which are culturally specific, and perennialists either deny this or maintain that experiences have significant nonconceptual aspects. But no one has attended carefully to the nature of this complicated term, "concept," on which so much of the debate hinges.

One influential player in the debates on religious experience who has addressed the nature of concepts explicitly is philosopher William Alston. Alston's book, *Perceiving God*, is a defense of the idea that religious experiences, which he understands as analogous to sensory perception, can contribute to the rationality of religious belief.[16] That is, for people who take themselves to have experiences of God, these experiences can lend support to making their beliefs in God reasonable. Just as is the case for Proudfoot and Katz, for Alston too concepts are an important part of the story. Alston admits that concepts and beliefs can affect perceptual experience, religious or otherwise. However, he does not think that concepts are essentially part of the experiences, unlike Proudfoot and Katz. So he remains agnostic on the debate between perennialists and constructivists as to whether there are experiences in which concepts are not involved.[17] should read: Alston admits that concepts and beliefs can affect a perceptual experience, religious or otherwise. However, he does not think that concepts are essentially part of the experiences, unlike Proudfoot and Katz. So he remains agnostic on the debate between perennialists and constructivists as to whether there are experiences in which concepts are involved. He writes, "Sensory experience essentially involves a *presentation* of objects to consciousness in a way that does not *necessarily* involve the application of general concepts to those objects . . . and it is this feature of perception that clearly distinguishes it from just thinking about an object, remembering it, or fantasizing about it."[18] To make sense of this position, then, and evaluate its plausibility over and against the position Proudfoot takes, we need to hear more about what concepts are. Alston does not have much to say on that topic in *Perceiving God*, but he does give us a bit more in a later text titled "Perception and Cognition." In that essay, Alston tells us, "To apply a concept to X is either to think of X as belonging to a certain kind or as possessing a certain property."[19] So to apply the concept "blue mug" to a particular object is to think of the object as a member of the class of mugs and to think of it as having the property of being blue.

But what are we to think of this "to think of"? What does it mean to think of objects in such ways? In our daily routines, we do not go around mentally talking to ourselves, saying the name of every kind of object we see. I do not walk into this room and silently recite to myself, "wall," "window," "table," "desk," and so on. That would be tedious indeed. Now Alston recognizes this, and he says that applying concepts can be "more or less implicit." But not so implicit as to be unconscious. He insists that conceptualization is an exercise of which we are conscious, at least on some level. So if Alston wants us to believe that it is possible to have a perceptual experience that does not involve concepts, it is crucial that he make us understand how to distinguish between a situation in which we are using a concept and one in which we are not. But all we have to go on is our ability to detect whether or not we are implicitly, on some level of consciousness, thinking of objects as members of kinds and as having properties. But do we have a reliable ability introspectively to detect such things? And if so, how would we know that we did? Alston does not give us much help here.

The contribution that I want to make to the debates about the nature of religious experience starts with a conception of concept that is thoroughly social practical in nature, not introspective. I will round out the social-practical philosophy of language that I discussed in chapter 4 here, discussing in more detail the role of perception in relation to language, meaning, and knowledge, and then applying this account of perception to religious experience. This philosophy of language and mind is in many respects indebted to Ludwig Wittgenstein. Wittgenstein situates our language-use in the context of our social practices, our various shared patterns of behavior that aim at achieving certain practical ends. This view rejects the idea that there is some bare relation between words and things, independent of our interests, goals, projects, and needs. This is what is in large part captured in Wittgenstein's saying, "The meaning of a word is its use in the language," and his appeal to such notions as a shared "form of life" as the context in which language achieves meaningfulness and the capacity to refer.[20]

Wittgenstein is a theoretical quietist, but Sellars and Brandom are themselves hardly timid when it comes to theorizing. Sellars develops his views most influentially in the essay, "Empiricism and the Philosophy of Mind," a piece famous for the rejection of what Sellars calls the "Myth of the Given."[21] According to the myth of the given, some experiential state, in and of itself and independent of other experiences and of the experiencer's knowledge and beliefs, can deliver a piece of knowledge to the experiencer. I can know that the necktie in front of me is green because I see a patch of green in my visual field, regardless of what else I know.[22] (One easily gets the impression that this sort of view is in operation in much of the perennialist literature on religious experience.) This view of the relation between knowledge and experience removes all social and cultural influence on the acquisition of knowledge derived from experience. In contrast, Sellars (and before him G. W. F. Hegel and John Dewey) emphasizes the role of socialization and context in determining just which bits of knowledge we acquire in response to our interactions with our environment. For me to judge that the necktie is green, for example, I have to regard myself in standard viewing conditions (as opposed to being in a room with lighting that makes blue things appear green). Any item of perceptual knowledge presupposes other knowledge.

In Brandom's interpretation and development of Sellars's views, perception has both a causal and a conceptual component. The causal component involves our capacity to respond differentially to different environmental conditions. This is a capacity that we share with all sorts of objects, including, for instance, thermometers and rods of iron. A thermometer is disposed to respond differently to a temperature of eighty degrees from a temperature of seventy degrees; and iron is disposed to respond to the presence of water by rusting. The human organism also is disposed to respond differentially to different environmental conditions. It has the capacity, for instance, to respond differently to the presence of a cat as opposed to the presence of a dog. For a human who has learned language, one way that such a person is disposed to respond differentially to nearby cats and dogs is to acquire a disposition to report, "That is a cat," in the one case, and, "That is a dog," in the other. Of course, acquiring and possessing a disposition to issue such reports does not mean that one actually goes around blurting out such statements in response to everything one sees, even mentally. To say that one has a disposition to say such things is just to say that one would make such a statement, should the occasion to do so arise, and, further, that one can, on the basis of acquiring the disposition, perform actions (such as exiting the room to avoid an allergic reaction) and make inferences (such as, "That is a dog; I'm at Gordon's house; I know Gordon has just one dog whose name is Sierra; therefore that is Sierra").

Once one has acquired language, one is a concept-user, since in this view we are to understand "grasping a concept as mastering the use of a word."[23] That means that we can say similar things about what is involved with concepts as we did in the last chapter about the meaning of terms. To master the use of a word is more than just to respond to the presence of a certain object by reciting its name, as we saw in chapter 4. Parrots can respond to the presence of a saltine by squawking "cracker," but they are not thereby language-users, and they have not grasped the concept of cracker. To qualify as grasping a concept, one must know the inferential relations in which the word stands. So to grasp or use any one concept one must know a whole lot of concepts. The person who knows what cracker means is able to make such judgments as "Crackers are edible," "Crackers are not carrots," "Crackers get mushy when wet," "Crackers are not living organisms," "Crackers are not numbers," and so on. And so if I see a cracker and acquire a disposition to make the observation report, "That is a cracker," I can infer such things as "That is edible." The ability to make inferences is the salient difference between a parrot and me. What is more, inferring is a normative undertaking. One can make proper or improper inferences. So a concept, then, is a norm of judgment.[24] The concept of cracker is constituted by its contribution to the inferential role of sentences in which it occurs, which is to say the proper inferences that are licensed by statements in which the concept occurs. Concepts are also constituted in part by the perceptual situations ("That is a cracker") and practical situations ("I will now eat this cracker") in which they play a role in perceiving and acting.

So concept-use requires both dispositions to respond differentially to different sorts of things and the capacity to issue reports and make judgments. As we saw in the last chapter, though, the judgments or beliefs that one comes to through perception and inference are not just a matter of dispositions and abilities to report, act, and infer but also a matter of normative social statuses. When we see Michael standing within plain view of Lucille, we can attribute to Michael the belief that Lucille is in the room, not because we think some strange entity called a belief resides in Michael's head, but because we treat people in such situations as responsible to speak and act in accordance with the fact that Lucille is in the room. We would expect him to say, "Yes," were he asked by a friend later if Lucille was at the party. We would expect him to point to Lucille, whom he knows is a physician, if a stranger were to ask whether there was a doctor in the house. Beliefs, then, are very much public affairs, not absolutely private states or entities.

In denying the myth of the given, we are denying that merely being in the presence of a visible cracker is sufficient to confer on an observer the piece of knowledge, "That is a cracker," in isolation from any other knowledge, beliefs, and concepts the observer has. Rather, to attain even such a basic piece of knowledge about the object before one, one must have suitably undergone a process of training and socialization, such that one acquires two sorts of skills: first, one must have been trained to key certain kinds of observation reports to certain kinds of stimuli—in our example, one must have been trained to respond to the visible presence of crackers by acquiring the disposition to report, "That is a cracker"—and, second, one must have acquired the skill of being able to make inferences about crackers. So acquiring knowledge about perceptible objects involves both a causal and a conceptual element. In arriving at the judgment, "That is a cracker," the causal process is that the visible presence of the cracker causes (with the help of socialization) the acquisition of a disposition to make the report, "That is a cracker." The conceptual element comes both in that the report, as a linguistic disposition, consists of concepts and in that the observer knows the inferential roles of the terms in the report. In conjunction with possessing the two skills of reporting and inferring, one must be in a social practice with others, subject to norms, in which one is held responsible by them for acting and speaking in certain ways, and in which one holds others responsible as well.

Importantly, for the person appropriately trained, the judgment "That is a cracker" is not inferred from anything. The person arrives at the belief causally, not inferentially. In that the judgment is not arrived by inferring it from some premise, we can speak of it as immediate. Immediate here does not imply the absence of cultural influence, however. Culture and concepts influence our perceptual beliefs, but they do so by way of preparation, not mediation. That is, our concepts do not stand between us and the world; rather they are culturally acquired ways of responding to the objects and events we encounter. The belief about the cracker is immediate and noninferential, but it is implicated in (and constituted by) inferential roles, since one cannot arrive at the judgment that one sees a cracker without already knowing what sorts of things one can infer about crackers.

We can say similar things about the immediacy of the judgments that we issue regarding our own states of emotion and belief and regarding other states of the self such as pain and pleasure, skin temperature, and the position of our body and limbs. It is important to mention this, because the primary models that have been used to analyze religious experience are perception (as in Alston's *Perceiving God*) and emotion (Proudfoot emphasizes this model). Beliefs about our emotional states are immediate in the same sense as our perceptual judgments are: they are not arrived at on the basis of inference (there are exceptions, such as being resentful or jealous unawares, until one infers it from one's own behavior).[25] In the case of self-awareness, as in perception, the judgments originate causally, not inferentially. In both the case of perception and of self-knowledge, the immediacy of the judgments does not imply that the judgments are infallible, incorrigible, or indubitable. A barn façade can noninferentially bring about the perceptual judgment, "That is a barn," which is false.

The capacity to respond to the objects in our environment that we sense by acquiring linguistic dispositions to report the presence of the objects is what marks off sapient animals, humans, from merely sentient animals. Sentience consists in the capacity to detect objects in the organism's environment (and to detect states of the organism itself) through the use of sensory organs. The human capacity for sapience presumes sentience but adds to this the ability to make judgments about the objects and to make inferences from these judgments to other judgments and to hold one another responsible to infer in accordance with the relevant norms. Brandom reserves the term "perception" for this sort of achievement, an achievement that is necessarily conceptual. A merely sentient organism can hear, smell, see, touch, and so on but not perceive.

So in this account, any sensory episode that one has the capacity to report—to talk about—is necessarily conceptual, because the employment of concepts in a sensory episode just is the acquisition of a capacity to report and to talk about the sensed object with one's peers, in combination with the capacity to respond practically to the object. This is a whole different way of thinking about what it is to employ a concept than those ways that have heretofore dominated the discussion of religious experience. Philosophers of religion and other scholars have tended to regard concepts as some sort of mentalistic filter into which raw sense data flow. The concept as filter model or something like it seems to be present in Katz (*"All* experience is processed through, organized by, and makes itself available to us in extremely complex epistemological ways" and "the forms of consciousness which the mystic brings to the experience set structured and limiting parameters on what the experience will be") and something comparable is in Russell T. McCutcheon ("The generic, indistinguishable stuff of the world gets to count as isolatable 'things' [i.e., items of discourse] only in light of competing, institutionalized systems of value, classification, and rank").[26] These are views that Donald Davidson describes in these terms: "Conceptual schemes, we are told, are ways of organizing experience; they are systems of categories that give form to the data of sensation." To views such as McCutcheon's, in which language organizes the "generic, indistinguishable stuff of the world," Davidson replies:

We cannot attach a clear meaning to the notion of organizing a single object (the world, nature etc.) unless that object is understood to contain or consist in other objects. Someone who sets out to organize a closet arranges the things in it. If you are told not to organize the shoes and shirts, but the closet itself, you would be bewildered. How would you organize the Pacific Ocean? Straighten out its shores, perhaps, or relocate its islands, or destroy its fish. . . . How about . . . experience? Can we think of a language organizing *it*? Much the same difficulties recur. The notion of organization applies only to pluralities.[27]

Conceptualization requires and involves reliable dispositions to respond differentially to different environmental conditions. If the stuff of the world were really indistinguishable, conceptualization could not get off the ground.

Mentalistic views of concepts (and perception and sensation) result in radical subjectivism. In such accounts, all the real work of sensing, perceiving, and conceptualizing occurs in the mental sphere, accessible to one individual at most: a veil behind which the internal workings are radically removed from the possibility of inspection by others. The subjectivism of these accounts has plagued the modern academic study of religion since its inception and has funded both Otto's attempt to deauthorize the religiously inexperienced from having any say about the nature of religious experience and Robert Sharf's consignment of the term "experience" to meaninglessness (see chapters 2 and 3). The social practical account of concepts, however, decisively breaks from this subjectivist tradition and locates concepts and perception in social practices, not some opaque mental space. To conceptualize something is to acquire dispositions to talk and reason about it and act in respect to it and to occupy the associated normative social status of being held responsible to talk and reason properly about it.

The linguistic dispositions involved in perception are public in another way, too, in that they are acquired through a process of training and habitutation, in short, socialization. We acquire the linguistic dispositions that we do in response to objects because we have seen others so speak about similar objects, and we have been, from a young age, instructed and corrected so to speak ourselves about similar objects. Even when we encounter a novel type of object, we rely on our socialization, either by employing more general terms ("the thing in my car's engine to the right of the carburetor"), by querying others for the proper term, or, if possible, by inferring the identity of the proper term from other things that we know ("I've never seen one of those before, but it has a curved tail, and they told me that here in Arizona I should watch out for scorpions, which have curved tails. So that must be a scorpion").

SOCIAL PRACTICES AND RELIGIOUS EXPERIENCES

To turn from scorpions to spirits, we can now apply this model to religious experience in a fairly straightforward way. Let's say someone reports that he has seen Kali, and a scholar wants to assess the significance of this claim. The scholar regards Kali as a religious object, even if she does not believe Kali exists, and so regards the report as a report of a religious experience. (This is true regardless of whether the reporter himself has a concept for religion. The act of classifying an experience as a religious experience depends on the concepts of the classifier.) In regarding this experience as a religious experience, the scholar is treating the experiencer as occupying a normative social status in relation to the event. The scholar regards the experiencer as responsible to speak and act as though he has seen Kali. For example, the scholar expects the experiencer to answer "Yes" to questions like "Have you ever seen Kali?" So the scholar regards the experiencer as having acquired a set of dispositions to act, speak, and infer in accord with the belief, "I saw Kali," and regards the experiencer as responsible to do so. So far, this is in the relevant ways just as it is in relation to ordinary sensory perception.

In regard to ordinary sensory perceptual events, however, the scholar may be more likely to adopt beliefs concerning the actual presence of the object. If the person reports, "I saw a mango lassi," the scholar will probably herself adopt the belief that there was a mango lassi in the room where the experiencer was. If the scholar does not believe that Kali exists or is agnostic about the goddess, however, then she will not adopt the belief that Kali was actually experienced by the individual. She expresses this reservation by speaking in such ways as, "He believes that he experienced Kali" instead of "He experienced Kali," whereas when it comes to mango lassis, the scholar will be willing to say things like, "He saw a mango lassi." This sort of attributing beliefs to others but withholding assent oneself is not peculiar to assessments of religion. This is a common pattern regarding anything for which the third party doubts that the experience is as the experiencer says that it is. If the scholar knows that a friend was making milkshakes that look just like mango lassis at the time and place that someone reported seeing a mango lassi, she withholds assent from the proposition, "He saw a lassi," admitting only, "He believes he saw a lassi." These are standard features of our ordinary practices of using language. If we think that the person is reliably capable of recognizing the object in question and we have no reason to doubt that the object in question was really present, we both attribute beliefs to others and adopt beliefs about the perceived objects. If we don't think the person is reliably capable of recognizing the object in question and/or we have reason to doubt that the object actually was present, then we attribute the perceptual belief to the person but withhold assent from the belief that the purported object was actually present.

The scholar may doubt that the experience report corresponds to an experience, thinking instead that the report is a fabrication, whether sincere or ill intentioned. However, in many cases, the scholar will not have reason to doubt that some sort of experience occurred, even if she doubts that it involved an actually existing god. In those cases where a scholar is willing to attribute an experience of some sort to the one reporting the experience, the scholar will suppose that the experiencer underwent some sort of causal process that led to an event that he thought was an experience of Kali. In speaking of causal conditions, I in no way mean to imply that the third party is obligated to affirm that the causal conditions that the experiencer thinks are responsible for the experience are the ones that actually are responsible. Like Proudfoot, I assume that experience reports generally imply some sort of causal explanation of the experience, often supernatural. When someone says, "I experienced Kali," it is implied that the person thinks that Kali exists and that Kali's activity is relevant to bringing about the experience. Also following Proudfoot, I do not regard it as obligatory that the observer accepts the experiencer's understanding of the causal conditions. The scholar could have any number of causal processes in mind: a hallucination, for example, or a dissociative state or an intense emotional state that the person mistakenly attributed to Kali's presence. The scholar who is religious herself and believes in the object reported, of course, may think that Kali actually is involved in the causal process of the experience. (I construe causality here broadly enough to include ordinary processes and also supernatural processes such as those involved in being affected by gods and other religious entities and states, if such processes there are.)

This notion of experience constitutes a radical break from the phenomenological tradition that has dominated the study of experience. The phenomenological tradition has placed at the center of its analysis the presence of certain phenomenal qualities, the sense of the sacred, the feeling of absolute dependence, the feeling of the numinous, or what have you. This institutes a mysterious realm inaccessible to all but the individual self and perhaps even opaque to that self, since self-consciousness is at least in certain cases notoriously elusive and misleading.[28] It is the privileging of states of self-consciousness and introspection, with little regard to the causal conditions underlying or producing such states, that has given the categories of religious experience and experience generally such bad names, as concepts too slippery and elusive to bear any analytical weight.[29] In contrast, by understanding religious experiences in terms that are intrasubjective and extrasubjective, like observable dispositions, causal conditions, and normative statuses, we make religious experiences in principle no more problematic than our ordinary, everyday sensory perceptions. The special problems that religious experiences pose are due to questions that we might have about the reality of the causes that the subject ascribes to the experience, not to any particular difficulties that inhere in the use of terms like "consciousness" and "awareness."

PERENNIALISM AND CONCEPTS

In many regards, the social practical account of religious experience that I have outlined sides with constructivists against perennialists. Many perennialists have proposed that there is a special kind of mystical experience in which the experiencer's concepts are not involved. Forman calls this a "pure consciousness event," which he thinks is the consciousness of nothing except for consciousness itself. In such a state, one is aware of no objects of experience but is in a state of "wakeful contentless consciousness."[30] One's concepts and beliefs are not involved in the experience. This whole perspective makes consciousness the central analytical principle and places a high degree of trust in the reliability of introspection. Forman and people like him think that one can, through introspection, know whether or not one is using concepts and even that one is in a state of wakeful contentless consciousness as opposed to being asleep. How is it possible that mystics can know that they have had an experience of nothing but their own consciousness? Forman answers: *I do not know how* I know that have been aware in a pure consciousness event. I just know by means of knowledge-by-identity that I was continuously awake. And that's all."[31] He appeals to three types of knowledge: knowledge-that, which is propositional in nature, such as I know that a banana is on the table; knowledge-by-acquaintance, which occurs merely by sensing the banana; and knowledge-by-identity, which is awareness of oneself. These latter two are not conceptual, whereas knowledge-that is conceptual, according to Forman.[32]

In a social practical view of concepts, the employment of concepts is not a mental event or process of which one necessarily is conscious. Rather, concept use is the acquisition or exercise of dispositions to speak, infer, and act in certain ways and it is the social status of being held responsible by one's conversation partners. So any experience that someone could report necessarily involves concepts, because acquiring dispositions to report that one has had an experience is an essential aspect of what it is to conceptualize an experience. To count as having a religious experience, one must be able to respond to the experience by acquiring a disposition to report having had the experience, and such a report will be issued in the terms that one has acquired through socialization and language learning. This view objects to the way that Forman wants to distinguish among conceptual knowledge-that from both nonconceptual knowledge-by-acquaintance and nonconceptual knowledge-by-identity. For any state of awareness to count as knowledge of any sort, one must be able to report it. To be able to report it, one must have acquired a sizable repertoire of concepts and beliefs. An experience that was not conceptual would be an experience that one could not report to anyone, even oneself. It would be an event that we did not notice, like the case of a bicyclist, deeply immersed in thought, who successfully navigates around a stick in her path but could not tell you that she had done so.

This may seem to be an unfair refutation of the perennialist position, since the conception of concept to which I appeal is perhaps quite different from that embraced by perennialists. The perennialists might complain that even if I am right about the social practical ways in which concepts and beliefs operate, this does not address their concerns or what their concept of concepts involves, which is the phenomenology of the experience at the moment of the experience. But even if I employ a different conception of concepts than the perennialists do, there is still a direct point of contention. One benefit for many perennialists to emphasizing the phenomenologically conceptless experience is to eliminate the aspects of experiences, like concepts and beliefs, that are culturally specific, so that the experience can be cross-culturally universal. But if I am right about the social practical operation of concepts, then regardless of what is phenomenologically occurring in the experience, cultural particularity is still involved. For one thing, this is true simply in virtue of the fact that the experiencer responds to the event as a religious or mystical experience. The experiencer, when having the ostensibly pure consciousness event, retains the necessary bodily posture and attention to persist in the state. The experiencer does not (typically) lie down and go to sleep, make a phone call, or strike up a casual conversation with a peer. Remaining in a pure consciousness event would require beliefs, whether consciously experienced or not, such as that extraordinary states of consciousness are desirable. Someone who thought that they were to be avoided at all costs would respond to the ecstatic moment quite differently. This is a similar point as that in Sellars's rejection of the myth of the given, when he points out that to count to oneself as perceiving a tie as green, one must take oneself to be in standard lighting conditions, as opposed, for example, to taking one's conditions to be such that unusual lighting is making blue objects appear as green ones. The phenomenology itself is not enough to make the experience what it is; one's background beliefs and attitudes count too.[33] To return to the supposed pure consciousness event, the experiencers, with their body and their attention, respond to what they are undergoing as to a pure consciousness event. Regardless of what things seem like during the experience, this practical and bodily classification of the event, which in many cases are a result of the techniques of preparation for the event, are culturally particular. Similar considerations apply to the value of the pure consciousness experience. Let's say, for the sake of argument, that the perennialists turned out to be right that there are cross-culturally identical experiences that do not involve any objects of awareness. Another key lesson from Sellars's rejection of the myth of the given is that nothing in the nature of the experience itself presents a reason to take it as any more significant than napping, chewing gum, or conversing with a friend. Objectless states of consciousness, should they occur, do not announce to their owner whether or why they matter. It is only the larger context of the beliefs and values of the tradition in which the experience occurs (or the beliefs and values of some other party who is assessing the experience) that assigns significance to it. Those beliefs and values are certainly products of historically particular processes of transmission. Forman claims that pure consciousness events have "a great deal to teach about the nature of human life and intelligence."[34] If they do, it is only because some individual or tradition holds certain beliefs about them and attributes a certain value to them, and such beliefs and values cannot be derived merely from the experiences themselves.

Perhaps, though, the deeper issue is that the perennialists' conception of concept, and knowledge for that matter, to the degree that they give us any inkling of what they mean by the terms, are too mentalistic and subjective to perform any analytic work. It is this sort of concept of concept that has given experience such a bad rap. If perennialists want to maintain that one can determine whether or not one has applied concepts in an experience, strictly through introspection, they owe us an account of concepts, nonconceptual knowledge, and introspective reliability that can make sense of their claims. If their account bifurcates consciousness from the social and public world, as it seems to, then those of us who have rejected Cartesianism will hardly find their account plausible.

PERENNIALISM AND CAUSES

It may be that there is another option for perennialists. If the strategy of arguing for a common religious experience on the basis of the experiencers' phenomenological descriptions does not succeed, perhaps an alternative would be to argue that, regardless of the phenomenology, there is some common causal origin of the experiences. My account keeps the causal conditions that bring about experiences on the table as a separate matter from the conceptual aspects of experiences; the causes are important in their own right in contributing to the occurrence of the experience. This serves as a corrective or at least a significantly different placement of emphasis to accounts like Proudfoot's and Katz's that emphasize the conceptual as the primary element in determining the nature of the experience (though Proudfoot certainly recognizes the importance of causes). While I agree with Proudfoot and Katz that concepts are necessarily involved in experiences, my account has no difficulty hand-ling those cases in which the conceptual element is at best a minor feature of the experience, as in extreme cases of ecstasy, pleasure, and pain.

Retaining the causal conditions as a matter fully worthy of attention in their own right preserves, in principle, a place for the common mystical experience. The common-core proponents have faltered in making their case precisely because of the inscrutable interiority to which they appeal. However, an alternative strategy would be to locate the common core not in any supposed phenomenal quality but in a set of causal conditions. Just as we can speak of different individuals from different cul-tures perceiving the same object but responding in vastly different manners, so also we could speak of some similar causal conditions, whether involving natural or su-pernatural processes, that mystics the world over encounter. A neuroscientist might think that some identical physiological state undergirds various experiences, regard-less of how the experiencers conceptualize them. A theist might think that God un-dergirds various experiences, regardless of how the experiencers conceptualize them. John Hick argues that "the Real" undergirds various experiences, theistic and non-theistic, which members of different religious traditions conceptualize differently.[35]

Proudfoot thinks proceeding in this fashion, privileging the causal conditions over the experiencer's concepts, will be to misidentify the experience:

> Attempts to differentiate a core from its [experiencers'] interpretations may cause the theorist to lose the very experience he is trying to analyze. . . . It might indeed be possible to produce cross-cultural documentation of some common physiological states or mental images in the experiences of mystics. But to focus on these, as some theorists have done, is not to delineate a core but to attend to something other than the experience. A decelerated heart rate may be common to some mystics and to all athletes at the height of training, and it may be a natural endowment of some individuals in contrast to others. Deautomatization . . . may occur as a consequence of a psychotic break, of find-ing oneself in a completely unfamiliar and possibly threatening environment, or of preparation through spiritual exercises. But to attend to such phenomena while disregarding the content of the mystic's beliefs and the expectations he or she brings to the experience is to err in one's priorities. What others have dismissed as interpretative overlay may be the distinguishing mark of the experience.[36]

I am in agreement with Proudfoot that it would be a mistake to mark two experi-ences as identical just on the basis of some common causal process. But a perennial-ist could still maintain that there is an important universalism in such common causes, even if the experiences themselves are not identical. Proudfoot says that a focus on the causes of the experience is "to err in one's priorities," but there could be different priorities and purposes in approaching experiences. The perennialists' priority may well be to find a common causal origin to experiences without regard for the experiencer's conceptualization of the experience.

This is not a position that I have any inclination to advocate. The standard procedure for the perennialists has been to supply textual evidence from mystical texts to argue that the texts are reporting the same phenomenal qualities, and I regard Katz's and others' arguments against this sort of proof-texting as devastating to that strategy. Nevertheless, if a perennialist had another argument to the effect that mystics in different times and places undergo similar causal processes, then one could in principle advocate a common core to mystical experiences. The constructivists' overemphasis on the conceptualizing activity of the experiencer unduly precludes this possibility. Having said that, the challenges facing an attempt to argue for a cross-culturally universal cause to religious experiences on some other basis than supposed phenomenological similarities are staunch indeed. Once we set aside the attempt to find the commonalities among the experiencers' conceptual reports, all that we are left with is the perennialists' metaphysical or physical assumptions, and if we do not subscribe to those already, we will not be likely to be convinced by what the perennialist infers from the assumptions. The burden on the perennialist, then, is to make a convincing case for the metaphysical or physical assumptions, and this is no small task.

INSIDERS, OUTSIDERS, AND MARY

The question about perennialism concerns one aspect of the problem of privacy: whether or not experiences are removed from the effects of cultural and historical context. The other aspect of the problem of privacy is the question of whether insiders— the experiencers themselves—are privileged in relation to outsiders when it comes to understanding the nature of the experiences. Are Otto and likeminded people correct that those who have not had an experience are vastly worse off in respect to knowledge about experiences? I will take up that question in this section.

To shed some light on the perspective of the outsider in relation to religious experiences, I will adapt a thought experiment from the work of philosopher Frank Jackson. Jackson's thought experiment involves an exceptionally intelligent color scientist named Mary who has lived her entire life in a monochromatic environment, consisting strictly of black, white, and shades of gray.[37] Notwithstanding that limitation, she has managed to learn every fact there is to be known about the physics and neuroscience of color perception. Then one day, Mary leaves the environment for the first time and sees colored objects. Previously, she has known everything that there is to know about the physical constitution of blue objects, the properties of light reflection, and the neurobiological behavior of the retina, optic nerve, and brain in response to the sight of a blue object. But now she has seen something blue, let's say a blue mug. Mary, despite her exhaustive physical knowledge, has achieved a new status. She now has undergone the causal process of being visually stimulated by a blue object, and she has now exercised the ability to discriminate visually blue objects from other objects.

Now if the basic elements in the case of Mary apply to religious experience, then we can draw two lessons from Jackson's thought experiment. First, it does make sense to speak of an asymmetrical relationship between the insider and the outsider. Someone who has had a religious experience can be in a significantly different situation in regard to the experience from the outsider. One who has been in a certain set of conditions and acquired an ability to respond to those situations verbally is in a different situation from one who has not. But, the second lesson that I want to draw is that the outsider can still in principle know a great deal about the nature of the religious experience. Against Otto, never having had a religious experience does not in and of itself leave one entirely ignorant of the nature of religious experiences. What Mary shows us is that one can know a great deal about a perceptual experience even if one has not had the experience in question or even any similar ones. Even before seeing any colors, Mary knew much about color perception, in fact, much more than any color perceiver knew. It is in principle possible for an outsider to know far more about the nature of a religious experience than the insider, even though the outsider has no first-hand acquaintance with the sort of experience at issue.

All this is true if the thought experiment has applicability to the study of religious experience. But that is a big if. We have at least one good reason to think that Mary's situation is not applicable to religious experience. What makes the thought experiment informative is that it illustrates that the outsider, the inexperienced, can have knowledge regarding the conditions that give rise to the experience of color, namely, the physical properties of light waves, of the surfaces of objects, and of the relevant organs of the human body. Now the thing about these physical processes is that there is widespread agreement, at least in our contemporary society, about the various properties and processes involved in the physics and biology of perception. This is in marked contrast to the case of religious experience, since there is no such widespread agreement regarding the conditions that give rise to religious experiences. Some observers attribute religious experiences to supernatural origins; others, to little known aspects of human consciousness; others, to an overactive imagination; others, to unconscious drives; and others, to features of the human brain. That level of disagreement on the conditions that give rise to the religious experience seems to frustrate any potential lessons that we might draw from the case of Mary. The insider/outsider problem looms larger than ever, and it seems like the only way to gain knowledge about a religious experience is to have one.

But on second thought, it is not entirely clear why the lack of consensus should prohibit discussion of the conditions that give rise to religious experiences. In fact, we do have a way of retaining the conditions as a matter for discussion, if the scholarly investigator is willing to make some judgments regarding the cause and nature of the experience. A number of such judgments are possible, but four are especially relevant. In response to a report of a religious experience, the scholarly inquirer could judge the experience to be veridical, an illusion, a hallucination, or a fabrication.[38]

To judge an experience veridical means that it is as the experiencer says that it is. If the experiencer's report involves a supernatural object or state and the inquirer judges it veridical, then the inquirer is endorsing the existence of that object or state. This is the position Alston, as a Christian, takes regarding religious experiences in the Christian tradition. Second, the inquirer could regard the experience as an illusion. An illusion occurs when you misperceive one thing for another, as when you see a coiled rope and think it to be a snake. So the experiencer experienced something, but not what he thought that he experienced. Perhaps he saw an odd reflection of light and took it for a spirit or perhaps, as Proudfoot suggests, someone attributes a heightened emotional state to the operations of the Holy Spirit. Third, the inquirer could think the experience was a hallucination. The experiencer hears a voice or sees a vision, but this is the product of his own psychological makeup. A fourth possibility is that the inquirer could think that the religious experience report was fabricated and that no experience occurred. The inquirer could deem the fabrication to be insincere, like the person who pretends to hear messages from God to gain money or status. On the other hand, the fabrication could be sincere. For instance, someone might somehow acquire a false memory, a memory of an event that never actually happened. The person may have wound up with this memory innocently, with no intent to deceive. This is what Sharf suggests in regard to UFO abduction reports, and he says that if such fabrications happen in regard to UFO survivors, we should expect them among the mystics too.[39] I will disregard the case of fabrication, since in that case there is no religious experience for the inquirer to understand, although the case of fabrication certainly presents many interesting questions for study in its own right.

I'll focus on the cases where the inquirer judges an experience veridical, illusory, or hallucinatory. Which of these an inquirer judges an experience to be depends on two factors: the type of experience being reported and the commitments of the inquirer. If St. Augustine reports receiving a message from God and a scholar does not believe God exists, then the scholar will be disinclined to treat the report as veridical. On the other hand, when Alston, a Christian, encounters Augustine's experience report, he will be disposed to assent to the veridicality of the report. All this is just to say that the judgment that an inquirer issues regarding the nature of a religious experience report is as much a product of the scholar's commitments and inclinations as it is of the type of experience reported. And since scholars come from various perspectives and backgrounds, two scholars may very well pass different judgments on the veridicality of the experience. In judging a particular report to be veridical or not, the scholar ought to be willing to make explicit her own commitments affecting the judgment and, if pressed, defend them.

Now the inquirer who is willing to judge experiences as veridical, illusory, or hallucinatory is in a position to discuss the conditions that gave rise to the experience. So, for example, take Alston as one who thinks a reported experience of God is veridical. The conditions that gave rise to the experience of God are the fact that God exists and that God is of such a nature and humans are of such a nature that it is possible for the human to become aware of God in some way. We do not here have a physical process as we do in regard to color perception, and in fact, as Alston suggests, we may not understand the causal mechanisms any better than someone in the Stone Age understood color perception, but that is not to say that people in the Stone Age did not perceive colors. In this case, our understanding of the nature of the experience is drawn, not just from the experience itself, but also from what the Christian tradition teaches about the nature of God and the nature of humanity. Similar things could be said regarding religious experiences in the other religious traditions. In each case, the causal conditions of the experience will be understood in terms drawn from the tradition in which the experience occurs.

Now consider the inquirer who judges an experience to be a hallucination or an illusion. And I should say we need not assume the only such inquirer would be irreligious or atheistic. Someone from one religious tradition may regard the experiences of an alternative tradition to be nonveridical just as much as an atheist does. Or religiously committed inquirers may judge, for whatever reason, a particular experience reported within their own tradition to be illusory or hallucinatory. I mention this so we do not assume that all and only religiously committed inquirers will judge religious experience reports to be veridical and all and only the irreligious will judge the reports to be nonveridical. At any rate, once we judge an experience to be illusory or hallucinatory, we can talk of the conditions that gave rise to the experience. In the case of illusion, our opinions regarding the conditions will be determined by what we think the real object of the religious experience was, for example, a misattributed emotional state. In the case of hallucination, the conditions responsible for the hallucination will be the experiencer's neurological and psychological state.

Obviously, judging the experience to be illusory or hallucinatory will affect how likely we are to accept the mystic's claim that the religious experience is utterly unlike ordinary experiences. We may very well have a basis to question or reject the notion of ineffability on these grounds. People are not infallible about what they are perceiving. First-hand acquaintance with something does not guarantee indubitable knowledge about the thing or its properties. Someone might tell you, "I've never seen a sunset like that before," but you know that he has forgotten that he was here at this very place last year and the atmospheric conditions were just as they are today. On this and many other matters, the scholar need not agree with the experiencer. Alternatively, we may think that a hallucination or illusion does involve highly unique objects, properties, or qualities and so defend ineffability on those grounds.

At any rate, the lesson to be learned is that by taking a stand on the cause and nature of the religious experience, the scholar is not confined to the experiencer's own take on the matter. Further, since the experiencers can be wholly mistaken as to the origin and nature of their own experiences, the experience report itself does not dictate how the scholar is to regard it, although the report may provide cues that suggest one causal explanation over another. However, there is asymmetry between the insider and the outsider. The insider who has undergone a particular sort of causal process has demonstrated capacities to identify that causal process and distinguish it from other states of awareness. The outsider has not exercised capacities like this. This asymmetry is not unique to religious experiences; it is a pervasive aspect of our everyday social lives, and for the most part we take such asymmetry for granted and do not regard it as problematic. One who has not bungee jumped, been severely depressed, drunk Westvleteren 12, given birth to a child, fallen in love, flown in an airplane, had sex, been in a car crash, read Dostoevsky, or been to a Radiohead concert is in a significantly different situation in respect to these events than people who have. Nevertheless, the outsider may come to a great deal of knowledge about the experience and in some respects very well may come to know far more about the experience than the experiencer does, just as Mary knows far more about color perception than any of the color perceivers do. The scholarly observer can attain knowledge about the experience through two means. First, the scholar can acquire knowledge about the inferential relations in which the key concepts in the experience report stand in the discourse of the religious practitioners. The inferential roles that terms like "Allah," "nirvana," "the Holy Spirit," and "Brahman" have are determined mostly by the discourses, textual and oral, in which these terms occur. These are publicly accessible and so understanding them gives insight into the nature of the object or condition purportedly experienced, just as Mary knows about what sorts of things are blue and what their properties are. Second, as we have seen, the scholar can acquire knowledge about the causal conditions in which the experiencer stands. While there is no doubt a difference between understanding a causal process and undergoing one, even one who has not undergone a process can know a great deal about it, as Mary shows.

We can understand now more fully the significance of Geertz's call, appropriated from phenomenology, to attend to the "native's point of view" in studying religion. Participating in a religious practice, as we have seen in the last chapter and this one, is a matter of possessing certain abilities: the mastery, for example, of the use of the concepts in the religion's vocabulary, the mastery of abilities to classify perceptual circumstances in certain ways, and the ability to act in response to circumstances in certain ways, whether the circumstances are ritual, societal, ethical, or aesthetic. These abilities are acquired through practices of socialization and repetition and, once acquired, can be deployed by the practitioner flexibly and contextually in response to new situations. The use of these abilities is oftentimes tacit and unconscious. However, the practitioners have a degree of knowledge about many of their own abilities simply in virtue of their familiarity with the circumstances in which they have utilized them. A novice could observe an expert chef for hours and still only slightly understand the various abilities that the chef possesses. The chef can report to the observer how she would cook a certain dish or what a certain ingredient contributes to the flavor profile of a range of dishes. There is an asymmetry between their knowledge of what is involved in culinary arts. However, if the kitchen observer is a trained chemist, there is much about the chef's activities that the observer understands far better than the chef. The chef might know that arrowroot thickens sauce but have the wrong idea about why it does, whereas the chemist knows better. If the observer of religious practices is versed in social theory, she may perceive social effects of a ritual that the practitioner does not.

We are now in a position, then, to honor the distinctive position that the insider has in relation to his own experiences, even while understanding that position to be one that is only achievable because of the experiencer's situatedness in a social-linguistic, public context. Furthermore, we can see that experiences are not inaccessible matters that transpire solely within consciousness. They involve causal processes that extend beyond and outside consciousness, and whatever knowledge that people come to about their experiences, they only come to because of their social-linguistic capacities to respond to things that affect them by taking a normative status that their peers recognize. The study of experience, then, can proceed in confidence. The term "experience" refers to matters that are public and/or social: dispositions, normative statuses, and causal processes.

Even the important private dimension that experiences have is socially constituted. Sharf has expressed worry that "all attempts to signify 'inner experience' are destined to remain 'well-meaning squirms that get us nowhere.'"[40] But this is not the case. The concept of religious experience does not pose any intractable problems and can refer quite sensibly to perceptual or emotional episodes that people undergo.

ANN TAVES'S *RELIGIOUS EXPERIENCE RECONSIDERED* AND SCIENTIFIC
APPROACHES TO RELIGION AND RELIGIOUS EXPERIENCE

Our discussion of experience thus far has been conducted in a conversation with philosophers, theologians, and scholars of religion. A whole other way to study the topic of experience draws from the sciences, in particular, neuroscience, cognitive science, and psychology. These disciplines have increasingly turned their attention to religion, generating a great deal of interest, among both scientists and humanists, in the possibility that they could shed a different sort of light on religion and religious experience than the methodologies of the humanities. A recent book on religious experience, Ann Taves's *Religious Experience Reconsidered*, does religious studies a great service by engaging with scientific investigations of religious experience, as she attempts to develop a scientifically informed theoretical understanding of religion and religious experience.[41] Taves's book counsels that we compare religious experience to related but nonreligious occurrences, like dreams and hallucinations. Furthermore, Taves makes a contribution to the science and religion dialogue because, as a historian, she brings a substantial theoretical discussion of religion, whereas one does not generally find that scientists themselves think extensively about the definition of religion. Because of the book's importance and the broad attention that it has received, I will attend to Taves's accounts of experience and religion and use her book as an occasion to offer a few general reflections about how scientific approaches relate to the social practical approach that I am developing.

Taves calls her theory of religion a "building-block approach to the study of religion and other special things." One of her aims is to redirect our attention from the concept of religion to what she calls "special things" and "paths." She says that the meanings of the words "religion," "religious," and "religions" are "unstable and contested" and "cannot be defined so as to specify anything uniquely."[42] She does not advise that we do away with the term "religion" but says that we should not fret over properly defining it and should instead give more analytical prominence to special things (instead of religious things) and paths (instead of religions). Taves sees the categories of specialness and paths as including religion but, more broad than just that, encompassing magic, spirituality, mysticism, sacredness, and associated things as well as other things that people value highly. "Departments of religious studies" in this scheme "might want to conceive of themselves as loci for studying special things and the ways people incorporate them into their lives."[43] In Taves's approach, there are particular things (experiences, objects, agents, and events) that people regard, in acts that she calls simple ascriptions, as "special." Special things are different from ordinary things, and they are of positive (or negative) value to those who regard them as special. The particular singularities that special things are can be incorporated into a "composite formation," examples of which include what we typically call religions. A composite formation involves a goal-oriented "path" into which the particular special things, the "simple formations," are incorporated.

This account raises important questions. First, there is a set of questions about specialness. One issue is the definitional criteria that Taves uses to designate specialness. One criterion that Taves employs is that special things are those that people refuse to commodify or exchange. However, her admission that people do in fact at times buy and sell what they regard as special undermines that criterion for specialness, leaving the status of the category unclear.[44] At other times, she speaks of specialness as distinct from ordinariness.[45] What this occludes is the way that so many things that we take to be special, caring for one's children, for example, are simultaneously as ordinary and as special as can be. Furthermore, by construing religion in terms of specialness, we threaten the insights of one of the most important recent developments in the study of religion: the study of lived religion (discussed more fully in chapter 7). The study of lived religion looks at how religion transpires in everyday life, the realm of the ordinary. Barbara Myerhoff's examination of the way that religion informs domestic chores for some Jewish women in matters as mundane as folding dishtowels challenges any attempt to distinguish religion from the ordinary.[46] Similarly, when Robert Orsi, a primary proponent of the study of "lived religion," recounts instances of Catholics who pour holy water into their radiators for protection, his point is to challenge any notion of religion as separate from the ordinary events of daily life.[47] Another problem with specialness is its breadth. If religious studies departments took Taves's advice and transformed themselves into "loci for studying special things" then in effect, they are departments of axiology, the study of value, because specialness is, as she says, "a function of value."[48] Parents regard their own children as singular and incommensurable with other values. Patriots regard their country in this way. Certainly it is important to compare religious valuations with these sorts of valuations, but the benefit of subsuming religion to the category of special value is unclear, and the risk is that once that move has been made, it would be a matter of contestation among philosophers and political scientists who study value whether religion is a form of valuation that deserves special or substantial treatment. Would the academic study of religion flourish or even survive in these newly formed departments of the study of special value? One reason that Taves wants to subsume religion to special things and paths is that this facilitates comparison of religious things with nonreligious things, in contrast to scholars who have insisted that religion is sui generis and incomparable with anything but other religious things. I side with Taves in rejecting that view of religion and comparison, but comparison does not require instituting formal taxonomic categories that subsume the items to be compared. All that it requires is the identification of similar features of two distinct items and inquiring as to what sort of ramifications attend the fact that they share these features. Conceiving of religions, as I do, as social practices that involve reference to gods, spirits, transcendent realms, salvation or liberation, and such matters and taking as paradigmatic examples of such social practices the roster of so-called world religions preserves a focus of study without presupposing in advance that the religious things in such practices are extraordinary or noncommodifiable.

Another set of questions concerns Taves's ideas about special things as building blocks that make up religions. To think of something, such as a particular religious experience, concept, or artifact, as a building block is to think of it as something that is distinct and self-contained and that retains its nature regardless of how it is arranged or rearranged in larger configurations. The building blocks that special things are, for Taves, serve as "component parts" that "can be assembled" in "disparate ways."[49] Taves acknowledges that she is "envisioning special things as elementary phenomena standing on their own," though it is important to her account that "individuals or groups . . . can also incorporate them into more elaborate formations that provide means for people to engage them on a more regular or continuous basis."[50] The building block conception of particular religious things stands in stark contrast to the view that I have been developing in this book. The practical or symbolic significance of any religious experience, concept, action, or object is, in my account, a product of the role that it plays in the religious practice (and indeed in the multiple other social practices that intersect with any religious practice). The significance, then, is holistically determined, and indeed the significance of any particular act, concept, or experience can vary according to the context in which it occurs. Even by the lights of Taves's own account, it is hard to see that the building block metaphor works. She admits that in a composite formation, like a religion, particular things get marked as special and assigned meaning and value according to the larger context of practice. She acknowledges that "people deem some things special and set them apart from others" in relation to "larger processes of meaning making and valuation."[51] For example, she notes, "In India, elaborate rituals transformed human-made statues into cult objects in which deities reside."[52] It makes no sense to speak of these statues (or the experience of them) as "elementary phenomena standing on their own." They only acquire religious significance because of the practical, ritual context in which they are produced as gods' residences. So the notion of a building block does not adequately capture the way that particular religious things operate in a religious tradition. The thrust of my own theory has been to show that the study of any particular religious ritual, artifact, or experience can only be understood properly by thickly describing the item in question in its broader context of relationships to multiple other items. I worry that scholars who accepted Taves's building block metaphor would think that they could look at particular things in isolation and think that they had understood them, without referencing or examining the various uses to which they are put in a broader religious practice. I am unsure whether Taves herself takes her use of the terminology of building blocks to license such an approach, but her language of component parts and elementary phenomena that can be assembled in various ways gives me pause. Scholars of religion must appreciate that a rapprochement between the humanities and the sciences will require them to accept the sort of quantifiable, decontextualized data that are produced in survey questionnaires and in laboratory experiments, but they should do so in the consciousness of the artificiality of such data. What they must not do is buy into the idea that decontextualized, self-contained items are the basic constituents in the practice of religion.

Even if I have misgivings about the theory of religion that Taves puts forth, I find her thoughts on religious experience and her attention to a broad scientific literature that includes the study of sleep paralysis, dreams, and trance states highly informative. Among her contributions to the study of experience is the way that she details the complex interplay between cultural beliefs and physiological processes. Her discussion of experience as "embodied behavior" and her corresponding rejection of any unbridgeable gap between a person's private consciousness and the public world are consonant with my own approach. Her study complements my philosophical investigations into the social practical context in which experiences occur with attention to the cognitive, psychological, and neuropsychological processes that correlate with conscious states.

Taves contributes to the debate between perennialists and constructivists a distinction between top–down mental processes, in which our (culturally specific) conceptual facility is prominent, and bottom–up mental processes, in which unconscious and largely universal cognitive systems process information that subsequently enters our conscious awareness.[53] This leads her to endorse the view that experiences are "a complex mixture of both biology and culture," in contrast to constructivists who think of experiences as exclusively cultural (note that this is not Proudfoot's view) and perennialists who think of experiences as exclusively biological.[54] She suggests:

Constructivist theories have been insensitive to the distinction between top-down and bottom-up processing and the differential role of cultural input along the gradient that interrelates them. If many of the experiences that people consider religious or mystical emerge from the bottom up, and thus are relatively (though of course not totally) culturally insensitive, this might explain (in part) why many who have had such experiences are resistant to the constructivist account.[55]

These thoughts indicate promising directions for future research into religious experiences, as research into the brain and cognition continues to burgeon.

I spoke above of the possibilities for a rapprochement between the humanistic and scientific study of religion, and Taves's book supplies a welcome occasion to make a few more remarks about the possible points of connection between a social practical theory of religion and cognitive science, neuroscience, and evolutionary psychology. To be sure, these scientific approaches to religion have proved highly controversial. Some people find in cognitive science and psychology a way to study religion with all the legitimacy of the scientific method, resting one's conclusions on the results of verified laboratory experiments. Others see the promise of an explanation for why religion exists. On the other side of the debates, people think that laboratory experimentation is not suited for understanding the complexities of human behavior and never will be. Moreover, they are worried that historical particularity will get swept aside in the search for universal features of human cognition. Many are somewhere in between, watching the debates transpire, not totally sure what to think of it all yet. What does a conception of religion as a social practice say about which of these camps we should inhabit?

On one level, cognitive science will clearly have a lot to say about religious practices and will ultimately prove to be compatible with a social practical theory because everything that religious practitioners do—they speak, move, perceive, eat, and so on—they do by means of their brains and the physiological systems that transmit information to and from their brains. However, this does not mean that an understanding of our cognitive systems is necessarily relevant to the study of religion, anymore than one would want a physiologist as a television commentator at a tennis match, explicating the sport in terms of optic nerves, cognitive object-recognition systems, and fast-twitch muscles. It would have been a detraction, not an added value, had Pierre Bourdieu gone into a lengthy digression about mirror neurons in his account of the significance of social imitation in the development of the habitus.[56] This is not to say that understanding our cognitive architecture is unimportant; it is just to say that most of our social theory, history, anthropology, and philosophy can get along just fine without it. In some contexts it is appropriate to speak about human behavior in terms of cognitive systems, and in some contexts it is appropriate to speak in other terms. A lot of the humanities and social sciences will be in the latter category. This is not to say that there is anything intrinsically incompatible about the two types of accounts; it is just that they serve different purposes.

However, there are three places where the potential for incompatibility between cognitive scientific and evolutionary psychological approaches, on the one hand, and the social practical approach I am advancing, on the other, is evident. The first has to do with the question of whether our cognition involves a so-called language of thought, a mental system of representations that is distinct from the language that we speak. Cognitive scientists largely hold the view that our minds do involve a representational system distinct from spoken language. They understand much of cognitive processing as processing information that consists of mental representations. Social practice theories tend to be skeptical of representational accounts of the mind, worried that such accounts will instantiate a bifurcation between the mind (with its internal representations) and the world. Richard Rorty, an influential proponent of social practice theory, for example, challenged the idea of the mind as a "mirror of nature" for much of his career.[57] Davidson, a significant influence on philosophy of religion and on social practice theories of the pragmatist variety, argues against the possibility that there could be thought without language.[58] Second is the issue of universality versus historical particularity. Social practice theorists, whether of the Bourdieuian, Butlerian, Foucaultian, or pragmatist variety, emphasize historical particularity and see our behavior as a product preeminently of social forces, not biological ones. Cognitive scientists, on the other hand, see the mind as a set of systems that are universal and to a large extent, biologically "hard-wired." The human brain evolved over millennia and is what it is, in terms of its capacities and how it processes information, in significant measure, for all members of the species. Of course they do not deny variety from individual to individual, but they welcome universal explanations of human behavior. Third, and related to the question of universality versus historical particularity, is the question of social power. For cognitive scientists and evolutionary psychologists, the architecture of the brain is what it is because of an evolutionary history that favored organisms that propagate their genes more effectively. Therefore, the sorts of explanations of human behavior that cognitive scientists and evolutionary psychologists tend to supply are in terms of natural selection and biology. Power theorists, however, see human behavior as in significant part a matter of strategies on the part of certain social groups to control others. These two different approaches to understanding human behavior result in bitter conflict. When Lawrence Summers, as the President of Harvard University, suggested the possibility that fewer women are scientists and mathematicians because of differing biological capacities between women and men, he was met with an uproar of opposition by people who would point instead to a long history of institutional sexism as the key explanatory factor.

I will say something about each of these three problem areas. In response to the contention over internal systems of representation, there are two possible avenues for rapprochement between the cognitive scientific approach and the social practical one. First is that there is a small number of people involved in cognitive science who question the reigning model of internal representation. Tim Van Gelder, for example, has argued that minds work not by internally representing their external environment and performing computations on these representations but rather as a dynamic, embodied system of adjustment and readjustment with the environment.[59] On the other hand, in the recent work of Robert Brandom, we have the willingness by a social practice theorist of the pragmatist variety, one influenced by both Rorty and Davidson, to countenance the idea of internal representations. Brandom wants to distinguish between personal representations, which are propositional and have the meaning that they do because of their inferential role in our social practices, and the subpersonal representations with which cognitive scientists deal. Brandom is fine with accounting for "the kind of attunement to their environment that intelligent nonlinguistic animals display—the way they can practically take or treat things as prey or predator, food, sexual partner or rival and cope with them accordingly" in terms of subpersonal representations.[60] Further, humans' practical attunement with the environment is the know-how in terms of which the know-that of personal, propositional representations must be explained. For the pragmatist, knowing-that is a form of knowing-how. So the pragmatist wants to explain personal level representations in terms of practical attunement with the environment. The job of cognitive scientists, Brandom says, is to explain the practical attunement in terms of subpersonal representations. These are compatible explanatory projects. The problem arises if someone wants to explain practical attunement in terms of personal level representations, that is, to explain knowing-how to interact with one's environment in terms of propositional knowledge (knowing-that). That would be incompatible with the philosophy of language that Brandom articulates.[61] So between people like Brandom and Van Gelder, we have some grounds for hope that the divide between social practice theory and cognitive science of religion on the matter of internal representations is traversable.

As for the issue of universalism, the achievement of a historicist sensibility was a hard fought achievement in the Western intellectual traditional, and a variety of essentialist and universalist philosophies (Platonism and Christianity chief among them) had to be overcome to get there. Under the guise of universalism went all manner of pernicious doctrines: sexist, racist, homophobic, and colonialist, to name a few. So it is understandable that social practice theorists would be wary of the reintroduction of universal explanation and universal notions of human nature, like we find in cognitive science and evolutionary psychology. On the other hand, it would be foolish to treat the human organism as though it accounted for nothing in explaining human behavior, as though people were nothing but a blank slate against which culture could scrawl whatever it wished. We are, after all, animals, and if we are willing to account for nonhuman animals' behavior in terms of tendencies that are genetically determined, it would be extraordinary to deny this altogether in the case of humans. The interplay of the tendencies, motives, capacities, and instincts that are genetically determined with the influence of socialization and enculturation is a matter that occupies a vast and contentious literature. These questions will not be settled for a long time. But the research of psychologists and cognitive scientists is an essential contribution to the debates, and social practice theorists should welcome their agendas. Furthermore, any comprehensive explanation of human behavior, if such were possible, would have to make reference to both human biology and processes of socialization. People are biologically constituted, but culture can override even strong drives like sex and hunger, as celibates and hunger-strikers demonstrate. So whatever contribution that biology makes to human behavior will in many cases be in terms of dispositions and predispositions (and many of these would be distributed unevenly across a population) that culture would activate or override in various ways. The full explanation would have to include both the biological predispositions and the cultural practices in which these predispositions express or do not express themselves.

When it comes to religion, we should be reluctant to rush to find the single thing that explains everything, whether it is a cognitive system that hyperactively detects agents, a god gene, a pattern of blood flow in a brain lobe, or a memorable meme. Religions are complex matters that vary widely across time and culture in how they are practiced. Minds are complicated systems, and cognitive systems work in conjunction with numerous other cognitive systems. But resisting the rush to find simplistic evolutionary psychological accounts of religion does not mean discounting such research altogether. Cognitive science of religion and evolutionary psychology of religion are in their early stages of development, and we should follow the growing body of research as it develops.

Similar considerations apply to the issue of power. Thus far, the cognitive science of religion and evolutionary psychology of religion have proceeded without much attention to matters of social power, and this is a mark against them, especially since these disciplines are themselves very much invested with power relations: financial, cultural, racial, and gender. But as cognitive science of religion and evolutionary psychology develop, we can expect and insist that questions about social power become a significant part of the agenda.

In short, there is much that remains to be seen about the utility of scientific research for the study of religion but certainly the potential should not be foreclosed.

To return to our examination of experience, the next and final task then is to show that experiences are thoroughly implicated in social power relations.

6

Experience and Power

EXPERIENCE AND POWER

In 1856, in what is now South Africa, a Xhosa teenager reported that she had received a message from ancestral spirits. They instructed her to tell her people that dead Xhosa would resurrect if they would slay all their cattle. Skeptical at first, they eventually complied, leading to the decimation of the Xhosa population and the end of their resistance to British colonists. Turning to the present day, charismatic and Pentecostal Christians have visions of God as a male, and these visions occur in a religious tradition that thinks that women should submit to men in church and family. Or consider the example anthropologist Barbara Myerhoff recounts, about an elderly Orthodox Jewish woman observing a prayer service being conducted in an adjoining room. As a woman, she cannot participate in the rituals, but even from her position of exclusion, she undergoes a powerful, emotional experience, the sort that would bind her to the very tradition that marginalizes her.[1] When Muslim women in Indonesia decide to begin wearing headscarves because of their anxiety about dying, they do so for personal reasons, but they are simultaneously participating in a global and politically inflected Islamic renewal movement. More generally, a long-standing criticism of mysticism and experiential religion is that it is apolitical; that is, people abandon the public realm of contestation over shared goods for the space of private devotion.

These sorts of examples demonstrate that religious experiences and social political power are interrelated in complex ways. However, many of those who have devoted themselves to the study of mysticism and religious experience in modern times have had almost nothing to say about social and political power. Mircea Eliade, a primary proponent of the experiential approach to religion, regards religious experience as something separate from power. He distinguishes religion as a creation of the human spirit from mere "gestures of protest and revolt."[2] Charles Long, like Eliade a phenomenologist of religion, also thinks of religious experience and political oppression as separate matters, as we saw in chapter 3. As for William James, many regard his decision to define religion individualistically as something that leads to a political quietism that does not challenge the status quo power structures.[3] More recently, the most important parties to the debates about constructivism and perennialism in the study of mysticism, W. T. Stace, G. William Barnard, Robert K. C. Forman, Wayne Proudfoot, and Steven Katz, do not substantially address issues of socio-political power in relation to experiences. So for much of the modern history of the study of mysticism, the tacit assumption has been that religious experiences and social power have little to do with each other.

In this chapter, I will programmatically respond to views that that either explicitly or through inattention treat experience as unrelated to social power. I will build on the preliminary discussion of experience and power in chapter 3. My goal is to catalog a number of important configurations that the relation between experience and power can take. These configurations recur cross-culturally (which is not to say there is something essential or timeless about experience, power, or their relationship). No significant stock-taking of scholarly views of experience and power has occurred, and this chapter intends to rectify this lack. The typology that I present here is by no means exhaustive. Also, the different configurations of experience and power described below are not mutually exclusive; indeed one configuration may very easily give rise to another or work in conjunction with another.

Happily, despite the long-lasting tendency to ignore power in discussions of experience, things have been changing as of late. Grace Jantzen, Robert Sharf, and Amy Hollywood have all published work in the past decade or so that features concerns about power prominently in their discussions of mysticism and religious experience.[4] Furthermore, the founding figures of social theory all had something to say about power and experience, even if they did not give the issue sustained attention. So we are not without resources for understanding the complicated relations between experience and power.

THE CONCEPT OF EXPERIENCE AS IDEOLOGICAL

The first relation between experience and power that will concern us is actually not so much about experiences themselves but rather about the relation between power and the concept of experience. The way that the concept is applied to some things and not others and the implications that follow from its application are of great significance. The most significant development in the philosophy of religious experience in the past few decades is Sharf's and Jantzen's elucidations of the ideological purposes to which the concept of experience can be put. By ideology here, following Terry Eagleton, I mean roughly "a body of meanings and values encoding certain interests relevant to social power."[5] Typically those who employ the meanings and values are unaware that they encode social power. Sharf and Jantzen have done for religious studies what Joan W. Scott did for history and gender studies in her influential essay, "The Evidence of Experience": show that "what counts as experience is neither self-evident nor straightforward; it is always contested, and always therefore political."[6]

I have discussed the particulars of Jantzen's and Sharf's arguments at some length in chapter 2, so here I will just recap a few significant points. Both Jantzen and Sharf detail two primary ways in which the term "experience" and its equivalents are ideological: first, in the way that religious communities use the terms and, second, in the way that scholars use the terms. A precursor to Sharf and Jantzen on these points is Proudfoot. In *Religious Experience*, Proudfoot argues that one important implication of Friedrich Schleiermacher's experiential approach to religion is that his way of conceiving religion serves to protect religion apologetically from the skeptical attitudes of modern philosophy and science. According to Proudfoot, Schleiermacher and those who followed in his footsteps want to locate religion in the recesses of subjectivity because that was a space that science could not assail.[7] Eliade, for example, conceives of religion as a sui generis type of experience and does so to preclude reductionist accounts of religion, as Russell McCutcheon argues.[8] Furthermore, the strategy in much of modern theology of rendering religion compatible with science can be a protectivist strategy. If pitting religion and science at odds means that people committed to naturalism will reject religion, then shedding the nonnaturalistic elements of religion is a way of reconceiving religion to make it amenable to the scientifically minded. This is protectivism of a sort, though not a matter of protecting religion by putting it off limits from science. Rather, religious practices are protected by rendering them naturalistic. In any case, if proponents of a religious tradition construe it as experiential in order to preserve the tradition in the face of challenges by naturalistic science and if they do so in a manner that is relevant to social power conflicts, then their definition of religion is ideological, in the sense at issue here.

Jantzen focuses on the Christian mystical tradition and its precursors in Greek and Roman religion, as we saw in chapter 2. Jantzen tells the story of the development and changes of the term "mystical" throughout this tradition. At every stage of the term's development, Jantzen argues, religious communities used the term in ways that excluded women. In early Christianity, the term "mystical" referred to the church's rituals and its Scriptures, which had a mystical significance that transcended their sensible qualities. Since women were excluded from the priesthood and were not likely to be literate, they were excluded from the mystical, relative to men. In the medieval era, when the term "mystical" acquired the experiential sense that it now has, the male priesthood carefully monitored women's claims to receive divine revelation, since the capacity to receive messages from God was a threat to the hierarchy. In the modern era, when religion became sequestered from the public, political realm, at least in the minds of the enlightenment philosophers and their progeny, women were allowed into the ranks of the mystics. Only now that religion's power had been (supposedly) defused could women participate fully in the mystical. However, the emphasis on the ineffability of religious experiences ensured that whatever mystical achievements that women attained would not threaten male authority, since mysticism, as something inexpressible, could not give rise to claims or demands.

For Jantzen, scholars' use of the category of the mystical is also sexist. Contemporary philosophers of religion, she says, accept unquestioningly an understanding of mysticism as "a subjective psychological state, perhaps a state of 'altered consciousness,' in which an individual undergoes a private intense experience, usually of a religious nature."[9] Jantzen says this is a modern conceptualization of the term. The historical mystics themselves understood the mystical as a long-term practice of cultivating an ongoing awareness of God, not as short-lived intense raptures. She acknowledges such raptures occurred but says that the mystics themselves oftentimes treated them with suspicion.[10] Thus, philosophers of religion are failing to attend to the mystics themselves (there is "hardly any serious study of the primary sources") and failing to attend to the dynamics of power that have accompanied the use of the designation mystical. "Where such issues are unnoticed," Jantzen charges, speaking about the interfusion of power with mysticism, "they are reinforced."[11] Furthermore, in buying into the Jamesian notion of experience as intense and brief raptures, scholars subscribe to a notion that

> plays directly into the hands of modern bourgeois political and gender assumptions. It keeps God (and women) safely out of politics and the public realm; it allows mysticism to flourish as a secret inner life, while those who nurture such an inner life can generally be counted on to prop up rather than to challenge the status quo of their workplaces, their gender roles, and the political systems by which they are governed, since their anxieties and angers will be allayed in the privacy of their own hearts' search for peace and tranquility.[12]

Jantzen thinks that the scholars' focus on discrete experiences leads to a misrepresentation of Christian mysticism, but it also construes mysticism as flash-in-the-pan, here-and-gone events that have no real impact on the social and political structure. Scholars, then, who employ this conception of mysticism uncritically are complicit in the quietism. In contrast, she advocates a recovery by feminists of the extended awareness model. The goal of contemporary feminists should be to "become divine" (where divinity is construed pantheistically).[13] An ongoing and progressively realized awareness of the divine would be integrally related to the individuals' pursuit of social justice, especially justice for women.

Sharf's examples of the ways that experience serves ideological purposes in religious communities come from Asian traditions. He discusses modern Theravāda and Zen Buddhist practices, which have specific understandings of particular meditative states and the phenomenology associated with those states. Despite the specification of phenomenological criteria for the various states, there is not agreement across schools as to how to classify particular experiences. Schools tend to deny the most significant experiences to their rivals and attribute them to themselves. Sharf concludes:

> A meditative state or liberative experience is identified not on the basis of privileged personal access to its distinctive phenomenology, but rather on the basis of eminently public criteria. Such judgments are inevitably predicated on prior ideological commitments shaped by one's vocation (monk or layperson), one's socioeconomic background (urban middle class or rural poor), one's political agenda (traditionalist or reformer), one's sectarian affiliation, one's education, and so forth. In the end, the Buddhist rhetoric of experience is both informed by, and wielded in, the interests of personal and institutional authority.[14]

In another essay, Sharf presents evidence that a group of intellectual-practitioners of nineteenth- and twentieth-century Zen, including D. T. Suzuki, advanced an idea of Zen and its experiences as uniquely expressive of the Japanese temperament, thus promoting a nationalistic attitude of Japanese superiority over China and the West.[15]

Scholars and practitioners of Asian religion use the category experience ideologically, in Sharf's view. He agrees with Proudfoot that the move to associate religion with a special type of experience is "recent and ideologically laden," motivated by the desire for "new grounds upon which to defend religion against secular and scientific critique" on the part of scholars of religion, in particular theologians and nontheologians like James who are friendly to religion.[16] Moreover, the concept of experience has a promise of forestalling "the objectification and commodification of personal life endemic to modern mass society," by contesting alienating tendencies to posit a "centerless physical world of 'objective facts' amenable to scientific study and technological mastery."[17] Asian intellectuals, many of them practitioners as well as scholars (like Suzuki), sought to construe Eastern religion as experiential with the result of granting privilege to the spiritual East over the materialistic West. Western intellectuals found "comfort" in the idea of a spiritual East, because they found in experiential Asian religion a mirror to their newly subjectivized Christianity. The discovery of an experiential core in Asian religion allowed them to conceive of religion, in its good, experiential form (as opposed to its bad, doctrinal, ritualistic, and institutional forms) as universal.[18] In other words, the reconceptualization of religion, in both the East and West, was not a neutral affair of objective inquiry, but one thoroughly fraught with desires (for cultural supremacy and for the preservation of religion in the face of scientific and modern encroachments).

The primary contribution to the effort of showing the connections between experience and power that Jantzen and Sharf make is not about experiences themselves but about discourse about experience. It is discourse about experience that has the ideological effects that we have been discussing, and it has these effects whether or not it refers to any actual experiences that people are having. This is an essential point to keep in mind, and it is an important corrective to the philosophy of mysticism in its tendency to focus on experiences and neglect attention to the rhetoric of experience as a matter for study in its own right. However, we need to remember not to lose sight of the experiences themselves as we attend to discourse. I have in previous chapters and elsewhere criticized Sharf for not having a sufficient account of the experiences themselves as an object of scholarly study. I will not reiterate my criticisms of him or my defense of the viability of the study of experiences here,[19] but I do want to point out that we can accept his claim that the category experience is frequently ideologically laden but reject the suggestion that the category has only ideological uses. That is, in addition to its ideological uses (and intertwined with them) it also has legitimate uses of designating states of consciousness that are religious in nature.

In response to Jantzen's concern about philosophers' use of the intense-episode conception of mysticism, I want to respond that we should have a broad enough conception of mysticism (and experience) to include both long-lasting, subtle experiential states and brief, intense episodes. Both occur, as Jantzen admits. While Jantzen is right to highlight the Christian mystics' pursuit of long-lasting states of awareness of God, she does somewhat downplay the episodic, intense experiences that are just as much a part of the mystical tradition. Furthermore, it is far from clear that those sorts of episodes have been apolitical, as Jantzen fears. At any rate, Marx, Weber, and Durkheim all have accounts of experience that give episodic experiences political relevance, whether for good or ill, as we shall see. This is to say that we can learn from Jantzen the importance of ongoing states of mystical awareness without sacrificing the importance of episodic ones.

Sharf and Jantzen have provided an invaluable service to the study of mysticism in emphasizing the ideological uses to which the concept has been used. I endorse their claims that the concepts mysticism, experience, and their equivalents can serve ideological purposes, including nationalistic ones, culturally supremacist ones, and sexist ones. We should not think that the concept experience has no uses besides ideological ones, but those who study religion should be alert to ideological uses of experience, both by scholars and by practitioners.

EXPERIENCE AS A MEANS TO PERSONAL POWER

One who undergoes religious experiences may acquire power within his or her community on that basis. Furthermore, those who stand in some relation to the experiencer can acquire power in a community or tradition because of their relation to the experiencer, even though they are not the ones who had the experience. This relationship between experience and power, where the appeal to experience bolsters one's status and power, will strike many as the most obvious, given the prevalence of legitimating experiences, for good and for ill, in history and in sacred texts: Moses received a mandate from God and became leader of Israel, Jesus began his ministry after the Holy Spirit descended upon him in the form of a dove, Siddhārtha Gautama achieved enlightenment under a pipal tree and then set about teaching the Four Noble Truths, the visions of Joan of Arc propelled her to military leadership, Joseph Smith received visitations from Moroni and founded what would become the Latter Day Saint movement, and Jim Jones acquired respect and loyalty in the People's Temple through faith healings and prophecies. In regard to trance and spirit possession, I. M. Lewis notes that "religious leaders turn to ecstasy when they seek to strengthen and legitimate their authority."[20] For the North American charismatic Christian women whom Marie Griffith describes in *God's Daughters*, it is the exercise of the gift of prophecy, the ability to convey messages of divine origin, that is "one of the most important ways that members may attain some kind of spiritual authority."[21] Of course an individual's claim to have had an experience is not self-authenticating. Such a claim only garners status for the experiencers if others are disposed to validate the experiences and so regard the experiencers and their teachings as deserving respect. When this does happen, though, experiences are a significant means to acquire a privileged status in a community.

The classical social theorist who advanced this configuration of experience and power is Max Weber. Weber thinks there are three basic types of authority

(*Herrschaft*) in groups, patriarchal, bureaucratic, and charismatic, and he discusses each at length. The patriarchal and bureaucratic leaders owe their power over their subordinates to the subordinates' respect for the patriarchal tradition or the bureaucratic institution and its rules. The charismatic leaders, however, derive their authority from a sense among their followers that the leaders have personal qualities that mark them off as exceptional or even supernatural.[22] Weber mentions prophets and magicians as primary examples of charismatic authorities. Both prophets and magicians receive revelations from divine or spiritual sources and have the authority that they do in their groups because of the revelations that they receive. These revelations often are experiential, involving ecstasy, for example.[23] So Weber sees a clear relation between experience and power.

Weber's insights about experience and power come not in an investigation of experience but in his study of authority. As a result, he tends to pit charismatic authority and its revelatory experiences against the status quo of institutions and social structures: "In a revolutionary and sovereign manner, charismatic domination [*Herrschaft*] transforms all values and breaks all traditional and rational norms: 'It has been written . . . , but *I* say unto you. . . . '"[24] This is no doubt an important insight. In many cases, the individual's religious experience, a message from God, for example, has been perceived as a threat by religious and political officials who wanted to preserve for themselves the right to speak on behalf of God. But we need to keep in mind that revelatory experiences are just as suited to confirm the status quo as disrupt it. Nevertheless, Weber deserves credit for noticing the connection between ecstatic experiences and the possession of power by the experiencer over other members of a community.

I have been speaking of experiences as conferring power on certain individuals, but experience reports can oftentimes do the job just as well whether an experience occurred or not. Whether or not people have an experience, if they claim that they have and people believe them, then that could suffice to bolster their power over the group. Further, people can claim about someone else that she or he has had an experience to bolster their own position in their group. They even can make such claims about figures who did not actually exist. Scriptural texts make claims such as that Moses encountered God on Sinai and that Siddhārtha Gautama experienced nirvana. Such texts can bolster the authority of contemporary religious leaders, whether or not Moses and Siddhārtha Gautama ever walked the earth. Recognizing that experience reports can do this work without experiences, however, does not imply that experiences are irrelevant. For those instances in which someone does have an experience, reports it, and acquires power over others for doing so, it matters that the experience is causally related to the report and to the acquisition of power. Again, the study of experience should attend to both experiences and experience reports.

EXPERIENCES CAN COMPENSATE FOR DEPRIVATION

Another relation to power that experiences can have is that they may serve as a compensation for deprivation, social or psychological, real or perceived. The famous expression of this view comes from Karl Marx in "A Contribution to the Critique of Hegel's Philosophy of Right: Introduction": "The wretchedness of *religion* is at once an *expression* of and a *protest* against real wretchedness. Religion is the sigh of the oppressed creature, the heart of a heartless world and the soul of soulless conditions. It is the *opium* of the people." Marx says that religion furnishes an "*illusory* happiness" and that once the oppressive economic conditions that give rise to the need for illusory happiness are removed, people will abandon their religion. They will no longer need it, as they will have achieved real happiness. Marx is speaking of religion in general here, but for our purposes it is important to note how experiential Marx's account of religion is (in the broad sense of experience that includes religious emotions). Religion is a sigh, a heart, and a soul, he says. It is a narcotic. It is happiness (though illusory). It is the enthusiasm that correlates with a view of the world in which humans are estranged from themselves, revolving around an imaginary deity while they should be revolving around themselves.[25] These are terms of emotion, and his point is that religion supplies an emotional satisfaction that helps people cope with their miserable circumstances.

Numerous deprivation theories have been proposed for experiential religion. They put forth experience either as something that provides psychological benefits to relieve misery or as something that helps one advance one's social position. As an example of psychological benefits, E. P. Thompson, a Marxist historian, refers to Wesleyan revivalism as "psychic masturbation," compensation for the grueling poverty of the English poor in the eighteenth century.[26] As for improving social conditions, Lewis in a classic study of spirit possession notes that trance is most common among people of marginalized social status, especially women. According to his deprivation theory, possession and trance episodes provide a means for the possessed to achieve beneficial social gains not otherwise available.[27] One study that draws from Lewis's deprivation theory is Aihwa Ong's account of women in Malaysia who have moved from the village to the city to take factory jobs. Ong interprets workplace possession trance among newly urbanized factory women as "the unconscious beginnings of an idiom of protest against labor discipline and male control in the modern industrial situation."[28] Brusco, whom I discussed in chapter 3, views conversion to Pentecostalism in Colombia as a means for women to better their family situation, since men who convert are instructed to stay sober, not to abuse their wives, and to work and earn money.[29] To return to Griffith's study of the charismatic Christian organization *God's Daughters*, one sort of deprivation that she mentions is familial: "Where no loving father is present, there is a protective, nurturing Father in Heaven; in place of uncommunicative and generally inadequate husbands, God or Jesus may act as the romantic lover-husband, ever faithful and solicitous of his beloved's needs."[30] In regard to conflicts and disappointments with one's husband, Griffith notes, "Prayer, the turning point in Aglow stories, marks the moment when a woman abandons all attempts to assert control over the conditions in her family life in favor of sacrificial obedience, acceptance, and gratitude."[31] In regard to conflicts and disappointments with authority figures and other members within Aglow, Griffith writes that one "can always return to God in prayer and seek immediate experience of divine reality. . . . Moreover, prayer helps heal even the bad feelings that emerge from the questioning of authority."[32] In each of these cases, the emotions that attend a sense of being mistreated are assuaged through prayer and its attendant spiritual experiences.

In psychology of religion, Lee A. Kirkpatrick has applied attachment theory to theistic religion. According to attachment theory, humans have an evolved psychological system to seek proximity to caregivers. This psychological system goes beyond the need for nutrition and aims for security and protection. A sense of insecurity or abandonment leads to behavior that seeks proximity to the caregiver.[33] The paradigmatic attachment relationship is between the infant and the parent or primary caregiver, but attachment theorists think that attachment relations persist into adulthood and toward figures other than one's parents. Kirkpatrick maintains that God serves as an attachment figure for people in theistic religions and that their need for security and care accounts for their conception of God as a loving parent. In particular, in times of distress caused by personal crisis, illness, injury, or grieving, people seek emotional comfort from God in prayer and worship.[34] Compensating for psychological or social deprivation may not be very relevant to social power structures. Various types of malaise may be due to misfortunes or disasters that have little to do with the distribution of a society's goods. However, even in the case of naturally caused misfortune, some people are more vulnerable than others and some have means to recover that others do not. Anyone can get sick, but the wealthy have disproportionate access to medical care. Anyone can lose property to a flood, but the wealthy can better protect their goods in advance and more quickly replace them when damaged. Other types of malaise are thoroughly social, including the structures and institutions by which some classes of people have access to wealth, education, and positions of leadership that others do not. So the concern, shared by Marxists and others, is that people who would otherwise be so miserable that they would have motivation to contest injustice, instead find satisfaction in their religious emotions and experiences. The possibility that they would act politically, then, goes unrealized, and the status quo perpetuates. A sick person might join a movement to expand health-care insurance but instead has ecstatic raptures in a religious ceremony. A woman might be angry enough to confront her husband for refusing to do any housecleaning, but instead her anger dissipates in her love for God as she prays.

On the other hand, if religious experiences energize religious practices that work to the advantage of an oppressed or marginalized group, then the possibility for transformative change exists. This is the case in Colombia, according to Brusco, since the experiential conversions to Pentecostalism result in an improved situation for Colombian women. And in India, women can complain about their husbands' misbehavior in the voice of deceased ancestors, whereas it would be socially costly for them to do so if they were not in a possession trance. Because the spirits complain, their husbands reform, and their social situation improves.[35]

We should not think of experiences as either resisting or supporting the status quo. Oftentimes they are more ambiguous, doing both at the same time. Robert Orsi articulates this eloquently in his study of American Catholicism:

> The saints could be dangerous enforcers of cultural structures, norms, and expectations. . . . At the same time, however . . . the very same figures who were called into play against [the socially disadvantaged] could become their allies in resistance and subversion. . . . Rarely is it a simple matter of either resistance or submission, but rather of negotiating compromises . . . the saints are never innocent, nor are the effects of their presence singular. . . . It is impossible to say that the saints and the Mother of God are either on the side of those with power in any social world or those without it. Instead . . . holy figures get caught up and implicated in struggles on earth. . . . How they are positioned, what they do for whom or to whom requires close local analysis, historical and social psychological study to figure out, because it varies from situation to situation.[36]

Griffith shows how experiences specifically can simultaneously subvert and support the patriarchal structures of conservative Christianity, as we saw in chapter 3. The women's experiences of God's love cement their commitment to male authority in church and family, but simultaneously provide a means to criticize negligent and abusive men: "While [Aglow women] are preoccupied with pleasing an undeniably male God, the very contrast in their vision between God and most earthly men slides into an expedient critique of the gender ideals preserving the status quo."[37] Or, for another example, Indonesian Muslim women who begin wearing the veil are simultaneously exercising autonomy in the face of disapproving parents while committing themselves more deeply to a patriarchal religion.

It is important to note that merely acknowledging the effects of experiences on social structures does not make one a functionalist. Functionalist explanations of religious behavior combine the idea that religious practices have a relevant psychological or social effect with the ideas that the relevant effect is unintended and that the effect accounts for the existence of the religious behavior. Brusco's account of Pentecostalism is functionalist. She holds not just that Pentecostalism and its experiences advance the situation of women, but also that it is this feature of the religion that accounts for the existence of the religious movement or at least that accounts for its wide appeal and explosive growth. Similarly, Lewis thinks that the explanation of the occurrence of spirit possession is that it improves the situation of women. He theorizes that women's possession cults are "thinly disguised protest movements directed against the dominant sex."[38] In support of this "sex-war" theory of possession, Lewis notes that, due to the special privilege granted to one who undergoes possession and the ability for one in a state of trance to do and say things otherwise inappropriate, possession gives a means to "press . . . claims for attention and respect" for those who have no other avenue to do so.[39]

Functionalist explanations face the challenge that they are out to explain the existence of something by its effects. But if the thing precedes its effects, how can the effects account for the thing? As Jon Elster points out, what the functionalist explanation needs to do is present a "feedback loop" from the consequences of the behavior in question to the occurrence of the behavior.[40] The functionalist will have to tell us a story of how the actual but not consciously intended consequences of a behavior relate to the intentions involved in the behavior. Another challenge, as Jean and John Comaroff note, is that the conditions that give rise to a pattern of behavior are not necessarily the same as those by which it persists. "Not only are the conditions that produce an historical phenomenon to be distinguished from those that sustain it, but any such phenomenon, once created, may acquire the capacity to affect the structures that gave rise to it."[41] Even if a religious practice arises because of the economic, social, or political gains that it brings about, once established, its goods may come to acquire intrinsic desirability and may even motivate individuals and whole communities to forsake the very gains originally responsible for the practice. Too often, functionalists do not fulfill the responsibility to provide a feedback loop as part of their explanation. The risk then is that the scholars have the freedom to project whatever sorts of explanations that they find interesting or appealing onto the community in question with little regard for how the supposed explanatory factor actually brings about what it is supposed to. The problem is that religious practices, like all practices, produce all manner of effects, so it is all too easy just to light upon the one effect that the theorist finds particularly salient, without identifying alternate effects and without justifying the selection of the favored effect over the alternatives.

So functionalist explanations have peculiar challenges that confront them, which is not to say that they do not have their proper place in certain situations. But we can talk about power-relevant effects of religious practices, whether intended or not, without committing ourselves to functionalism. People's religious experiences can have compensatory or redressing consequences in relation to the suffering that results from power imbalances. People may seek experiences for those very consequences, but frequently they seek them for other reasons. In any case, the fact that the experiences have these effects is an important relation between experience and power.

EXPERIENCE AND THE CULTIVATION OF POLITICAL AGENCY

People may seek experiences in part for their political consequences. In premodern religious traditions (and continuing into the modern era), contemplative and meditative programs, such as those in Buddhist and Christian monasteries, commonly had as one of their aims the cultivation of moral virtue. A goal of the meditative lifestyle, which would include experiences but certainly was not limited to them, would be to grow in one's compassion, for example, or to strengthen desires regarded as pure or godlike and enervate immoral desires. In the modern era, many have expanded this practice to include not just the cultivation of moral character but also of political agency. By cultivating political agency I mean the intentional effort over time to develop oneself into a person who has a set of politically relevant emotions and dispositions to act.

So, for example, engaged Buddhism sees meditation and meditative experiences as relevant to political action. Engaged Buddhism is a twentieth-century movement in Eastern and Western Buddhism that applies Buddhist practice and teaching to social and political issues, including war and violence, political suppression, poverty, and environmental degradation. Some key representatives of engaged Buddhism are the Dalai Lama, Thich Nhat Hanh, and Aung San Suu Kyi. Meditation fosters key Buddhist virtues like compassion, loving-kindness, and the inner peace that comes with nonattachment. Engaged Buddhists regard such results as appropriate emotions and motivations not just for interpersonal relationships but for large-scale political issues. Further, meditation weakens dispositions that are socially harmful and that would hinder effective activism, like craving, hatred, delusion, and self-centeredness.[42]

Jantzen, as we have already seen, advocates a "broad sense of experience" as opposed to brief and intense raptures. The broad sense of experience is the "gradual transformation of all of life in charity, through the lifelong journey of purification, enlightenment, and union [with God]."[43] Jantzen sees this sense of mysticism as that which the premodern Christian mystics, such as Bernard of Clairvaux and Julian of Norwich, endorsed and pursued. But in the modern era, she proposes a version of this broad sense of experience for the formation and flourishing of feminists. She is cautious in recommending a feminist appropriation of the Christian mystical tradition, because of the racism, classism, sexism, and heterosexism in that tradition. But she also recognizes the mystics' "creative and courageous efforts at pushing back the boundaries of thought and action so that liberation could be achieved" and hopes that contemporary women could "use our experiences creatively in feminist/womanist philosophies of religion that preserve vital connections to the urgent issues of social justice."[44]

One of Jantzen's primary foils is James. She attributes to him the popularity of the intense, brief episode conception of experience that dominates the contemporary philosophy of mysticism. She thinks of this conception as a "privatized, inward spirituality which soothes and tranquillises and promotes an inner harmony that is content to leave the public and political world as it is."[45] In contrast to Jantzen, I regard James's conception of experience as very much concerned with the transformation of the public and political world. To make this case fully would require more of an effort than I can exert here, but I will make some remarks to indicate why I think that James, like engaged Buddhists, Jantzen, and others, views religious experience as an important component of the cultivation of selves into political subjects. In *Varieties of Religious Experience*, James presents the moral life as a life of struggle. Morality requires foregoing one's selfish desires for the sake of others, but self-centeredness is a strong and constant pull. Morality, then, requires ongoing efforts to discipline and overcome one's selfishness. Thus, he can call the moral life a "strenuous life" and even liken it to war.[46] James thinks that over the long haul, with nothing more than their own resources, people will not be able to sustain the strenuous attitude. They will eventually lapse and fail to meet the demands of morality. Religious experiences, however, supply a motivational energy that people cannot obtain through any other means, and so the religious person is uniquely capable of fulfilling the moral life. Religion provides access to a "new sphere of power," a "higher happiness" that "keeps a lower form of unhappiness in check."[47] In other words, religion supplies a satisfaction that renders one willing to undergo the sacrifices that morality requires. What makes James's views on these points relevant to political subjectivity is that James holds a broad conception of morality that includes political values. In "The Moral Philosopher and the Moral Life," for example, he says that he is speaking of morality, but under that heading he mentions social and political matters such as warfare, capital punishment, the institution of marriage, property rights, the distribution of wealth, political equality, economic modes of production, anarchism, and socialism.[48] So James thinks that religion, and religious experience specifically, plays an essential role in developing agents who are capable of giving themselves to social and political goods.

Sarah Coakley is another important figure who thinks of experiences as integral to the development of political agency. In *Powers and Submission*, she advocates a form of contemplation, wordless prayer, in which one encounters God and is transformed by the encounter. In wordless prayer, people forego their own agendas and demands and "'make space' for God to be God."[49] This "self-emptying" is "the place of the self's transformation and expansion into God." The controversial aspect of this proposal is the risk that in embracing an attitude of vulnerability before and submission to God, one could engender attitudes of vulnerability and submission to humans that would lead to oppression or domination. Coakley takes pains to resist this interpretation of her proposal. She insists that the "power-in-vulnerability" that she recommends, "the willed effacement to a gentle omnipotence," is the "undoing" of masculinism. Masculinism involves the effort to exert control, characteristic of sexism, so in foregoing control one is contesting masculinist attitudes. The result of the contemplation that Coakley advocates is "personal empowerment, prophetic resistance, courage in the face of oppression, and the destruction of false idolatry."[50]

For Coakley, Jantzen, James, and engaged Buddhists, religious experiences contribute to efforts to transform political structures in progressive ways. Experiences could, however, have just the opposite effect. This is Jantzen's primary concern about the widespread acceptance of the privatized, subjective notion of religious experience that is prevalent in contemporary scholarship. Her worry is that such a notion of mysticism emphasizes the importance of a "secret inner life" that "keeps God (and women) safely out of politics and the public realm."[51] Certainly this has been the case not just for how scholars conceive of mysticism but oftentimes also for how it is practiced. It would be an error to think of mysticism as always a withdrawal from the public realm into the interior recesses of the prayer closet and the human heart, but it is true that those who are devoted to prayer and contemplation are spending time that could be spent in other ways, such as in political activism. Coakley, Jantzen, and engaged Buddhists want to emphasize political activism as a consequence of the contemplative life, but this is hardly the case for all who give themselves to meditation and experiential prayer.

EXPERIENCE AS FOSTERING GROUP SOLIDARITY AND GROUP IDENTITY

For Durkheim, experiences of "collective effervescence," as he calls group ecstasies that practitioners undergo during religious rituals, are an important way of bringing about and expressing group solidarity and the emotional bonds that reinforce it.

Durkheim's reflections come from reports of indigenous Australian religious practices. He comments,

> The very act of congregating is an exceptionally powerful stimulant. Once the individuals are gathered together, a sort of electricity is generated from their closeness and quickly launches them to an extraordinary height of exaltation. Every emotion expressed resonates without interference in consciousnesses that are wide open to external impressions, each one echoing the others. . . . Since passions so heated and so free from all control cannot help but spill over, from every side there are nothing but wild movements, shouts, downright howls, and deafening noises of all kinds that further intensify the state they are expressing. . . . The effervescence becomes so intense that it leads to outlandish behavior; the passions unleashed are so torrential that nothing can hold them. People are so far outside the ordinary conditions of life, and so conscious of the fact, that they feel a certain need to set themselves above and beyond ordinary morality. . . . If it is added that the ceremonies are generally held at night, in the midst of shadows pierced here and there by firelight, we can easily imagine the effect that scenes like these are bound to have on the minds of all those who take part. They bring about such an intense hyperexcitement of physical and mental life as a whole that they cannot be borne for very long. The celebrant who takes the leading role eventually falls exhausted to the ground.[52]

These times of festival and ecstasy punctuate the profane, "languid" world of daily life with the abrupt entry into "relations with extraordinary powers that excite . . . to the point of frenzy." This is the sacred world, in which ecstatic frenzy puts practitioners into contact with forces above and beyond them and associates these forces with the tribal totem or some other symbol that unbeknownst to the practitioners is a representation of their society.[53] The result is to foster the emotional bonds that contribute to group solidarity. In addition to the ecstatic festival and its collective effervescence, Durkheim acknowledges a wide range of emotions that foster solidarity. Endorsing James's presentation of the importance of religious experience in *Varieties*, Durkheim thinks himself to have shown in *Elementary Forms of Religious Life* that the "reality—which mythologies have represented in so many different forms, but which is the objective, universal, and eternal cause of those *sui generis* sensations of which religious experience is made—is society." Society—in the unrecognized form of religious symbols—awakens "that feeling of support, safety, and protective guidance which binds the man of faith to his cult. It is this reality that makes him rise above himself."[54]

Durkheim does not emphasize how significant such group solidarity is for socio-political power relations, but it is an important implication of his thought about religion. A sense of group solidarity, bolstered by periodic bouts of collective effervescence, perpetuates the ingroup/outgroup distinctions that are the stuff of ethnic and national conflict. Furthermore, group loyalty can supercede subgroup loyalties (like class or gender solidarity) that could lend themselves toward improving the status of the subgroup. Durkheim generally thinks of the group solidarity that festivals and religious emotions bring about as a good thing, and he worries about the disinterest in religion and its rituals in his own time.[55] However, scholars subsequent to Durkheim have noted the sinister dimensions of solidarity. Karen Fields, Durkheim's translator, points out that the rallies of the Nazis and the Ku Klux Klan had Durkheimian effects, leading the participants to "impute to themselves shared inborn essences and fabulous collective identities."[56] Marcel Mauss, a Durkheimian, admitted as well that twentieth-century fascism provided a "verification through evil" of the Durkheimian principles of collectivity, whereas Durkheim, Mauss himself, and others had been expecting a "verification through goodness." French philosopher Leon Brunschvicg remarks, "Nuremberg is religion according to Durkheim, society adoring itself."[57]

René Girard also has a theory of the ecstatic festival and group solidarity. His account of ecstatic festivals is one application of his theory of mimetic violence and scapegoating. For Girard, people imitate each other's desire for various objects and imitate each other's attempts to acquire them. This mimesis leads to violence, since they end up desiring and competing for the same goods, and so they resort to force. The resolution of this situation is to transfer the violent urges that the group members have for each other to a scapegoat. The group unites violently against the scapegoat, and, after the attack, their unity persists, at least for a time. This process occurs in various contexts and is also represented in literature, myths, and rituals. The ecstatic festival is one such ritual, involving a "theatrical reenactment of a mimetic crisis in which the differences that constitute the society are dissolved." A sacrifice occurs, and the community "purifies itself of its own disorder [the result of mimetic rivalry] through the unanimous immolation of a victim."[58] So here the ecstatic, communal religious experience of the group leads to violence, real or symbolic, against a victim, real or symbolic. The ultimate result, here as for Durkheim, is group solidarity, which is a matter of power, here as for Durkheim.

EXPERIENCES AND INSTITUTIONAL STRUCTURE

Religions typically involve institutions, as Bruce Lincoln points out in the definition of religion that he offers in the first chapter of *Holy Terrors*. A religious institution "regulates religious discourse, practices, and community, reproducing them over time and modifying them as necessary, while asserting their eternal validity and transcendent value."[59] Such institutions incorporate power relations in various manners: in their authority structure, both official and unofficial, in their finances, and in the meanings that they perpetuate in their religious discourse (since meaning and power are intertwined, as we saw in chapter 4). Religious experiences can make a substantial contribution to the existence and structure of a religious institution, and in doing so play a role in sustaining and/or disrupting the power relationships in that community. This is a more indirect contribution to power that religious experiences make than the previous configurations mentioned, but it is worth mentioning. For religious traditions and groups that place an especially high value on religious experiences and emotions, the experiences will contribute to the structure of the religions' institutions. Pentecostalism, a highly experiential religion, is a good example here. If religious experiences are a key aspect of any viable explanation of the existence and growth of revivalistic movements such as Pentecostalism, as Daniel Míguez and R. Andrew Chesnut argue that they are (as we saw in chapter 3), then experiences help maintain the operations of power and the functioning of authority in the religious community. They can also disrupt the institution's hierarchy. Unlike Míguez and Chesnut, Griffith is not interested in offering explanatory theories about the origination and growth of Women's Aglow. Nevertheless, it is impossible to read her account of the importance of experiences in the lives of Aglow women and not regard such experiences as a principal explanatory factor for their initiation into and continued participation in Women's Aglow.[60] If this is correct, then the experiences make a noteworthy contribution to the various power operations that infuse Women's Aglow, a hierarchically structured organization, as well as the economic, familial, and gender norms that the organization promotes. Experience not only could be a factor in determining whether an individual participates in the organization, it also undoubtedly plays a role in determining the strength of a woman's commitment to the organization, as reflected in tangible practices such as her willingness to give financially, regularly attend meetings, and recruit others, to the more intangible, such as the extent to which Women's Aglow, its activities, and its teachings shape her personal identity.

Experiences may not just facilitate the personal attachment of individuals to religious communities, they may also directly affect the structure of religious institutions, rituals, and ceremonies. Edward L. Cleary writes, "Pentecostals' experience of God is a primary and ongoing aspect of their religion. The structures of their worship are designed to enhance these experiences on a routine basis through expressive, intense, and performance-oriented liturgies."[61] The structure of spirit possession ceremonies, too, is oriented entirely toward the trance episodes produced therein.

EXPERIENCE AND SOCIAL CLASSIFICATION

In many cases, the content of religious visions and auditions involve social categories, like race, gender, and sexual orientation. People experience Kali as female and God as male. African American slaves experienced God as white, as we saw in chapter 3. In such cases, it is plausible to suppose that the experiences are shaped by the experiencer's preexisting attitudes toward the social categories present in the experience. Furthermore, it is plausible to suppose that the experiences would reinforce or disrupt the experiencer's preexisting attitudes. It is an established result of contemporary feminist theology that the pervasive tendency in monotheistic traditions to speak of God as male has contributed substantially to the historic and continuing subordination of women to men.[62] Whereas many noteworthy studies have examined the topic of sexism and God-talk, fewer have given any sustained treatment to the topic of sexism and experiencing God. For a number of reasons, this topic deserves attention. First, whereas the number of recognized and celebrated mystics or spiritual adepts in history is small in relation to the wider body of religious practitioners in any given tradition, the mystics have had a tremendous impact on the thought and practice of their religious traditions. Mystics like Bernard of Clairvaux, Meister Eckhart, Teresa of Avila, John of the Cross, and many others have exercised enormous influence on Christianity, and all of them conceived of and oftentimes envisioned God primarily in male terms. Second, even though the mystics are few, experiencing God is an important part of the lives of a much wider swath of religious practitioners. Exceptional experiences, like visions and auditions, and more subtle encounters, like having a sense of God's presence or love, are hardly the exclusive preserve of the mystical greats. In particular times and places, experiential spirituality became prominent among the masses, like the Great Awakenings of England and North America, not to mention contemporary movements like Pentecostalism and neo-paganism. In various surveys of the general populace—noteworthy ones being conducted in the United States, Great Britain, and Australia—a significant percentage of people answer the question of whether they have had religious or mystical experiences affirmatively. For one example, in a series of surveys in the United States in the 1980s that the General Social Survey of the National Opinion Research Center conducted, 40 percent gave an affirmative response to the question, "Have you ever felt as though you were close to a powerful spiritual force that seemed to lift you out of yourself."[63] For both the mystics and the masses, God is often explicitly encountered as a male. In other cases, the content of the experience does not involve the imagery of bodily forms but something more subtle, like a sense of God's love and presence. Even such subtle encounters are often gendered. For example, we see this especially in bridegroom mysticism, a phenomenon that goes all the way back to Origen in the third century, in which God is encountered in erotic terms as a male principle to the female principle of the experiencer's soul. Even in the cases where gender is not an obvious, specific aspect of the experience, Christians still conceive of and speak of the object of such experiences as a male God.

Given the strength and influence of mystical traditions and religious experiences generally, it comes as a real surprise to notice how little attention scholars have given to the potential effects that religious experiences might have on social relations. For those who experience God as male, for example, maleness and authority would be linked in a particularly vivid way. Experiencing God and speaking of God, however entwined, are quite different things. As Job so memorably puts it, after seeing God in the whirlwind, "I had heard of you by the hearing of the ear, but now my eye sees you." In many cases, having had firsthand acquaintance with something makes that thing lucid in one's imagination and memory in a way that merely talking about it cannot. Many religious experiences no doubt do not have the clarity and distinctness to affect the experiencer in this way. A religious experience is often subtle and indeterminate, leaving the experiencer unsure as to the veridicality, nature, and importance of the experience. In a great number of cases, however, experiences are distinct, impressive, and memorable, leaving the experiencer with a sense of certainty regarding the reality or significance of the experience. It is hard to believe that this would not affect one's views on gender and authority in one's social life.

If a person experiences God as a father, this relation to God is hierarchical and serves as a model for the normative relationship between people and their earthly fathers and between women and their husbands and other males. So experiencing God as a powerful male legitimates the corresponding human male figures' power. Similar considerations would apply to slaves and slave-owners who experience God as white. Experiences could just as well be subversive, however. In the *Panarion*, an encyclopedia of Christian heresies, Epiphanius of Salamis (d. 403) writes of Priscilla, a principal prophet of the Montanist group in the second century CE, the following: "'In a vision,' she said, 'Christ came to me in the form of a woman in a bright garment, endowed me with wisdom, and revealed to me that this place is holy, and it is here that Jerusalem is to descend from heaven.'"[64] Epiphanius finds in this clear evidence that the Montanists are heretics. It is significant that Priscilla's vision of Jesus as a woman occurred in a context that promoted female equality. Elisabeth of Schönau (1129–1165), widely read in medieval times even if somewhat obscure today, was a Benedictine nun who began having visionary experiences, which were recorded by her fellow nuns and her brother Ekbert. In an extraordinary vision, Elisabeth says, according to her scribe,

> While we were celebrating the vigil of the birth of the Lord . . . I came into a trance and I saw, as it were, a sun of marvelous brightness in the sky. In the middle of the sun was the likeness of a virgin whose appearance was particularly beautiful and desirable to see. She was sitting with her hair spread over her shoulders, a crown of the most resplendent gold on her head, and a golden cup in her right hand. A splendor of great brightness came forth from the sun, by which she was surrounded on all sides, and from her it seemed to fill first the place of our dwelling, and then after a while spread out little by little to fill the whole world.[65]

Elisabeth asks an angel who appears to her shortly thereafter the significance of the vision, and he tells her that the woman is the humanity of Christ; the sun, his divinity. This must have raised some eyebrows, because Elisabeth reports that when several days later John the Evangelist appeared to her, "I asked him, as I had been advised, and said, 'Why my lord, was the humanity of the Lord Savior shown to me in the form of a virgin and not in a masculine form?'" John replies that Christ appeared as a woman to enable a double symbolic significance, so that the vision can apply both to Christ and to the Virgin Mary. The implied exchange ("as I had been advised") between Elisabeth and her interlocutor, presumably Ekbert, clearly exhibits the social resistance to female images of God.

Just as one's cultural milieu affects the nature of the religious experience, so that a Christian has a vision of Christ or Mary, whereas a Hindu has a vision of Krishna or Kali, and each typically receives auditory messages in her or his native tongue, so the power structures in one's cultural and social milieu affect the nature of the religious experience. In a society where men are regarded as superior to women, it is no surprise that Christians would experience the most supreme being in the universe as Father, Son, and King. If we regard the genderedness of God in an experience as a product of the psychology of the experiencer then the psychological mechanisms involved in the experience transmit the social hierarchy into the experience, much as they transmit the experiencer's broader religious, linguistic, and cultural orientation into the experience. A second thing that we can say confidently is that the experiences involving social categories affect the experiencer's attitude toward social groups. The experiences are not merely inert repositories of cultural and social attitudes; they have the capacity to affect the experiencer's attitudes. When an individual who regards men as socially superior to women experiences God as a male, such an experience would reinforce the person's patriarchal attitudes, just as consistently encountering men in positions of social power reinforces attitudes.

EXPERIENCE AND THE POLITICAL BODY

One way in which preexisting attitudes toward whatever social classifications are present in an experience can affect the experience and vice versa is through the formation and exercise of bodily dispositions. Owing to the work of Michel Foucault, Judith Butler, and Pierre Bourdieu, discussed in chapter 2, the body has become a central category of analysis in religious studies. All three of these regard it as a mistake to think of power as something that is limited to one or a few sectors of a society. We should not think of power as something that the king, president, parliament, multinational corporation, army, or university possesses and exercises against the masses, who do not have power. Rather, power is diffused throughout the entire society, and it reaches all the way to the minute gestures of our bodies. The focus on the body has led to a rich and productive body of research in religious studies.[66] Bodily habits are related to power in various ways. For Foucault and his followers, bodily disciplines create subjects and their emotions and desires, and any regime of power will regard certain desires as legitimate and appropriate and others as subversive, and thus particular power regimes will foster bodily habits with the requisite desires and attitudes toward the regime. For Butler, gender identity is a matter of the repeated performance of actions with one's body that are appropriate to the prevailing gender norms. For Bourdieu, different social groups have distinctive patterns of bodily gestures and comportment, and having such a distinctive pattern of bodily gestures (the habitus) gives one a taken-for-granted sense that one's social identity and its relation to other social identities is natural and unquestionable. So if bodily habits are relevant to social power and experiences are relevant to bodily habits, this is another important way in which experiences are related to power.

In the contemporary study of religious experience, one of the most important texts linking the body and religious experience is Hollywood's "Practice, Belief, and Feminist Philosophy of Religion."[67] Hollywood's book *Sensible Ecstasy* is better known, but that work emphasizes psychoanalytic accounts of mysticism, not bodily habits.[68] In "Practice, Belief, and Feminist Philosophy of Religion" Hollywood picks up a line of thought that Mauss began. Mauss writes, "I believe precisely that at the bottom of all our mystical states there are body techniques which we have not studied, but which were studied fully in China and India, even in very remote periods. This socio-biological study should be made. I think that there are necessarily biological means of entering into 'communion with God.'"[69] Talal Asad develops this further, commenting on Mauss's essay, "The possibility is opened up of inquiring into the ways in which embodied practices (including language in use) form a precondition for varieties of religious experience."[70] Following Mauss and Asad, Hollywood presents a model according to which the discipline of bodily habits that transpires in social practices forms particular types of subjects, with particular types of habits. In particular, rituals accomplish this: "They create certain kinds of subjects, dispositions, moods, emotions, and desires."[71]

Importantly, the discipline of the body enables religious subjects to have certain sorts of experiences. Hollywood discusses three examples: Margaret Ebner (1291–1351), a German Dominican nun, the Egyptian Muslim women in Saba Mahmood's *Politics of Piety*, and the charismatic Christian women in Griffith's *God's Daughters*. In Ebner's case, she engages in the bodily practice of kissing every cross that she encounters and pressing it to her heart. Subsequently, she has a dream in which she sees Christ on the cross, and he gives her blood flowing from his heart to drink. She then has an experience of sharing in the suffering of Christ's Passion. Hollywood describes this as a "movement from actively pursued practice to unconsciously enacted experience."[72] As for the charismatic women of Griffith's study, Hollywood questions Griffith's seeming acceptance at face value of the spontaneity of the women's experiences of God at their meetings. The women might think that their experiences are spontaneous, but this would be to miss "the way in which the formalized movement from music and prayer to testimonials and then back to music and individualized prayer works to generate the tears, prophecies, and effusions of the spirit experienced by the Aglow women." Their practice "engender[s] an experience" of God, Hollywood says.[73] Particular practices give rise to particular types of experience.

We see a similar model according to which bodily practices give rise to particular types of experiences in Mahmood (experience in the broad sense of religiously inflected emotion). Mahmood's *Politics of Piety* is a fine study, masterfully interweaving a substantial amount of social theory and philosophy with first-hand ethnographic evidence. She approaches her topic through the lens of social practice theory, informed by Butler, Foucault, Bourdieu, and Aristotle. The participants in the Egyptian women's mosque movement, another expression of the transnational Islamic renewal, are involved in a practice of cultivating Islamic virtues by disciplining themselves into various bodily practices, such as prayer, mosque attendance, and wearing the veil or *hilbab*.[74] Mahmood discusses a number of emotions that fall under the rubric of religious experience, including sincerity, humility ("tenderness of the heart appropriate to the state of being in the presence of God"), and virtuous fear and awe.[75] One of the things that Mahmood wants to accomplish by focusing on bodily practices is to revise a standard way that many people think about agency and action, as actions proceeding from inner dispositions. The relation is just the reverse, Mahmood tells us. The actions, such as prayer and veiling, produce the inner dispositions, including emotional ones: "Instead of innate human desires eliciting outward forms of conduct, it is the sequence of practices and actions one is engaged in that determines one's desires and emotions. In other words, action does not issue forth from natural feelings but *creates* them."[76]

Hollywood, Mahmood, Asad, and Mauss have considerably advanced the study of experience by highlighting the connection between bodily habits and religious experiences. And while I agree with much of what they say about bodily practices and experiences, I would want to say one thing to supplement them. All four of these scholars speak of the causal relation between practices and experiences as unidirectional: bodily practices give rise to experiences, instead of the other way around. I do not mean to imply that they regard experiences as separate from or somehow outside of practices; they are explicit that experiences occur within bodily practices, as one facet of practice among other facets. Nevertheless, the impression one receives is that the experiences are determined by the other facets of practice and do not affect the other facets of practice. It is not, to be sure, that Hollywood, Mahmood, Asad, or Mauss deny that experiences can affect practices; they do not address the issue in these texts. A full account of experience as constituted by bodily practices should see experiences as both affected by bodily disciplines and as affecting them.

Bodily practices do give rise to religious emotions, as Mahmood says, but religious emotions can also give rise to bodily practices. The line between bodily practices and inner dispositions is not unidirectional from disposition to practice, but neither is it unidirectional the other way, as Mahmood states. Rather the relationship is bidirectional and complex, and Suzanne Brenner's account of emotions giving rise to bodily practices is as legitimate in principle as Mahmood's account, which goes the other way. In Brenner's account of Indonesian Muslim women who begin wearing the veil, the bodily practice of wearing Islamic dress is preceded by existential anxiety, the fear of death, and a sense of sinfulness.[77] For Griffith, even if Hollywood is correct that the bodily practices in the Women's Aglow worship services engender experiences of God, so also the experiences of God engender bodily practices. The women experience God and Jesus as a father and/or lover and as a male authority figure, and the experiences give rise to and strengthen bodily dispositions to relate to men in their lives—husbands, fathers, and pastors—as authority figures. In *God's Daughters*, Griffith juxtaposes accounts of women adopting a deferential posture toward God in prayer with their adopting a deferential posture toward their husbands in the home. We see this, for example, in one scene that Griffith depicts, in which a woman is urged by a male, her brother, to go to church and then, at the invitation of a male pastor, kneels and prays to a male God, converting to Christianity in so doing.[78] We can surmise that religious experiences such as this one reinforce, maintain, and naturalize the woman's habitual dispositions to defer to men. In the case of Ebner, too, her experiential identification with Christ would have affected her bodily practices. Hollywood notes that Ebner's experiential identification with Christ involved a "cross-gender identification" and a "gender fluidity that renders culturally plausible the valorization of women's suffering bodies." The subversive implications of these sorts of experiences were not lost on the authorities of the time, who wanted women to identify with Mary, not Christ. The mystical experiences of suffering with Christ would lead to ascetical bodily practices being associated with Christ's suffering, and this is something that men were eager to control and limit, even to the point of limiting bodily and spiritual suffering to men.[79] Such examples indicate that experiences, bodily habits, and social power are all complexly intertwined, and scholars of experience should not conceive of experiences as something mentalistic and interior and thus unrelated to power but as something that transpires within bodily practices, affected by bodily practices and affecting them, and very much related to power.

7

Conclusion

A SINGLE VISION: RELIGION AS A SOCIAL PRACTICE

Chinese domestic rituals that honor ancestors typically take place before an altar, on which tablets, images, and incense burners are arranged. The rituals include daily incense lightings and, on some occasions, food offerings. The altars and rituals are rife with symbolic meaning. The offerings and incense burnings are gestures of respect and veneration. Tablets represent ancestors and images represent deities. The positioning of the tablets and images represents the relative status of the gods and ancestors. The items are carefully arranged on the altars so that the tablets of the most esteemed ancestors are given the most honored place on the altar. In addition to symbolic meaning, these rituals involve social power. The altars were not long ago nearly universally present in Chinese households but now are far less so in urban households, so there are significant social differences between those observing the rituals and those not. Women perform daily rituals, but men conduct the food offerings on special occasions, so the rituals reflect and reinforce gender differences. Furthermore, the rituals reflect and reinforce societal structures, since a tablet's location on the altar, and whether it is included or excluded from the altar, is determined by the deceased person's relation to the family. The rituals similarly reflect and reinforce the importance of familial obligations to an individual's social identity. Further, the rituals involve experiences. The individuals conducting the rituals may experience a range of religiously significant emotions:

reverence, desperation, and gratitude and even disappointment or anger at unfulfilled petitions.[1]

In the Chinese domestic rituals we see these three factors—experience, meaning, and power—occur. The same is true for religious practices more generally. Religious people report having experiences. The experiences could involve the sorts of emotions just mentioned in the Chinese domestic rituals, like reverence, gratitude, and disappointment. Or the experiences could involve direct awareness of a god, a spirit, nirvana, or something else religious in nature. Religions incorporate meanings. Religious artifacts, for example, often have representational meaning. Practitioners adopt postures that represent reverence for their object of worship. They use words and sentences that are themselves symbolic. Religions are infused with power. Religious practices are organized in ways that privilege certain individuals and groups over others. The priest is in a position of power over the laypeople, for example. Men are often allowed access to certain rituals that women are not, and they occupy certain offices that women cannot. Religious rituals, ceremonies, and texts can reinforce ethnocentrism, nationalism, and other sorts of chauvinism.

The student of religion, then, does well in a study of any given religious community to attend to the three things: experiences, symbolic meaning, and power. A comprehensive understanding of any religious community must have something to say about all three.

The academic study of religion, however, has thus far not had a good theoretical account that could undergird and inform studies that attend to experiences, meanings, and power together. The most influential approaches in religious studies in the last hundred years have been devoted to one or, at best, two of these categories. Phenomenologists of religion, for example, focus on the subjective experience of religion, and they have resources to account for the study of religious meaning too. They have faltered on the issue of social power, however. Further, the phenomenologists' account of experience and meaning cannot specify with sufficient precision how it is that we can access other people's experiences and meanings. There is a gap between the observer and what the practitioner understands and feels, and the phenomenologists do not explain adequately how to bridge that gap. Yet another issue with the phenomenology of religion is that many of its adherents tend to treat religions the world over as involving some universalistic common core, like the sense of the sacred. If we consider symbolic anthropology of religion, does it fare better than phenomenology of religion? Symbolic anthropology gives us an account of religious meanings but stumbles on both experience and power. Also, the primary representative of symbolic anthropology, Clifford Geertz, gives an account of meaning that is at times social-practical in nature but at other times problematically mentalistic. These days, the most influential approaches to the study of religion focus on power, owing to Michel Foucault and other social theorists. Power approaches provide insights into how social power pervades religious practices and forms people into certain sorts of subjects, but these accounts dismiss experiences and meanings.

So if we think of religion as first and foremost an experiential matter, we are confronted with the problem of how the student of religion can access others' minds and feelings. And what if we think of religion as basically about meaning? This gets us no further than taking experience as most basic. Meanings do not inhere in the things that serve as symbols, so they must in some sense be in people's heads, if meanings are what is basic. And how do we observe what is inside people's heads? If social power is the basic thing, then we lose the ability to ascertain the broad range of values and motives in religious practices. Not everything in human life boils down to domination, resistance, and hierarchy.

In the preceding chapters, I have been articulating my recommendation in response to these challenges, which is to understand religion as a social practice and to understand each of our three key concepts, experience, meaning, and power, as social practical in nature. In this chapter, I will take stock of the theory that the preceding chapters of this book have developed, and then I will attend to the academic study of religion as it is presently configured and say something about what it would look like for the various subfields of religious studies to conduct their work informed by a social practical theory of religion like this one.

The analytical utility to conceiving of religion as a social practice stems from the fact that when we attend to religion with a social practical lens, we are taking what people *do*, as opposed to what they think, mean, or experience, as the basic thing in religion. A social practice, to borrow selectively from Alasdair MacIntyre's conception of the term, is a "coherent and complex form of socially established cooperative human activity through which goods internal to that form of activity are realized in the course of trying to achieve those standards of excellence which are appropriate to, and partially definitive of, that form of activity."[2] Two things that I would emphasize from this description of practices are, first, that what we are talking about is shared and coordinated patterns of behavior. Second, this behavior is subject to norms. What MacIntyre calls "standards of excellence," I will refer to as norms. The idea is that the participants in the social practice evaluate each other's performances as appropriate or inappropriate. So students of religion who take social practices as basic will view the study of religion as attending to the two most significant things that constitute a social practice: behavior and norms. To study religion is to attend both to human behavior and its products and to the norms that govern behavior. In general, we are looking at shared patterns of behavior, which is what makes the activity social, as opposed to individual. However, people who have been socialized into shared patterns of behavior can implement their own distinctive and individual normed patterns of behavior, and when attending to religious leaders, for example, it will be important to distinguish the patterns of behavior that are appropriate only for one or a select few members of a religious community. Religious leaders, for example, oftentimes have distinctive patterns of behavior that are proper for them but not others. Even such individual patterns of behavior, though, will be coordinated with the behavior of others. So whether in respect to the individual or the group, we attend to the way that people act in certain sorts of situations.

What then does the concept of norms contribute to the study of social practices? Normed patterns of behavior are pervasive throughout social life. In my own society, the norm when we greet someone is to clasp right hands and shake. A norm when someone gives an academic lecture is for the audience to sit quietly and attentively. A norm in a friendship is to listen sympathetically when one's friend is recounting a frustrating day. The norm for those who drive their cars in the United States is stay on the right side of the road. A norm when we play chess is to move the knight two spaces in one direction and one space in a perpendicular direction. If someone violates any of these norms, there will be repercussions. The repercussions might be minor, such as a rude glance at an audience member who is talking during an academic lecture. They might be more significant. A friendship might dissolve if one party is an impatient listener and an effusive talker. People who drive on the wrong side of the road could get stopped and ticketed by the police (if they do not wreck first!). We socialize newcomers to a social practice by instructing them, praising their appropriate performances, and correcting their misdeeds. More often, people internalize norms by way of observation and imitation, conscious or not.

Norms pervade religious communities too. There are right ways and wrong ways to conduct rituals and ceremonies. A Muslim who performs salat (daily prayer) without first achieving ritual purity by washing is violating a ritual norm. An Orthodox Jew who performs manual labor on the Sabbath is violating a norm. In many churches, Protestant Christians who do not bow their head and close their eyes while praying are violating a norm. Violations of religious norms will at the very least garner disapproval from one's coreligionists and in certain cases could lead to expulsion from the religious community or worse.

Norms themselves can be understood in terms of behavior. A norm is in operation when people assessing a given action either actually do or at least have a tendency to behave in a way that expresses approval or disapproval in respect to the action, regarding it as proper or improper. These expressions can take various forms, including utterances like "well done" or "try again" to more subtle gestures like a small nod or cocked eyebrow. In many cases, when behavior is in accordance with norms, no one consciously evaluates the performances, but you know that the norms are still in operation because, if a violation occurred, disapproval would result. To understand behavior and norms, then, you have to grasp the counterfactual aspects of a practice (what would result if people were to act in a certain way, even though they actually do not) as much as the factual aspects. In many cases, there is widespread implicit or explicit agreement on the norms that are operative in a social practice. This is not necessary, however. Disagreement about norms and correspondingly about whether a particular performance in a practice is proper or not is common. Norms are essentially contestable, but this does not preclude them from possessing the significance that they do in social practices or the study of practices.

Another vital feature of the view that takes religion to be a social practice is that social practices do not transpire in isolation from other social practices but any given social practice intersects numerous other social practices. The social practice of religion is not hermetically insulated but intersects the social practices of medicine, law, language use, architecture, education, and many more besides. Any given religious act, then, can be evaluated for its significance in relation not just to the religious social practice in which it occurs but any of these others.

Practice, then, is the basic idea in the study of religion, not experience or meaning. But to regard practices as basic does not exclude attention to experiences and meanings. Instead, we should understand experiences and meanings in terms of practices. Take religious experiences. We should not understand them as the basic constituent of religions, in the way that we find in certain passages in William James and in phenomenologists of religion like Mircea Eliade and Rudolf Otto. Experiences are social practical in nature because they are not private, internal events, thoroughly subjective in nature. Experiences, religious or otherwise, are a matter of perceiving or sensing something and responding to what is perceived or sensed. The response is as much a part of the experience as the perceived object; an object to which we did not respond in any way would be one that we did not notice. The way that we respond to many situations—in terms of our bodily postures, our emotions, our conceptual classification, and our evaluative judgments—has to do with the way that we are socialized and habituated. In the relevant cases, we respond to what we perceive similarly to the way that others in our social group respond to similar things. Even our idiosyncrasies are improvisations against shared patterns of behavior. To attribute an experience to someone is to think that the person underwent some sort of perceptual event and to hold the person responsible to speak and act in ways consistent with the way that people typically behave after undergoing such events. If someone gasps and smiles and then turns to us to report that he has just had the most wonderful experience of God's love (and we do not think he is faking it), we attribute a religious experience to him. We think that he underwent a perceptual event of some sort, whether or not we agree with him that it is divine in origin. We expect him to speak and act in a way consistent with someone who takes himself to have experienced God's love. It would be weird if immediately after reporting an experience of God's love, he denied the existence of God. We would think he had violated the norms of speech, which govern what sorts of statements appropriately cohere with any given assertion. Since it is incompatible to assert both that one has experienced God's love and that God does not exist, we would be puzzled and try to figure out whether he was confused or whether we were misunderstanding him in some way. In these ways, experiences are social practical in nature and even their private aspect depends on public, shared norms.

Meaning, too, is social practical in nature. The meanings of our linguistic and nonlinguistic symbols are not mentalistic or problematically subjective. Rather, they have to do with the norms that govern our assertions and how our assertions relate to our actions. Our symbols represent things, and they do so because of the way that we institute them and respond to them when we encounter them. The representational capacity of our symbols is not a mysterious one-to-one relationship between the symbols and the objects that they represent but emerges from the ways in which our actions and attitudes toward the symbols coordinate with our actions and attitudes toward what the symbols represent. All of this transpires in a larger social practical context. As Ludwig Wittgenstein said, meaning is use. The meaning of a symbol is determined by the role that it plays in our social practices, that is, the distinctive contribution that the symbol makes to the overall pattern of speaking, perceiving, and acting in which the symbol is involved. To hang a sign that reads "Open" on the door of a restaurant is to employ a symbol that represents that the situation is such that someone entering the door will find that there are people inside who are preparing and serving food in exchange for money. We expect the employees and the visitors to act in accordance with the various norms involved in food preparation and consumption. The sign indicates the described situation because we have instituted it to indicate as much. To turn to religion, people grasp the meaning of the assertion "I experienced God's love" if they evidence the requisite skills and attitudes involved in holding the asserter responsible to speak and act in ways that cohere with such assertions.

Earlier I mentioned the view that religion is at base a matter of meaning. Closely related to this view is the popular view that religion is primarily a matter of beliefs. In this view, the proper answer to the question "What is Mormonism?" or "What is Sikhism?" begins with "Mormons believe . . ." or "Sikhs believe. . . ." But if religion is primarily a matter of belief, problems result. First, we are tacitly privileging creedal religions, like Christianity, that place an emphasis on adherence to correct doctrine over religions that emphasize rituals more so than beliefs. Second, we have to give an account of what a belief is, in the first place, and if we are taking beliefs as the basic element in religion, this is not easy to do. Here as with experiences and meanings more generally, we can't peer into people's minds and detect discrete units, identifiable as beliefs, swimming around inside their skulls.

In the social practical account of religion that I propose, a belief is something that we attribute to people (including ourselves) when we hold them responsible to speak and act in certain ways. We expect them, in many cases, to assert the belief in question in appropriate circumstances. If a Jew believes that she has as an ethical obligation of *tikkun olam*, repairing the world, we would expect her to say so if asked. If a Buddhist believes that there is no permanent, persisting self, we would expect him to say so if asked. We expect him not just to assert the particular belief in question; we expect him to say other things in keeping with that belief. If a Catholic Christian believes that the mother of Jesus is a saint, we expect the person to say related things, such as that Mary is a saint. We also attribute beliefs to people on the basis of their behavior, even when they don't assert the beliefs directly. If we see a Muslim use sand to purify himself before prayer, we can attribute to him the belief that there is not sufficient water available, since we know that he would use water were it available. We attribute this belief to him on the basis of his behavior. So in these and other cases, we see that we can understand beliefs in terms of normed behavior: the behavior involved in saying certain things and acting in certain ways. As a product of normed behavior, beliefs are inherently social and practical. We expect people to conform to the relevant norms in question on the basis of the things they say and do. The way that we hold people responsible varies if they are near or far, living or dead, but we are still holding remote and dead people responsible when we evaluate the evidence of things that they said and did and attribute beliefs to them. The popular understanding of religion primarily as a matter of belief is wrong. But it is just as wrong to think that religion does not involve beliefs or that we can study religion without attending to beliefs. Taking practices as basic lets us give belief its proper due, not more or less.

Just as we can construe experiences and meanings as based in social practices, so also power. The norms that govern religious behavior have important and wide-ranging ramifications for how power is distributed in a religious community. The norms associated with the assertion of the author of the New Testament book of 1 Timothy, "I permit no woman to teach or have authority over a man," have led many Christian congregations to prohibit women from preaching. Many religious traditions reserve certain rituals exclusively for members of one gender and thus support differentiated roles for women and men in the community. Such differentiated roles coincide with the exclusion of women from certain offices.

We should understand power as social practical. Social power is acquired and exercised in the context of social practices. Social practices do not distribute goods,

privileges, resources, and roles evenly to all the participants. Some practitioners receive more goods than others and play different roles in the practice than others.
Social practices transpire oftentimes in such a way as to make the unequal distribution of goods seem natural, appropriate, and legitimate. Further, the means by
which power is exercised are social practical in nature. This is true for exercises of
power that are not explicitly coercive and for those that are. Policing and soldiering
are social practices. Domestic violence occurs in gendered social practices according
to which violence and masculinity are linked. Even in natural disasters, social practical arrangements of power are at issue, since some groups are more vulnerable to
disaster than others, and some have resources to recover from disaster better than
others.

A vision of religion as social practical encompasses all three of the grand traditions of theorizing religion in the twentieth and twenty-first centuries: religion as
experience, as meaning, and as social power. To conceive religion as social practice
requires that we correct certain assumptions that these traditions have had. For instance, we must correct the experiential tradition when it appeals to a notion of
subjectivity that is divorced from the public and social. We must also correct the experiential approach for treating religious experiences as universal and transcultural.
We must correct the meaning approach at those moments when it is mentalistic. We
must correct the power approach for focusing on discourse, practices, and bodies to
the exclusion of meaning and experience.

The social practical vision of religion also insists that we view experience, meaning, and power as thoroughly intertwined, and it gives us the resources to understand the ways in which they are interrelated. If experiences, meanings, and power
are all happening in the context of social practices then there are no compartmental-
ized realms in which any of them can subsist in hermetic isolation from the others.
They all play out on the same field, thoroughly intermixed with each other.

For example, experience is entangled with meaning. People apply concepts to their
experiences. If they did not, they could not report having had the experience. The
fact that people apply concepts to their experiences shows that experiences are closely
associated with meaning, since concepts are meaningful. People respond to the experiences the way that they do because of the way that they classify them. People's experiences affect how they conceive of and speak about what they experience. People
do not just respond to their experiences (and prepare for them) conceptually; they
also do so bodily. In many cases, their socially acquired bodily habits serve as the occasion of an experience and are affected by experiences. Experiences of compassion
and loving-kindness in meditation lead to (and are occasioned by) bodily habits that
express compassion and loving-kindness. Experiences of effervescent solidarity lead
to (and are occasioned by) bodily habits that conform to the group's norms.

The interrelations among one's concept use, one's experiences, and one's bodily habits ensure that experiences are not just entangled with meaning but also with power. For one thing, concept use is itself infused with power. This is true in relation to experiences in particular but also in general. Meaning, whether that of our linguistic terms or our nonlinguistic symbols, is thoroughly social practical and thoroughly a matter of power. The way that we apply concepts and the inferences that we make from the claims that we hear and utter are infused with power. Beliefs are constituted by meanings, beliefs lead to actions, and actions perpetuate, institute, and disrupt power structures. Our terms encode evaluative attitudes and our use of these terms reflects those attitudes, leading us to make differential judgments about people and their abilities according to their race, class, sex, sexual orientation, and ethnicity. Some groups exercise more influence over the way that we use our concepts and symbols than others. In these ways and others besides, power is at work throughout the systems of meaning we employ. So my conceptual responses to experiences are power-laden. If I experience God as male, I may infer that men are rightly to exercise power over women. Conversely, if I regard my gender as superior, I will experience God as friendly to my gender or even as possessing the characteristics of my gender. Similar thoughts apply to matters of race and nation. Bodily habits, too, are related to both experience and power. If a Ku Klux Klan member experiences an effervescent solidarity with his fellow white compatriots, such experiences will strengthen bodily habits that differentiate between blacks and whites and that undergird and perpetuate hatred for and violence against African Americans.

Once we take social practices as basic, we can stop speaking as though analyses of experience, meaning, and power are mutually exclusive. There is no longer good reason for scholars to say that they are unconcerned with symbolic meaning and that their focus is instead on what religious practices do. They should not speak of religious experiences as unfit for scholarly study, as a passé topic or as a strictly ideological notion. We should in fact preserve experience as a scholarly category and meaning too. We can do so without reverting to the days when phenomenologists of religion and symbolic anthropologists employed those concepts under problematic assumptions, without adequate attention to power and bodily practices.

Preserving the categories experience and meaning allows us to retain what is valuable from earlier approaches to the study of religion that have now fallen by the wayside. For example, we do not need to follow William James in thinking that religion is, at its core, experiential. But we can acknowledge experiences when they occur in religious practices and regard them as fit objects for study. Even the much-maligned phenomenology of religion approach has valuable insights that we can hold on to once we have divested the approach of its perennialism, its subjectivism, and its problematic appeals to empathy. The thing that the phenomenologists did well was attend to the practitioners' point of view and pay painstaking attention to the practitioners' accounts of what it is like for them to practice their religion. Studying religion is not limited to interpreting such accounts, but when we do encounter them, we should be willing to take them seriously. We can best retain what is valuable in phenomenology of religion in the methodology of Geertzian thick description, once we have sorted through Geertz's corpus to weed out the mentalistic moments therein, holding on to his Wittgensteinian moments. Appropriating Geertz in this way does not mean subscribing to an essentialist, sui generis conception of religion that treats religion as separate from politics. Rather, we can attend to first-hand descriptions of what it is like to practice religion keeping in mind that the descriptions and the corresponding emotions, experiences, beliefs, and actions are thoroughly invested with power. To understand the descriptions of religious life, we do not have to have privileged access to someone else's head and heart, whether through empathy, sympathy, or intuition. Rather, we have to grasp the concepts the practitioners employ, which is to say, to understand what their terms refer to and what the inferential roles of the terms are in the practitioners' discourse.

The power approach is alive and well and does not need rehabilitation, though we do need to articulate the concern with power in a way that does not give rise to the sorts of suspicions that Geertz has: that people who attend to power and bodily disciplines are power-reductionists, seeing in religious practices nothing but the operation of power in a struggle that pits every social group against the others.[3] Such power plays occur, of course, but so do actions and behaviors that have other ends besides advancing or preserving group or individual status.

One of the vital contributions of the power approach to religious studies has been the critical attention to the politics of classification that proponents of that approach have forwarded. The power approach has not just insisted on investigating power as it operates in religions; it insists that we acknowledge that power is operating in academic scholarship. Academic scholarship proceeds in a way, in its discourse and in its institutional arrangements, to privilege certain groups and exclude others within the academic guild and without. Further, scholarship itself is an operation of power over and against those whom the scholar is studying. One way that scholarship exercises power is in its classificatory schemes. Instituting a classificatory concept and then including some items and excluding others enables operations of power, since the distinction allows different attitudes for included things than the excluded ones. If Europeans esteem religion and regard superstition as uncivilized, then a distinction between superstition and religion can authorize colonial oppression of communities that they regard as superstitious. The social practical approach here accommodates this insight. The account of language that

I have been developing sees the meaning of our terms as a product of social practices, and this is as true for scholars' terms as for religious practitioners'. What this means is that the distinction between religion and nonreligion, natural and supernatural, Judaism and non-Judaism, ritual and nonritual, and so forth does not inhere in the social and physical world, independently of human interests or the interests more specifically of those employing the terms. There is no one right answer to the question of whether some disputed activity counts as religious or not. For some scholarly purposes a shrine to Elvis Presley might count; for others, not. Our practical interests determine how and why we classify. This is Foucault's seminal insight. "Power and knowledge directly imply one another. . . . There is no power relation without the correlative constitution of a field of knowledge, nor any knowledge that does not presuppose and constitute at the same time power relations."⁴ However, the insight can be taken too far, and it is when people speak as though scholarly classification had no purpose other than the operation of social power. Such a view reflects an extraordinarily impoverished and simplistic understanding of human life. We must account for power but also for a whole range of other motives, drives, and ways of valuing: curiosity, wonder, appreciation, respect, admiration, and aversion in addition to utilitarian and practical needs. Any of these can operate in conjunction with exercises of power, but this is not to say that they are reducible to such exercises. Merely to point out that a particular scholarly concept has been implicated in domination or exploitation does not suffice to dismiss the concept as though it has no other possible purposes.

Another vital contribution of power approaches to religious studies and the academy more generally has been their agenda to contest oppression and domination. Many versions of the power approach have an intellectual genealogy that traces back, by one path or another, to Karl Marx, and many practitioners of the power approach share his sense that the point of philosophy (and other disciplines) is not just to interpret the world but to change it. In scholarship on religion, one of the things that these sorts of projects strive to do is provide analyses that shed light on the situation of dominated social groups so that political actors might use the analyses to improve the lot of the dominated. Another aim has been to highlight features of academic culture, present or historic, that has reflected and perpetuated unjust power structures to contest the role scholarship plays in fostering injustice. My social practice theory is available for these aims. It would challenge any analysis that sought to analyze power without attending to meaning or experience, but in doing so the idea would be to enhance such intellectual political projects, not undermine them. The theory that I advance is particularly well suited for intellectual political projects that take the form of a particular sort of social criticism, which has as its goal the analysis of the norms implicit in social practices in order to make them explicit so that we can scrutinize them. An effective sort of scrutiny is to criticize particular commitments that a social group has implicit in its social practice in light of other commitments that it has. This is immanent criticism, which looks for incompatibilities and tensions within a social practice instead of appealing to principles external to the practice to criticize it. So, for example, a political culture that expresses an explicit commitment to political equality but that allows wealthy people to influence campaigns inordinately is guilty of internal contradiction.[5] There are other reasons to incorporate power into the study of religion besides political contestation, however. The descriptive and explanatory tasks of religious studies have not always done a good job of attending to power and various lines of social difference. An adequate description or explanation of religious practices should take account of the way that practices vary by social location.

Meaning, power, and experience, then, can all be accommodated in a social practical framework. Such a framework allows us to detail with some precision the complex ways in which they interplay with each other. A social practical vision of religion refuses to privilege any of the terms experience, power, and meaning above the others or to downplay the significance of any of the three. It can account for meaning and experience without referencing mysterious realms of mentalistic subjectivity, divorced from the public and the social. It can account for power without reducing everything of significance in society to mere plays of power. The social practical framework, then, is uniquely capable of providing a sufficiently comprehensive theory of religion.

THE STUDY OF RELIGION AS A SOCIAL PRACTICE

But what good is a theory of religion, anyway? Theorizing is one way to study religion, but how does it relate to other ways? In addition to theory of religion, the contemporary study of religion comprises historical work, ethnography, textual studies, philosophy of religion, religious ethics, the study of religious thought, and other subfields as well. In the remainder of this chapter, I will examine what the study of religion, in its various guises, would be like if informed by the social practical theory of religion advanced in this book.

The first subfield of religious studies I will consider is the one in which this book is an entry: theory of religion. Theory of religion in the broadest sense deals with questions about the nature of religion and how best to study it. These are closely related questions, since what you think religion is about will determine how you go about studying it, and how you study religion implicitly reveals what you think religion is. Thus, scholars often use the term "theory of religion" and the term "methods in religious studies" more or less interchangeably.

This subfield occupies a strange place in the contemporary academy. On the one hand, it is pervasive. Many religion departments and programs offer courses in methods and theory and departments have a widely held expectation that new professors of religious studies will have had training in the topic. But faculty positions with a primary focus in methods and theory are few and far between, and in many cases the important contributors to the scholarly conversation on theory and method in religious studies have their primary appointment in some other subfield or even some other field, such as anthropology. In such a situation, opinions about the significance of theory vary widely, with some thinking it central and essential to the study of religion and others assigning it little or no importance.

One thing that theorists of religion do is proffer explanations of why there are religious practices. Such explanations may be cognitive scientific, neuroscientific, psychological, social, or economic. Other theorists eschew explanation and make a case that the study of religion is properly descriptive, not explanatory. In my view, theory of religion should be construed as broad enough to endorse both explanation and description, and we should not think of it as limited to debates between proponents of explanation and description. More broadly, we should think of it as the critical analysis of the assumptions and key concepts involved in the practice and study of religion. Some of the assumptions operative in the study of religion might pertain to certain types of explanations, but the list of relevant assumptions is much broader. It includes the sorts of things that the scholar attends to when observing religious communities and their products. What do we see when we look at a religious community? Do we attend to psychological processes? Gender? Race? Ethnicity? Nationality? Sexuality? Class? Ritual? Belief? Material artifacts? Children? No one study can attend to every potentially relevant aspect of a religious community, but some studies are culpable for their systematic ignorance of such matters. For example, one of the contributions of feminist studies of religion has been to point out how systematically religious studies has over the course of its history ignored or devalued women's religion and treated men's religiosity as universal. When theorists analyze key concepts, they attend to a whole host of categories that scholars employ, including but hardly limited to ritual, sacredness, profaneness, secularity, belief, doctrine, personhood, community, pilgrimage, shrine, culture, society, nun, monk, priest, temple, god, spirit, possession, shaman, magic, purity, ethics, spiritual, artifact, tradition, holiness, saint, heaven, prayer, worship, supernatural, death, impermanence, submission, illusion, asceticism, nature, conflict, disability, childhood, suffering, liberation, performance, sacrifice, time, gift, sin, text, gender, race, ghost, duty, scripture, ancestor, revelation, myth, reason, ideology, play, soul, rebirth, politics, and on and on. The ideas that have been the focus of this book are prominent key concepts in the study of religion: experience, meaning, power, and practice. Furthermore, there are the concepts by which we designate the various religions (Buddhism, Judaism, Islam, Christianity, Hinduism, and so on), and a set of concepts for the key figures, events, texts, artifacts, and rituals in each religion. And of course, perhaps most important, religion itself is a key concept that deserves particular attention. The use of all these concepts and more is essential to the study of religion as a whole. We couldn't study religious communities without employing them. But the concepts themselves are problematic and contestable in various ways. They all have particular histories of usage in particular social and linguistic contexts. Even within these contexts, the terms' proper application is not self-evident or innocent, and their complexities are only exacerbated when they are applied cross-culturally and in comparative studies.

Any given study, whether historical, textual, or something else, will involve assumptions and key concepts, even if only implicitly, and so every study has an underlying theory of religion, even if only implicitly. So the question is not whether or not any particular scholar of religion is employing a theory of religion, but how well he or she is. The best case for the legitimacy and indispensability of theory of religion to the discipline as a whole is the fact that theories of religion are implicitly involved in the study of religion generally. So the study of religion will be much improved if the assumptions and concepts involved implicitly are explicitly identified, clarified, and criticized. In fact, many of the breakthroughs in the study of religion have occurred as people have stepped back from attending to religious communities and attended reflexively to the nature of the scholarly task. Several of these breakthroughs have been central to the account of the study of religion that I have provided in this book. The breakthrough that corrected the centrality of experience and the breakthrough that corrected the tendency of interpretive approaches to misconstrue or ignore social power both occurred because scholars performed the theoretical task of reflecting critically on scholarship. Religious studies is much improved for these theoretical projects and the accompanying breakthroughs as well as for the smaller advances that have come from the reflexive task of taking scholarship itself as an object of study.

The scholarly skills involved in analyzing the assumptions and concepts that guide the study of religion are not the same as the skills involved in historical, ethnographic, or textual studies. Familiarity with philosophy and social theory are requisite features for excellence in theory of religion, since philosophers excel at the sort of conceptual analysis needed to examine key concepts and social theory provides the tools to analyze the social realities of religious communities and the way scholarship accounts for them. In an era of specialization, few individuals are capable of dedicating the time necessary to develop the historical, ethnographic, or textual skills and also facility with philosophy and social theory. This highlights the need for dialogue, interaction, and interdependence between theorists and textual, historical, and ethnographic scholars.

One of the best cases for the existence of religious studies as a distinct academic field, as opposed to giving up the study of religion to departments of history, area studies, and anthropology, is the way that religious studies departments explicitly attend to the contested and problematic nature of the concept of religion and other key concepts and also explicitly attend to the history of the theory of religion. These are things that the theory of religion has contributed to the broader discourse in religious studies. Groundbreaking and excellent studies of religion occur frequently outside of religious studies departments, but this does not detract from the cultivation of such excellence that only comes with institutionalizing the study of religion in distinct departments and programs.

So much for a statement about what theory of religion in general has to offer the field of religious studies. I will turn now to some specific reflections about the contribution that the social practical theory of religion developed in this book can make to the study of religion in its various subfields. In whatever subfield, the standard that my theory of religion establishes is that any particular religious event, action, agent, or artifact must be understood in relation to its situatedness in the religious practice as a whole and indeed in its situatedness in the other social practices that intersect the religious practice. This is a version of what Geertz called thick description, but whereas for Geertz, thick description meant describing a particular symbol in relation to a larger web of symbols, for me, thick description should mean describing a particular religious thing, symbol or not, in relation to the larger practices in which the thing occurs. In doing this sort of thick description, scholars should conceive of a religious practice as something that involves experiences, meaning, and power. I will apply these insights now to the various subfields in religious studies.

What would it look like to study religion historically and ethnographically in a way compatible with a social practical theory of religion of the sort I propose? The first thing to say, given the emphasis that I have given to the three key concepts, experience, meaning, and power, is that historians and ethnographers should approach the subjects of their studies with an awareness of the prevalence of and significance of these three aspects of religious practices. This does not mean that every single study needs to explicitly thematize or address all three of these factors. No one study can do everything, after all. And the available evidence might not give us access to all three aspects in some cases. The evidence from some historical religious people may be too scant to extrapolate much about their experiences, for example. But in many cases, the experiences, meanings, and power that infuse religious practices are available to the scholar in some way or another and the decision to exclude one or more of these factors should be just that: a decision, as opposed to an oversight. Further, in studying any one of these things, the scholar should be aware that each of the three aspects is invested with the others. So here again, a decision in a particular study to treat one aspect but leave out its relations to the others should be one that is consciously made and not inadvertent. Scholars should treat experiences as social items, causally linked to other features of the experiencers' social practices. Scholars should not conduct their studies unreflectively treating experiences as epiphenomena but instead should view them as things that people desire, seek, and avoid—things that condition people's lives and their communities even as their lives and their communities condition the experiences. So scholars should be willing to take descriptions of emotions and experiences as *referring to* emotions and experiences, things with causal properties in their own right (excepting those cases where the evidence suggests that the experience reports do not actually refer to experiences). Scholars should be willing to regard experiences as religious goods in their own right and should not unreflectively treat experience reports as nothing but discourse.

My social practical theory of religion has two further methodological implications for historical and ethnographic studies, each drawn from a major twentieth-century theoretical school: the first, as mentioned above, is an endorsement of Geertz's idea of thick description, and the second is the phenomenology of religion's (and Geertz's) idea of practitioner-oriented description. Ethnography and, to the extent possible, history are at their best when they consist of "exceedingly extended acquaintances with extremely small matters."[6] If a practice is, as MacIntyre says, a "coherent and complex form of socially established cooperative human activity," then grasping the complexity will require sustained attention to the details of the practice. This is especially true because though practices must be somewhat coherent if they are to be recognizable to practitioners or observers, the coherence is not without fissures. Social practices are, in Geertz's words, "strange, irregular, and in-explicit . . . full of ellipses, incoherencies, suspicious emendations, and tendentious commentaries."[7] The overarching coherence of a practice allows for all manner of tension, confusion, and contradiction within it. In the social practical perspective, to understand a religious community is to be familiar with the community's activities and the norms that govern them. Since these norms are more often than not implicit and pertain as much to nonlinguistic things (body posture, for example, or clothing style) as to linguistic things like spoken utterances, a competent grasp of a community's norms takes an extensive encounter with the community or the evidence it left behind. In the account of norms and meaning that I have been developing, the significance of an action or object is determined by the role that it plays in the social practice, which is to say, its distinctive contribution to the practitioners' overall pattern of norm-governed activity. Since this is the case, no action or object can be understood in isolation from the broader social practice in which it occurs. The significance of any action or object is holistic in nature, that is, determined by its relation to a whole host of other actions and objects, and grasping the role that something plays in a social practice requires understanding the relation between that action or object and a great many other actions and objects. Furthermore, the view that the meaning of some utterance, action, or artifact is a product of the way that it is used challenges us not to assume that the meaning of any particular religious term, ritual, or artifact is stable and consistent across its occurrences. Once terms, rituals, and artifacts are socially instituted as meaningful, they are available for a wide variety of uses, and different people can use them in different ways, or even the same person can use them in different ways at different times. Covenant, for example, was a concept in colonial New England that served as "an elastic category capable of accommodating very different goals," according to Anne S. Brown and David D. Hall.[8] So grasping the meaning of a term or the significance of a ritual is not merely a matter of attending to the term or ritual itself but to the various ways in which the term or ritual is employed by various persons at different times for different purposes. Thick description is the designation for this sort of sustained attention to the details of the role of actions and objects in their social practical context.

The rootedness of doings, sayings, and objects in their surrounding context and the corresponding methodology of thick description give strong reasons not to engage in an activity that has been historically central to religious studies: the comparative study of religion. And indeed the social practice theory here rules out certain forms of the comparative study of religion, those that depend on some universal core to religion, like a phenomenologically identical sense of the sacred. However, despite the cautionary lessons that thick description has for comparative projects, we should not reject comparison altogether. Comparison, after all, and the factors that constitute comparison, resemblance and difference, are ubiquitous.[9] Any concept that we apply to two or more different items is comparative in nature, implicitly regarding them as similar to each other in certain regards and different in certain regards from those things to which we would not apply the concept. And any two items recognizable to us will share a whole host of properties, starting with the property of being recognizable to us. If we deny that there is one necessary or most appropriate way to classify the social or natural world and if we deny that our classifications are independent of human interests and aims, we can acknowledge that grouping distinct items under a common classification is appropriate or not given the interests, aims, and context of the classifier. For the context of religious studies, the relevant interests and aims will be about facilitating projects of inquiry that have the potential to expand our knowledge. When I. M. Lewis groups together a host of spirit possession rituals and ceremonies from different religions and locations, he does so by ascertaining features of these rituals that by his lights resemble each other: specifically, they involve ecstatic states of mind.[10] Ecstasy is his classificatory concept, not that of the people undergoing it, and it is in accordance with his own sense of the proper criteria for counting something as ecstatic or not that he makes the grouping. Having done so, he is in a position to notice another resemblance that these rituals have: women far more frequently undergo ecstatic spirit possession than men. This is a noteworthy finding, and it invites further inquiry as to the factors responsible for this fact. Given the wide range of examples that Lewis uses (and his disinterest in interpreting meaning), his treatment of the various rituals is superficial (though we should not think comparison is necessarily superficial). Janice Boddy's study of a particular community's involvement in spirit possession is thickly descriptive and focused on the interpretation of meaning, aspects of her methodology that allow her to give a far more compelling account of the particularities of spirit possession among Sudanese Muslims than any of the accounts that Lewis gives.[11] It also allows her to contest the functionalist explanation of female participation in ecstatic rituals that Lewis offers, according to which gender uplift is the explanatory factor. This does not negate the virtues of comparison that Lewis supplies, even if his particular explanation of gender differences is wrong. The relevant virtue in his comparative study is the way that it opens up interesting questions and lines of inquiry about gender differences in ecstatic rituals that ultimately can only be verified through thickly descriptive studies. With thick description as the standard, we have to acknowledge that few scholars will be able to obtain the linguistic and historical background to describe thickly multiple communities in a comparative study, which highlights, yet again, the need for collaboration, interaction, and interdependence among religion scholars.

The final methodological concern related to ethnographic and historical studies that I will mention, accounting for the practitioners' own accounts of their religious practices, is a plank of the phenomenology of religion. Since "phenomenology," as a term, refers to the study of the way that things appear to a conscious subject, the phenomenology of religion is the study of how religious people experience their religion. Geertz inherited practitioner-oriented description from the phenomenologists, talking about the study of religion as something that must account for the "native's point of view."[12] The first reason that attention to practitioners' accounts of their practices is essential to a social practical approach to religious studies is that the practitioners have a type of familiarity with the norms that observers do not: through a process of socialization, the practitioners have internalized the norms that govern their religious practices while the observers have not (unless the observers themselves go through a process of socialization into the practices), so the practitioners can report on what sorts of performances are appropriate and not in a broad range of factual and counterfactual cases. Second, a primary constituent of social practices (alongside nonhuman animals and material objects) is human actions. Actions, as opposed to accidents, are intentional. In many cases, a person's intentions are clear enough to the observer. Taking a drink has quenching thirst as its intention. But in a social context that is unfamiliar to an observer, the intentions for many actions will be unclear, and the actors and their fellow practitioners are in a unique position to report the intentions. Acknowledging the reality of this sort of self-knowledge and the importance of practitioners' reports of their own intentions does not imply that motives are always transparent to actors. We are in many cases perfectly clear about our motives and in many other cases ignorant. A theory of religion should not err by denying either of these facts. An observer who hears an actor's testimony about the intentions for an action is not restricted to accepting the reported intentions as the real cause of the action. The observer may decide that factors unknown to the actor are the real cause of the action. The actor may claim that fidelity to God is the reason for performing a ritual, whereas the observer suspects that buttressing male privilege is the real reason. Even in such cases, though, the real explanation of the action must operate through the intentions and motives of the actor, so a full explanation of the ritual in terms of gender would have to account for how the ritual's gender effects produce certain motives and intentions in actors. Even in such a functionalist explanation, then, attention to the practitioners' account is necessary. So even scholars who are interested in unintended effects of religious actions cannot afford to ignore the intended effects. There may be cases where the practitioners' own accounts of their religious practices are inaccessible, and there may be studies with limited focuses for which such accounts are unnecessary, but nevertheless for the discipline of religious studies as a whole, the practitioner's point of view is an indispensable resource.

As we saw in chapter 4, an understanding of social practices as normed behaviors allows us to respond to criticisms of ethnography in general and the ethnographic method of participant-observation in particular. Tomoko Masuzawa, for example, criticizes cultural anthropology in these terms:

> The reality of "culture as a complex whole," its intelligibility to the disciplined observer, and, in fact, all that is vested in the so-called anthropological notion of culture is contingent on the singular point of participant observation and the vigilantly empiricist prose generated from that position. Once the staying power supposedly endemic to the seat of observation is questioned or hypothetically denied, once the heightened rhetoric of empirical reality and self-evidence of data (with all the moralizing phrases that go into this rhetoric) is relaxed, and once the position of the observer ceases to be

supercharged—or, in psychoanalytic terms, hypercathected and fetishized—the gossamer reality of the "complex whole" will likely begin to appear no more substantial than the phrase itself.[13]

Masuzawa suggests that historiography should not be a matter of narrativizing "a certain wholeness of a past" in "thick descriptions," but rather "outwitting" such narratives to let "forgotten moments . . . flare up."[14] While I agree with Masuzawa about the importance of attending to forgotten moments, a social practical theory of religion allows for us to conceive of ethnography and participant observation in ways that escape her criticism. By dropping the notion of culture as a complex whole and focusing instead on social practices, we do not have to worry about identifying something so singular and all-encompassing as a culture or even a society. Any number of social practices could intersperse a given society, and many will extend beyond the borders of the society. Any given individual will participate in a number of social practices. In the course of a single day, a college student who goes to a prayer meeting, to class, to a doctor's appointment, and to a basketball game participates in social practices of education, medicine, religion, and sports. Each of these is distinctly identifiable, even if the practices intersect in complex ways, and each has its own "practical logic."[15] It does not serve much analytical purpose to lump these together into a single thing that we might designate as a culture. And what about the status of the ethnographer as participant observer? Masuzawa wants to read that status in terms of its history in European colonial and missionary efforts, a history that led to an "ideology" of the participant observer as the "Archimedean point," a "seat of observation" before whom the complex, whole of culture stands as objective data, self-evident and self-authenticating.[16] While I accept this account of the history of ethnography, the historical origin of the disciplines of ethnography and history is not the only model according to which we can understand or practice them in their contemporary forms. An alternative model is to see ethnography and historiography as rooted in two activities that are pervasive and essential to social life in general: observation of the things that people say and do and attribution of beliefs to them. No cooperative human social undertaking could take place without the participants in the undertaking performing these sorts of observations and attributions. The activities are ubiquitous.[17] So the anthropologist and historian are not doing something categorically different from what every competent member of social life does. To be sure, there are particular complications related to cross-cultural encounters: prejudice, desires for and aversions to foreignness on the part of both the anthropologists and their interlocutors, mistrust, and power differentials complicate the observations and attributions to a greater or lesser extent and require specialized training and special reflexivity. But the core aspects of the anthropological (and historical) tasks are just those that constitute social interaction in general. Once we demystify belief by providing a social practical account, attributing beliefs and understanding actions in terms of beliefs and desires should be uncontroversial matters, given their ubiquity and indispensability to social life. Since beliefs, actions, and material objects have the status that they do because of their role in social practices, the significance of these things is socially and publicly available. The job of the anthropologist and historian is to discern the norms that govern the uses of the utterances, actions, and objects in social practices. These norms, as we have seen, are essentially social. Discerning norms may be quite difficult in particular cases, and there might be reasons, given the challenges particular to cross-cultural exchanges, to be tentative about one's anthropological conclusions. But we can understand the possibility for success in ethnographic and historical investigation without positing some fancy "seat of observation" or "Archimedean point" of participant observation. Every language-using member of a social group is a seat of observation in a noncontroversial sense, in that all of them attribute beliefs and motives to all of those with whom they interact socially. When anthropologists take their place as yet another seat of observation among the others, this is not necessarily an ideological (in the pejorative sense of the term) undertaking. It can be so, of course, for various reasons, but the mere fact that anthropology (and the academy in general) has a sordid past, implicated in colonial domination, does not make it so in principle.

There is one final thing to say about history and ethnography before turning to other subfields, which is to point out that the contemporary interest in the study of "lived religion"—"religion as people actually do and imagine it in the circumstances of their everyday lives"—is consonant with this book's social practical theory of religion in many ways.[18] Indeed, my theory of religion has been inspired in significant part through reflections on the merits of a number of studies that I would call studies of lived religion, such as those of R. Marie Griffith, Robert Orsi, Albert Raboteau, and Janice Boddy. Indeed, Griffith and Orsi have been explicitly linked to the term as prime exemplars of the approach.[19] Lived religion scholarship shares key terms, such as "practice," with my theory, as well as key influences, such as Geertz and the phenomenology of religion.[20] The study of lived religion is a corrective to trends in historiography that take the official doctrines or rituals of a religion and its leaders to represent the tradition. As opposed to the official and intellectual versions of a tradition and to religion as practiced in designated religious spaces, scholars of lived religion are interested in how religion plays out in the everyday lives of the practitioners. Unlike some studies of popular religion that bifurcate official religion from lay religion, scholars of lived religion avoid such distinctions and attend to the complex interactions between official religion and ordinary practitioners.[21] The intellectual activity of theologians and the official proclamations of religious elites are of course products of social practices in their own right, and so studies of those matters are not excluded by the theory of religion that I promote, but even then recognition of the way that the official versions of a religious tradition are rooted in and connected to a larger context is salutary. We should see official religion as one facet of a religious tradition, among others, not the privileged expression of it.

The emphasis on religion as a "web . . . of relationships between heaven and earth," in Orsi's words, is another aspect of scholarship on lived religion that makes it a fit methodology for the theory of religion here.[22] As Orsi describes it, studying religion as a network of relationships among religious practitioners and sacred figures, real or imagined, facilitates an acknowledgment of the messy complexity of religious life. The relationships with divine figures in a religious practice "have all the complexities—all the hopes, evasions, love, fear, denial, projections, misunderstandings, and so on—of relationships between humans."[23] These complexities are laden with social power: "The saints could be dangerous enforcers of cultural structures, norms, and expectations" but also "allies in resistance and subversion," Orsi says about the Catholics whom he studies.[24] This allows for just the sort of attentiveness that my theory advocates, an expectation that when we turn to religion, we will find experiences, meanings, and power intertwined with each other. Furthermore, highlighting the way that religious practices institute and perpetuate relationships among humans and their gods allows us to account for some of the most important internal goods of religious practices, the "goods internal to that form of activity" that are "realized" in the cooperative human activities that MacIntyre defines as practices. Goods internal to a practice are ones that can only be obtained by participating in the practice, as opposed to goods external to the practice. If we value a cello concerto for the virtuosity of the composer and beauty of the performance, those are goods internal to the practice of music. The fame and money that come to a renowned cellist are external goods. Functionalist explanations of religion explain things in terms of external goods, like gender subordination or class uplift. The stated motives and aims of religious practitioners, however, are oftentimes couched in terms of internal goods, like fidelity to an ancestor or love for a god. Rituals have as their aim in many cases maintaining or strengthening the practitioners' relation to a divine being. Orsi's emphasis on religion as a network of religion works well with my social practice theory in accounting for the intentional actions of religious practitioners. The attention that scholars of lived religion give to the internal goods constituted in relationships helps us to do so.

I will turn my attention to textual studies now. One thing that scholars of lived religion and of material culture encourage us to do is to approach religious texts as objects that have numerous uses other than the meaning of their verbal contents. This is surely right, but it does not invalidate attention to the interpretation of the texts. Even if religious practitioners do many things with texts besides interpret them, they do in fact interpret them. We should not altogether "eschew the herme-neutical obsession with the non-material, symbolic, or spiritual *content* of a body of work" like post-hermeneutical scholars suggest but rather approach texts both as possessors of symbolic content and as material artifacts whose circumstances of production, circulation, and use are legitimate topics of inquiry alongside herme-neutical ones.[25]

But what about textual meaning and the interpretation of it? Does meaning, in any objective sense, reside in texts? Is it merely a product of the response of the reader? Or is it located in the fusion that occurs when the horizons of the text and the interpreters meet, as Gadamer would have it? Do texts have authors, or has author-ship died? Any brief answer to these questions will be necessarily inadequate, and I have treated some of these questions in more depth in chapter 4, but I will venture to indicate quickly some directions that we could go to address these concerns in a way that justifies textual interpretation as a legitimate discipline.

In a significant way, meaning does reside in the texts themselves. (For simplic-ity's sake, I will limit this discussion to a particular type of writing, assertive sentences, without meaning to imply that that is the only relevant sort of speech act.) As described in chapter 4, the meaning of a sentence is the role that it plays in inferences, and the meaning of the terms in the sentences is their contribution to the inferential role of the sentences in which they occur. These inferential roles are norms: inferring is a normative activity because there are proper and improper things one can infer from or to any given sentence. So, the sentences themselves that constitute a text have meaningful content. However, this mean-ing is not exclusively located in the text or in the sentences that constitute the text; the meaning is the joint product of the text and some larger context. There are an infinite number of sentences that we can infer from and to any one sen-tence, and so if the meaning of a sentence is its role in relation to whatever can be inferred from it and to it, then meaning is holistic indeed. Further, an indefinite number of contexts could be specified in relation to a text. A context could be as specific as the individual person who is interpreting the text or who authored it or, more broadly, the society in which the text was written or is being inter-preted. In Revelation in the Christian Bible, we find this assertion, describing the setting where John had a revelatory vision: "I, John, your brother who share with you in Jesus the persecution and the kingdom and the patient endurance, was on the island called Patmos because of the word of God and the testimony of Jesus." In today's context, an interpreter could offer the following infer-ence: "According to the author of Revelation, John had a vision on the island that *Forbes Magazine* in 2009 rated the most idyllic place to live in Europe."

Obviously, that inference would not have been available to the ancient context. This is to say, to determine meaning, it matters not just what is asserted but also what the beliefs are of the person interpreting the assertion. This interaction between the text and the interpreter ensures that meaning is not objective in the sense that it is independent of interpretive context, but neither is it thoroughly subjective. If an interpreter in our day stated that according to Revelation, John's vision occurred in *Forbes Magazine*'s third-most idyllic place to live in Europe in 2009, the person would be wrong, and objectively so. The fact that interpretation is relative to context does not mean anything goes.

If we conceive of a particular interpretive undertaking as ascertaining the author's (or editor's or redactor's) intention, then what we mean is that the relevant context for the interpretation is the author's own beliefs and attitudes. We would be constraining ourselves to attribute to the author of the text things that the author actually would have been able to acknowledge and avow. The more that we know about what the author believed, the better we will be able to do this. But what of the widely shared reports of the death of the author? The person who inscribes markings on paper is performing actions, and just like any action, the action can be understood by attributing beliefs and intentions to the actor. In inscribing marks on paper, though, the author is employing words and sentences that are not strictly his or her own province. The words and sentences are dependent on their role in social practices for the meaning that they have. Authors are only able to issue assertions insofar as they have been socialized into the practice of language use, a social practice that precedes, exceeds, and succeeds them. Indeed, we can even say that people are constituted by the social practices that they inhabit, perhaps especially language, insofar as people's identity depends on and is in significant part constituted by the norms and behavioral dispositions that they have internalized. So if authors are supposed to be discrete entities, possessing their own vocabulary and intentions independently of their social context, then the author is dead. Or at least such an idea of authorhood is. But if authors are actors among other actors, constituted by the social practices that they inhabit, then it is perfectly sensible to speak of authors and their intentions and to have as one interpretive goal the aim of discovering the authors' intention, that is, the aim of attributing to authors beliefs that they would acknowledge and avow.

Uncovering authorial intent is one possible interpretive goal, but hardly the only one. In fact, there is an indefinite number of interpretive goals, and the success of an interpretation should be judged in light of its goals. As Jeffrey Stout says, "Take as your frame of reference the history of Scotland, and Hume's *Dialogues* will have one 'meaning.' Concern yourself with dialogue as genre, critiques of religion, or psychobiography and it will have another."[26] A Marxist analysis, gender analysis, or postcolonial reading will approach a text with distinctive aims and standards. There is no one method of interpretation and no one answer to the question, "What is the meaning of this text?" But given certain aims and a certain text, there are standards of objectivity that make some readings better than others, and some interpretive claims correct and others incorrect.

Leaving textual studies, we can turn now to another major subfield, philosophy of religion. Philosophers work with concepts and arguments. Philosophers of religion employ resources from the discipline of philosophy to perform a number of types of analysis, such as rationally reconstructing a text's ideas; critically evaluating a text's ideas to see in what respects it is plausible or implausible, either in respect to its original context or today's; arguing in favor of or against a text's ideas; relating a text's ideas conceptually to other texts' ideas; and constructively developing one's own ideas on a topic. Philosophy of religion in its current guise has two significant divisions: there is a division between philosophy of religion as it is practiced in philosophy departments and philosophy of religion as it is practiced in religious studies departments, and there is a division between philosophy of religion that draws from analytic philosophy (people like W. V. Quine and David Lewis being primary exemplars of that style of philosophy) and that which draws from post-Heideggerian Continental philosophy (represented in the work of people like Jacques Derrida and Jean-Luc Marion). Because of the vitality of the Society of Christian Philosophers in the discipline of philosophy (and other factors as well), philosophy of religion in anglophone philosophy departments is disproportionately devoted to the philosophical investigation of topics drawn from Christian theology and monotheism. It also tends to be conducted far more in the analytic vein than the Continental vein.

There is nothing in the social practice approach to rule out the philosophical investigation of such abstract questions as the logical coherence of the Trinity or Incarnation. These pursuits are explorations of the inferential relations of various assertions that Christian theologians have made, and a social practical theory of language that construes the meaning of assertions as determined by the inferential role that they play happily licenses such inquiries. However, the social practical emphasis on the holistic evaluation of assertions, theological and philosophical or not, in their social context encourages new trends in the philosophy of religion. One such trend would be to evaluate philosophical and theological problems in relation to their implications for lived religion. Indeed, to treat theological concepts without reference to their social practical context will be artificial to a significant degree, in my account, since the very meaning of the concept is a product not just of the assertions and writings in which it appears but of the holistic role of the concept in its religious practice. So, for example, in one essay, Amy Hollywood discusses topics in the philosophy of religion, such as belief, objects of religious belief, and religious experience, in relation to social theory and with substantial reference to the religious practices of a fourteenth-century German nun, Margaret Ebner.[27] In her book, Grace Jantzen investigates the history of the concepts of mysticism and the mystical with attention to the way that those concepts have affected the institutional and practical situation of women.[28] Jantzen's attention to sexism in the history and study of Christian mysticism highlights a historic lacuna in philosophy of religion in that it attends to intellectual problems without acknowledging the ways that the topics (and the philosophical study of them) are implicated in relations of social power.[29] One of the correctives to philosophy of religion that my approach would counsel is to attend specifically to relations of power while situating philosophical ideas in their historical and social context. To relate philosophical topics effectively to lived religion, familiarity with social theory, history, and ethnography is a valuable skill for a philosopher of religion to have, and my social practical theory of religion welcomes philosophical investigations that are worked out in relation to religious practices, as reported by historians and ethnographers. Philosophers of religion in religious studies departments are well situated to receive this sort of training, since social theory, ethnography, and history are central to religious studies but not to philosophy. Having said that, scholars in philosophy departments excel at conceptual analysis, clarity of expression, and rigor of argumentation. Philosophy of religion at its best will incorporate the excellences of both disciplines, and it is not well served if practitioners of each version fail to appreciate the excellences of the other.

If philosophy of religion goes in these directions, it will be impinging on the territory that has traditionally belonged to theory of religion, since it will be doing one of the primary tasks that theorists of religion do: examining key concepts involved in the practice of religion. I see this as a welcome development, and blurring the boundary between philosophy of religion and theory of religion will result in more conceptual sophistication in theory of religion (many of the most influential works of which have been written by people untrained in philosophy) and more lived religion in philosophy of religion. Once more, we see the need for collaboration, interaction, and interdependence across subdisciplinary divides in religious studies. Theorists and philosophers depend on ethnographers and historians for (mediated, to be sure) access to lived religion, and the latter depend on the former for disciplined reflection on the assumptions and concepts that undergird the practice and study of religion.

Finally, I will turn to the subfields of religious ethics and theology or, as the latter is sometimes called, religious thought. These are the most controversial subfields in religious studies, because much of the intellectual work in these subfields is done self-consciously from a confessional standpoint. For some, this fact alone rules out these subfields from legitimacy, since in their mind, the academic study of religion should limit itself to descriptive and explanatory tasks and leave aside evaluative and constructive ones.[30] What shall we think about these complicated issues? First, it is important to point out that in many cases, what passes for theology and religious ethics is not constructive or evaluative but more along the lines of intellectual history, trying to determine what some historical figure's views on the good life or the proper relation between humans and the divine are, for example. But in other cases, theology and religious ethics are done with the intent to offer proposals about how contemporary religious people should think about religious matters or how they should conduct their moral lives. The Buddhist intellectual may offer a proposal as to how contemporary Buddhists should think of the tenet of nonself, and the Jewish ethicist may offer a proposal as to how contemporary Jews should apply a particular Talmudic injunction. These problems and their controversies involve issues far beyond the scope of this book, but it is worth pointing out that evaluative and constructive intellectual projects have been at the heart of the humanities throughout the Western intellectual tradition's history and have been at the heart of the academic mission throughout its history. Constructive proposals for individuals and societies are found throughout the academy and find special institutional home in political theory (in the political science department) and ethics (in the philosophy department). Outside those subfields, it is not uncommon for sociological or historical works to throw in a few pages of constructive suggestions in the conclusion of what was otherwise a straightforwardly descriptive analysis. We benefit from the inclusion of moral vision in the social sciences. Would Michelle Alexander's seminal analysis of the racialization of criminal justice policies, *New Jim Crow*, really have been better without its moral edge and its policy prescriptions?[31]

So perhaps the issue is not that descriptive and explanatory projects are permissible and constructive and evaluative ones not. Perhaps the issue has to do with the fact that, in theology and religious ethics, the constructive and evaluative projects start from religious commitments. Is the issue here specifically that they are religious? Or merely that they are particular? It would be too damaging to academic discourse in general to rule commitments inadmissible merely because they are particular. Kantianism is a particular perspective, as is utilitarianism, yet we welcome constructive ethical projects under those banners. Feminism and critical race theory have particular commitments, in terms of their aims and methodologies, that are not universally shared. Yet we welcome constructive ethical projects under those banners. In these post-foundationalist days, many disciplines welcome projects that proceed from premises that are not universally shared. Christian philosopher Nicholas Wolterstorff makes a similar point:

Once upon a time, lasting until not long ago, philosophers assumed that philosophy, like religion, had to be rationally grounded in certitudes; they understood the methodology of their discipline as foundationalist. . . . Seldom
anymore does the analytic philosopher assume that he is obligated *qua* philosopher to ground rationally what he says in certitudes. . . . The philosopher,
approaching the practice of philosophy from his life in the everyday, finds
himself believing many things, both large and small. Perhaps he finds himself
believing in physicalism. He then regards the challenge facing him as a philosopher not to be that of discarding all those convictions unless he can rationally
ground them in certitudes; the challenge facing him is that of working out
the nature and implications of his physicalist convictions in various areas of
thought, doing so in such a way as to cope not only with the complications
that arise in his own mind but with the objections lodged against his line of
thought by others. In principle these objections might prove so powerful that
he gives up his physicalism. In place of the old foundationalist picture, the picture of the academic enterprise now being taken for granted by philosophers in
the analytic tradition is what I call *dialogic pluralism*. The academic enterprise
is a dialogue among persons of differing perspectives.[32]

If this is an accurate designation of the academic enterprise in many fields, not just
philosophy, then it is unclear why scholars of religious studies should not be permitted to participate in it on such terms. Furthermore, one need not be committed to a
particular set of premises to take an interest in or explore the inferential significance
of those premises. That is why nontheists like Stout can make valuable contributions
to Christian ethics.

The primary challenges facing religious ethics and theology in the academy, then,
may be not so much principled reasons to reject religious premises from intellectual
and ethical inquiry but rather the practical problems that face their projects: for
a project to succeed in the academy, it must be of significant interest to a pluralistic audience. Projects that take for granted a set of religious commitments will not
garner the interest of many who do not share the commitments. The risk then is that
theology and religious ethics will remain sequestered and insular. The burden on
religious ethicists and theologians is to clarify to a broad audience the stakes of their
projects in such a way that it is clear why the pluralistic audience should see the project as significant. This is the same burden, of course, that all academic research faces,
but religious intellectuals will face a particular challenge to the extent that their
peers in the academy do not take religious commitments to be worth their consideration. In societies where many members of the populace themselves have religious
commitments, there are obvious reasons to be interested in intellectual projects that

explore and critically analyze the inferential relationships of those commitments, but for various reasons, this consideration does not generate much interest in theology outside of seminaries, divinity schools, and religious colleges.

With those thoughts in mind, what would the contribution of my social practical theory be to religious ethics and theology? Here some of the same considerations discussed in relation to philosophy of religion apply. My social practical theory of religion can countenance studies that treat doctrines or ethical principles in abstraction from their surrounding social context, but it insistently reminds us that there is something artificial about such treatments, and it encourages theological and ethical work that assesses and constructively generates theological doctrines and ethical principles with attention to the historical and social situatedness of the doctrines and principles.

In this, my social practical theory of religion has affinity with the methodology of certain strands of post-liberal theology. George Lindbeck, who draws from Wittgenstein and Geertz, is right to attend to the significance of doctrine in its context of use and to reject the strand of modern theology that sees experience as the basis of theological reflection, experiential-expressivism as he calls it.[33] Another post-liberal, Hans Frei, asks us to conceive of Christian theology not so much as a variant of history or philosophy but of anthropology. The Christian community, Frei says, is a type of culture, and the task of the theologian is to interpret the culture, much the same way that Geertz says anthropologists are to interpret culture. The Christian church has a sacred text and "formal or, more likely, informal rules" (I would say explicit and implicit norms) as to how its speech and action are to conform to the sacred text. The job of the theologian is observe Christian practices with an eye toward articulating these rules and, when they are implicit, rendering them explicit.[34] Both Frei's theologian and the interpretive anthropologist have as their job describing the religious practices of a particular community. The theologian and not (generally speaking) the anthropologist avows the key religious commitments of the community in question, but in terms of their interest in the community's practices, its utterances, and the implications of those utterances, there can be a great deal of overlap in their methodologies. Both Frei and Lindbeck, then, see theology as subordinate to the community's religious practices. The religious community is what is prior and generative; the theologians' job is just to formalize and render intelligible what the community is doing. A recent and sophisticated development of the idea that religion is a social practice and theology is reflection on that practice is Kevin Hector's *Theology without Metaphysics*.[35] Hector uses a similar social practical account of language as the one in the present book to argue that religious speech is capable of referring to God, even if God is transcendent of human practices. He supplies a far more sophisticated account of the referentiality and truthfulness of religious speech than Frei and Lindbeck, and he addresses a key shortcoming in their work, their lack of a critical role for the theologian in relation to the community's practices, by avowing and accounting for the theologian's role as a critic of unjust religious practices, not just a reporter of them.[36]

The preceding reflections on the various subfields are from comprehensive, but hopefully they convey enough to give an idea about the value of these various subdisciplines and the place of a social practical theory of religion in them. Further, I hope that they shed light on the advantages of the theory that I describe. The social practical theory in this book helps us identify exemplary studies across the various subfields of religious studies and articulate why they are so effective. Further it makes explicit and extends the implicit theory in these studies, for example, studies on lived religion. The social practical vision of religion also challenges studies and approaches that systematically neglect experience, meaning, or power, and it endorses important features of each of the three major approaches to the study of religion over the last hundred years. However much we may think that any of the three approaches has had shortcomings and faults, each has also had valuable insights. We can preserve the viable contributions of each and correct its problems. Doing so puts us in the best position to grapple with religion in all its complexity.

INTRO

1. William James, *The Varieties of Religious Experience* (Cambridge, Mass.: Harvard University Press, 1985).

2. Mircea Eliade, *The Quest: History and Meaning in Religion* (Chicago: University of Chicago Press, 1969), 6. Quoted in Rosalind Shaw, "Feminist Anthropology and the Gendering of Religious Studies," in *The Insider/Outsider Problem in the Study of Religion*, ed. Russell T. McCutcheon (New York: Cassell, 1999), 107–108.

3. Talal Asad, *Genealogies of Religion: Discipline and Reasons of Power in Christianity and Islam* (Baltimore: Johns Hopkins University Press, 1993), 110.

4. Arun Micheelsen, "'I Don't Do Systems': An Interview with Clifford Geertz," *Method & Theory in the Study of Religion* 14, no. 1 (2002): 9.

5. Saba Mahmood, *Politics of Piety: The Islamic Revival and the Feminist Subject* (Princeton, N.J.: Princeton University Press, 2005), 188.

6. Russell T. McCutcheon, *Manufacturing Religion: The Discourse on Sui Generis Religion and the Politics of Nostalgia* (New York: Oxford University Press, 2003); Shaw, "Feminist Anthropology and the Gendering of Religious Studies."

7. Robert H. Sharf, "Experience," in *Critical Terms for Religious Studies*, ed. Mark C. Taylor (Chicago: University of Chicago Press, 1998).

8. Seyla Benhabib, *Situating the Self: Gender, Community, and Postmodernism in Contemporary Ethics* (Cambridge: Polity Press, 1992), 208.

9. Ann Taves, *Religious Experience Reconsidered: A Building-Block Approach to the Study of Religion and Other Special Things* (Princeton, N.J.: Princeton University Press, 2009), xiii–xiv; Leigh Eric Schmidt, "The Making of Modern 'Mysticism,'" *Journal of the American Academy of*

Religion 71, no. 2 (June 1, 2003): 273; Harold D. Roth, "Against Cognitive Imperialism: A Call for a Non-Ethnocentric Approach to Cognitive Science and Religious Studies," *Religion East & West* 8 (2008): 7.

10. Sharf, "Experience," 113–114.

11. Taves, *Religious Experience Reconsidered*, xiii–xiv.

12. Sharf, "Experience"; Grace Jantzen, *Power, Gender and Christian Mysticism* (Cambridge: Cambridge University Press, 1995).

13. Sharf, "Experience," 113–114.

14. Ludwig Wittgenstein, *Philosophical Investigations: The German Text, with a Revised English Translation*, trans. G. E. M. Anscombe, 3rd ed. (Oxford: Blackwell, 2001).

15. Wilfrid Sellars, *Empiricism and the Philosophy of Mind* (Cambridge, Mass: Harvard University Press, 1997); Robert Brandom, *Making It Explicit: Reasoning, Representing, and Discursive Commitment* (Cambridge, Mass: Harvard University Press, 1994).

16. Clifford Geertz, *The Interpretation of Cultures* (New York: Basic Books, 1973), 91.

17. Elizabeth Cady Stanton, *The Woman's Bible* (Boston: Northeastern University Press, 1993).

18. Revised and published as chapter 1 of Asad, *Genealogies of Religion*.

19. David Chidester, "Material Terms for the Study of Religion," *Journal of the American Academy of Religion* 68, no. 2 (2000): 378.

20. Paul J. Griffiths explains in a brief but helpful summary of the development of the concept religion that, as early modern Europeans discovered non-European cultures, the term "religion" expanded from having a strictly Christian referent to a wider one. Paul Griffiths, "The Very Idea of Religion," *First Things* 103, no. 1 (2000): 30–35. See also Jonathan Z. Smith, "Religion, Religions, Religious," in *Critical Terms for Religious Studies*, ed. Mark C. Taylor (Chicago: University of Chicago Press, 1998), 269–284. For a fuller account of the development of the concept of religion, see Wilfred Cantwell Smith, *The Meaning and End of Religion* (San Francisco: Harper & Row, 1978).

21. Smith, *The Meaning and End of Religion*; Denys Turner, "Doing Theology in the University," in *Fields of Faith: Theology and Religious Studies for the Twenty-first Century*, eds. David Ford, Ben Quash, and Janet Martin Soskice (Cambridge: Cambridge University Press, 2005); Timothy Fitzgerald, *The Ideology of Religious Studies* (New York: Oxford University Press, 2000).

22. Bruce Lincoln, *Holy Terrors: Thinking about Religion after September 11* (Chicago: University Of Chicago Press, 2003).

23. I owe this point to Jeff Stout.

CHAPTER 1

1. Alfred North Whitehead, *Religion in the* James, *The Varieties of Religious Experience*, 34; *Making* (Cambridge: Cambridge University Press, 2011), 37.

2. This is the sense of the term that concerns Joan W. Scott in her celebrated essay, "The Evidence of Experience," *Critical Inquiry* 17, no. 4 (1991): 773–797.

3. Anthony B. Pinn, *The African American Religious Experience in America* (Westport, Conn.: Greenwood, 2006).

4. See, for example, William P. Alston, *Perceiving God: The Epistemology of Religious Experience* (Ithaca, N.Y.: Cornell University Press, 1991).

5. Friedrich Schleiermacher, *On Religion: Speeches to Its Cultured Despisers*, trans. Richard Crouter (New York: Cambridge University Press, 1996); Friedrich Schleiermacher, *The Christian Faith*, ed. H. R. Mackintosh and James Stuart Stewart, 2nd ed. (Edinburgh: T & T Clark, 1999).

6. See Hans-Georg Gadamer, *Truth and Method*, trans. Joel Weinsheimer and Donald G. Marshall, 2nd ed. (London: Continuum, 2004), 63–64 and 64n121.

7. Schleiermacher, *On Religion*, 12. Crouter translates from the first edition, which was originally published in 1799.

8. Schleiermacher, *The Christian Faith*, sec. 8. It is important not to overstate the common element in all religions for Schleiermacher and not to understate the influence of historical and social context. The feeling of absolute dependence "can be named and reflected upon in isolation from other feelings," Andrew Dole explains, but it "in fact occurs only as a concomitant of people's awareness of their particular circumstances," so "all of the features that distinguish religions from each other—in fact, everything about piety other than the bare feeling of absolute dependence—will be contingent, a product of the environment within which religion develops." Andrew Dole, *Schleiermacher on Religion and the Natural Order* (New York: Oxford University Press, 2010), 93–94.

9. Dole, *Schleiermacher on Religion and the Natural Order.*

10. See Robert D. Richardson, "Schleiermacher and the Transcendentalists," in *Transient and Permanent: The Transcendentalist Movement and Its Contexts*, ed. Charles Capper and Conrad Edick Wright (Boston: Massachusetts Historical Society, 1999), 121–147.

11. Though it is too much to say, as Richard King does, that Schleiermacher "heavily influenced" James. Richard King, *Orientalism and Religion: Postcolonial Theory, India and "the Mystic East"* (London: Routledge, 1999), 22. Grace Jantzen says, "The extent of Schleiermacher's influence [on James] is insufficiently noticed," but she does not supply any evidence that Schleiermacher had a direct influence on James. Grace M. Jantzen, "Could There Be a Mystical Core of Religion?," *Religious Studies* 26, no. 1 (1990): 59–60.

12. James, *The Varieties of Religious Experience*, 32.

13. Ibid., 332.

14. Ibid., 31.

15. Andrew Dole, "Schleiermacher and Otto on Religion," *Religious Studies* 40, no. 4 (2004): 400.

16. Rudolf Otto, *The Idea of the Holy: An Inquiry into the Non-Rational Factor in the Idea of the Divine and Its Relation to the Rational*, trans. John W. Harvey, 2nd ed. (New York: Oxford University Press, 1958), 7.

17. Ibid., 6.

18. Mircea Eliade, *The Sacred and the Profane: The Nature of Religion,* trans. Willard R. Trask (New York: Harcourt, 1959), 216.

19. See D. G. Hart, *The University Gets Religion: Religious Studies in American Higher Education* (Baltimore, Md.: Johns Hopkins University Press, 1999), chaps. 5 and 6.

20. Representative works are: G. van der Leeuw, *Religion in Essence & Manifestation: A Study in Phenomenology*, trans. John Evan Turner (London: G. Allen & Unwin, 1938); Eliade, *The Sacred and the Profane*; Ninian Smart, *The Phenomenon of Religion* (New York: Herder and Herder, 1973); Charles H. Long, *Significations: Signs, Symbols, and Images in the Interpretation of Religion* (Philadelphia: Fortress Press, 1986).

21. Eliade, *The Sacred and the Profane*, 12.

22. Mircea Eliade, *A History of Religious Ideas*, trans. Willard R. Trask, 3 vols. (Chicago: University of Chicago Press, 1978–1985), 1: xiii.

23. Eliade, *The Quest*, i.

24. Benhabib, *Situating the Self*, 208.

25. Friedrich Schleiermacher, *Hermeneutics: The Handwritten Manuscripts*, ed. Heinz Kimmerle, trans. James Duke and James Forstman (Missoula, Mont.: Scholars Press, 1977).

26. See "The Methodological Foundations of Sociology" and "'Objectivity' in Social Science" in Max Weber, *Sociological Writings*, ed. Wolf V. Heydebrand (New York: Continuum, 1994), chaps. 27 and 28.

27. Martin Heidegger, *Being and Time*, trans. Joan Stambaugh (Albany: State University of New York Press, 1996); Hubert L. Dreyfus, *Being-in-the-world: A Commentary on Heidegger's Being and Time, Division I* (Cambridge, Mass.: MIT Press, 1991), 16–29.

28. Gadamer, *Truth and Method*, 270.

29. Ibid., 272.

30. Paul Ricoeur, "The Model of the Text: Meaningful Action Considered as a Text," in *From Text to Action*, trans. Kathleen Blamey and John B. Thompson (Evanston, Ill.: Northwestern University Press, 1991), 144–167.

31. Paul Ricoeur, *Freud and Philosophy: An Essay on Interpretation*, trans. Denis Savage (New Haven, Conn.: Yale University Press, 1970); Paul Ricoeur, *The Symbolism of Evil*, trans. Emerson Buchanan, 1st ed. (New York: Harper & Row, 1967).

32. See Sumner B. Twiss and Walter H. Conser, "Introduction," in *Experience of the Sacred: Readings in the Phenomenology of Religion*, ed. Sumner B. Twiss and Walter H. Conser (Hanover, N.H.: Brown University Press, published by University Press of New England, 1992), 1–74.

33. Clifford Geertz, *Interpretation of Cultures*. This paragraph includes material from Stephen S. Bush, "Are Meanings the Name of the Game?," *Religion Compass* 6, no. 12 (2012): 525–533.

34. Geertz, *Interpretation of Cultures*, 13.

35. Ibid., 91.

36. Fred Inglis, *Clifford Geertz: Culture, Custom and Ethics* (Cambridge, UK: Polity Press, 2000), 42.

37. Geertz, *Interpretation of Cultures*, 5.

38. Ibid., 89.

39. Ibid., 9–10.

40. Ibid., 9, 452.

41. Ibid., 91.

42. Ibid., 90; emphasis in original.

43. Ibid., 100.

44. Ibid., 93–94.

45. Tomoko Masuzawa, "Culture," in *Critical Terms for Religious Studies*, ed. Mark C. Taylor (Chicago: University of Chicago Press, 1998), 80–81.

46. Geertz, *Interpretation of Cultures*, 112.

47. Clifford Geertz, *Person, Time, and Conduct in Bali: An Essay in Cultural Analysis* (New Haven, Conn.: Southeast Asia Studies, Yale University, 1966), 7; Micheelsen, "'I Don't Do Systems,'" 4–5.

48. Otto, *The Idea of the Holy*, 7.

49. For example, see Smart, *The Phenomenon of Religion*, 71.

50. Ibid., 31.

51. Geertz, *Interpretation of Cultures*, 91. Also, "The focus is now neither on subjective life as such nor on outward behavior as such, but on the socially available 'systems of significance'—beliefs, rites, meaningful objects—in terms of which subjective life is ordered and outward behavior guided." Clifford Geertz, *Islam Observed: Religious Development in Morocco and Indonesia*, Phoenix ed. (Chicago: University of Chicago Press, 1971), 95.

52. Geertz does appeal to experiences as a basic factor in his explanation of how religion influences human behavior in ibid., 107–116. His account here is not particularly compelling, and it does not factor in his most influential methodological treatises, those contained in *Interpretation of Cultures*.

53. Micheelsen, "'I Don't Do Systems,'" 4.

54. Geertz, *Interpretation of Cultures*, 21, 23.

55. Ibid., 25.

56. Ibid., 21.

57. Aldous Huxley, *The Perennial Philosophy*, 1st ed. (New York: Harper, 1945).

58. Steven T. Katz, "Language, Epistemology, and Mysticism," in *Mysticism and Philosophical Analysis*, ed. Steven T. Katz (London: Sheldon Press, 1978); Wayne Proudfoot, *Religious Experience* (Berkeley: University of California Press, 1985).

CHAPTER 2

1. Kevin Schilbrack, "Religion, Models of, and Reality: Are We Through with Geertz?," *Journal of the American Academy of Religion* 73, no. 2 (2005): 429–452.

2. Lincoln, *Holy Terrors*, 1; Jeffrey C. Alexander and Philip Smith, "Introduction: The Rise and Fall of Clifford Geertz," in *Interpreting Clifford Geertz: Cultural Investigation in the Social Sciences*, ed. Jeffrey C. Alexander, Philip Smith, and Matthew Norton (New York: Palgrave Macmillan, 2011).

3. Benhabib, *Situating the Self*, 208; emphasis in original.

4. James C. Scott, *Weapons of the Weak: Everyday Forms of Peasant Resistance* (New Haven, Conn.: Yale University Press, 1985).

5. Max Weber, *Economy and Society: An Outline of Interpretive Sociology*, ed. Guenther Roth and Claus Wittich, trans. Ephraim Fischoff et al, 2 vols. (Berkeley: University of California Press, 1978), 1:215.

6. Michel Foucault, *Discipline & Punish: The Birth of the Prison*, trans. Alan Sheridan, 2nd Vintage ed. (New York: Vintage, 1995); Michel Foucault, *The Birth of the Clinic: An Archaeology of Medical Perception*, trans. A. M. Sheridan Smith, 1st American ed. (New York: Pantheon Books, 1973); Michel Foucault, *The History of Sexuality*, trans. Robert Hurley, Vintage Books ed. (New York: Vintage Books, 1990); Michel Foucault, *Madness and Civilization: A History of Insanity in the Age of Reason*, trans. Richard Howard (New York: Vintage Books, 1988).

7. Foucault, *Discipline and Punish*, 27.

8. Michel Foucault, "Truth and Power," in *Power/Knowledge: Selected Interviews and Other Writings, 1972–1977*, ed. Colin Gordon, 1st American ed. (New York: Pantheon Books, 1980), 131.

9. Frantz Fanon, *The Wretched of the Earth*, trans. Richard Philcox (New York: Grove, 2004).

10. Edward W. Said, *Orientalism*, 25th Anniversary ed. (New York: Vintage Books, 2003); Gayatri Chakravorty Spivak, "Can the Subaltern Speak?," in *Marxism and the Interpretation of Culture*, ed. Cary Nelson and Lawrence Grossberg (Urbana: University of Illinois Press, 1988), 271–313.

11. Spivak, "Can the Subaltern Speak?," 308.

12. Robert Young, *White Mythologies: Writing History and the West* (London: Routledge, 1990), 1.

13. Jantzen, *Power, Gender and Christian Mysticism*.

14. Asad, *Genealogies of Religion*.

15. Ibid., 28–29.

16. Ibid., 44.

17. Ibid., 47–48.

18. Ibid., 35, see also 53 and 43, where he faults Geertz for insisting "on the primacy of meaning without regard to the processes by which meanings are constructed."

19. Mircea Eliade, *The Sacred and the Profane*, chap. 2; Bruce Lincoln, *Theorizing Myth: Narrative, Ideology, and Scholarship* (Chicago: University of Chicago Press, 1999).

20. Catherine M. Bell, *Ritual Theory, Ritual Practice* (New York: Oxford University Press, 1992).

21. Nancy B. Jay, *Throughout Your Generations Forever: Sacrifice, Religion, and Paternity* (Chicago: University of Chicago Press, 1992), 40.

22. R. Marie Griffith, *God's Daughters: Evangelical Women and the Power of Submission* (Berkeley: University of California Press, 1997).

23. Mahmood, *Politics of Piety*.

24. Mark C. Carnes, *Secret Ritual and Manhood in Victorian America* (New Haven, Conn.: Yale University Press, 1989).

25. Mark D. Jordan, *The Invention of Sodomy in Christian Theology* (Chicago: University of Chicago Press, 1997), 163.

26. Eddie S. Glaude, *Exodus!: Religion, Race, and Nation in Early Nineteenth-Century Black America* (Chicago: University of Chicago Press, 2000).

27. Evelyn Brooks Higginbotham, *Righteous Discontent: The Women's Movement in the Black Baptist Church, 1880–1920* (Cambridge, Mass: Harvard University Press, 1993), 2.

28. King, *Orientalism and Religion*.

29. David Chidester, *Savage Systems: Colonialism and Comparative Religion in Southern Africa* (Charlottesville: University Press of Virginia, 1996), xiii.

30. Ibid., 14.

31. Tomoko Masuzawa, *The Invention of World Religions, Or, How European Universalism Was Preserved in the Language of Pluralism* (Chicago: University of Chicago Press, 2005).

32. Fitzgerald, *The Ideology of Religious Studies*.

33. Talal Asad, "Thinking about Religion, Belief, and Politics," in *The Cambridge Companion to Religious Studies*, ed. Robert A. Orsi (Cambridge: Cambridge University Press, 2012), 39.

34. Chidester, "Material Terms for the Study of Religion," 378.

35. Donald S. Lopez, Jr., "Belief," in *Critical Terms for Religious Studies*, ed. Mark C. Taylor (Chicago: University of Chicago Press, 1998), 30–31.

36. Ibid., 28.

37. Ibid., 34. This echoes Asad's criticism of Geertz for subscribing to a "modern, privatized Christian" concept of belief and understanding belief as essential to religion. Asad, *Genealogies of Religion*, 47. In a more recent essay, Asad offers this connection between the concept of belief and power: "The modern *idea* of religious belief (protected as a right in the individual and regulated institutionally) is a critical function of the liberal-democratic nation-state," a state that demands exclusive loyalty and "nationalistic fervor" from its citizens and governs them according to bureaucratic rationality. Asad, "Thinking about Religion, Belief, and Politics," 56–57.

38. Vincent Crapanzano, "Hermes' Dilemma: The Masking of Subversion in Ethnographic Description," in *Writing Culture: The Poetics and Politics of Ethnography: A School of American Research Advanced Seminar*, ed. James Clifford and George E. Marcus, 25th anniversary ed. (Berkeley: University of California Press, 2010), 70, 74.

39. James Clifford, *The Predicament of Culture: Twentieth-Century Ethnography, Literature, and Art* (Cambridge, Mass.: Harvard University Press, 1988), 40.

40. Masuzawa, "Culture," 87.

41. Asad, *Genealogies of Religion*, 35.

42. Ibid., 83, 110.

43. Mahmood, *Politics of Piety*, 188; see also 29 and 122.

44. Sharf, "Ritual," 250.

45. Masuzawa, "Culture," 88.

46. Russell T. McCutcheon, *Critics Not Caretakers: Redescribing the Public Study of Religion* (Albany: State University of New York Press, 2001), 7.

47. Masuzawa, "Culture," 91.

48. Schmidt, "The Making of Modern 'Mysticism,'"273.

49. Taves, *Religious Experience Reconsidered*, xiii–xiv.

50. Gadamer, *Truth and Method*, 346.

51. Michel Foucault, *The Order of Things: An Archaeology of the Human Sciences* (London: Routledge, 2005), xv.

52. Scott, "The Evidence of Experience," 797.

53. Others who have done important work bringing power concerns to bear on the study of mysticism include Amy Hollywood and Jeffrey Kripal, who have examined mysticism in relation to gender and sexual orientation, respectively. Amy Hollywood, *Sensible Ecstasy: Mysticism, Sexual Difference, and the Demands of History* (Chicago: University of Chicago Press, 2002); Jeffrey J. Kripal, *Kali's Child: The Mystical and the Erotic in the Life and Teachings of Ramakrishna* (Chicago: University of Chicago Press, 1995).

54. James, *The Varieties of Religious Experience*, chap. 16.

55. Jantzen, *Power, Gender and Christian Mysticism*, 23.

56. Ibid., 326.

57. I discuss Sharf's account of experience more extensively in Stephen S. Bush, "Are Experiences Too Private to Study?," *Journal of Religion* 92, no. 2 (April 2012): 199–223.

58. Robert H. Sharf, "The Zen of Japanese Nationalism," in *Curators of the Buddha: The Study of Buddhism under Colonialism*, ed. Donald S. Lopez Jr. (Chicago: University of Chicago Press, 1995), 124.

59. Robert H. Sharf, "Buddhist Modernism and the Rhetoric of Meditative Experience," *Numen* 42, no. 3 (1995): 241.

60. Ibid., 249.

61. Ibid., 27–28.

62. Ibid., 259–265.

63. Wayne Proudfoot, *Religious Experience*, xiii.

64. Andrew Dole has challenged this understanding of Schleiermacher in Dole, *Schleiermacher on Religion and the Natural Order*.

65. Robert H. Sharf, "Experience," in *Critical Terms for Religious Studies*, ed. Mark C. Taylor (Chicago: University of Chicago Press, 1998), 113–114.

66. Ibid.

67. Ibid., 113.

68. Sharf, "Buddhist Modernism," 260.

69. Jantzen, *Power, Gender and Christian Mysticism*; Sharf, "Experience"; Sharf, "The Zen of Japanese Nationalism"; Sharf, "Buddhist Modernism"; Robert H. Sharf, "Whose Zen?: Zen Nationalism Revisited," in *Rude Awakenings: Zen, the Kyoto School, and the Question of Nationalism*, ed. James W. Heisig and John C. Maraldo (Honolulu: University of Hawai'i Press, 1995).

70. Sharf, "Experience," 110. Russell T. McCutcheon follows Sharf in criticizing the category of religious experience and suggests, instead of taking experiences as objects of study, that we focus instead on "discourse on experience" and "understand the discourse on experience as an all too human construction that accomplishes specific rhetorical work in specific social groups." McCutcheon, *Critics Not Caretakers*, 9–10.

71. Sharf, "Experience," 111.

72. Mircea Eliade, *Rites and Symbols of Initiation: The Mysteries of Birth and Rebirth* (New York: Harper & Row, 1965); Valerie Saiving, "Androcentrism in Religious Studies," *Journal of Religion* 56, no. 2 (1976): 177–197.

73. Carol P. Christ, "Mircea Eliade and the Feminist Paradigm Shift," *Journal of Feminist Studies in Religion* 7, no. 2 (Fall 1991): 94.

74. Ibid., 82.

75. Shaw, "Feminist Anthropology and the Gendering of Religious Studies," 106–107.

76. Ibid., 110.

77. Taves, *Religious Experience Reconsidered*; Courtney Bender and Ann Taves, "Introduction: Things of Value," in *What Matters?: Ethnographies of Value in a Not so Secular Age*, ed. Courtney Bender and Ann Taves (New York: Columbia University Press, 2012), 19–22; Courtney Bender, *The New Metaphysicals: Spirituality and the American Religious Imagination* (Chicago: University of Chicago Press, 2010).

78. Schilbrack, "Religion, Models Of, and Reality"; Kevin Schilbrack, "The Social Construction of 'Religion' and Its Limits: A Critical Reading of Timothy Fitzgerald," *Method and Theory in the Study of Religion* 24(2012): 97–117.

79. Asad, *Genealogies of Religion*, 29.

80. Lincoln, *Holy Terrors*, 2.

81. Terry F. Godlove Jr., "Saving Belief: On the New Materialism in Religious Studies," in *Radical Interpretation in Religion*, ed. Nancy Frankenberry (Cambridge: Cambridge University Press, 2002), 10–24. See also Kevin Schilbrack, *Philosophy and the Study of Religions: A Manifesto* (Malden, Mass.: Wiley Blackwell, 2014), chap. 3.

82. Arun Micheelsen, "'I Don't Do Systems,'" 9–10.

83. G. Scott Davis, *Believing and Acting: The Pragmatic Turn in Comparative Religion and Ethics* (Oxford: Oxford University Press, 2012), 4, 17.

84. Ibid., 9, 143.

85. Robert A. Orsi, *Between Heaven and Earth: The Religious Worlds People Make and the Scholars Who Study Them* (Princeton, N.J.: Princeton University Press, 2005), 197–198.

86. Robert A. Orsi, "Belief," *Material Religion: Journal of Objects, Art and Belief* 7, no. 1 (2011): 14.

CHAPTER 3

1. Clifford Geertz, *Available Light: Anthropological Reflections on Philosophical Topics* (Princeton, N.J.: Princeton University Press, 2001), 178.

2. Martin Jay, *Songs of Experience: Modern American and European Variations on a Universal Theme* (Berkeley: University of California Press, 2005), 121.

3. Geertz, *Available Light*, 184.

4. G. Scott Davis, *Believing and Acting*, 21, 173. The article in question is Robert H. Sharf, "Zen and Japanese Nationalism," *History of Religions* 33, no. 1 (1993): 1–43; revised and reprinted as Sharf, "The Zen of Japanese Nationalism."

5. Robert A. Orsi, *Between Heaven and Earth*, 4.

6. Robert A. Orsi, ed., *The Cambridge Companion to Religious Studies* (Cambridge: Cambridge University Press, 2012). R. Marie Griffith's essay on sexuality discusses gender in relation to "the recent sexual turn in religious studies," but the importance of gender is not limited to its role in sexuality, obviously, and should not be subsumed under that topic. R. Marie Griffith, "Sexing Religion," in *The Cambridge Companion to Religious Studies*, ed. Robert A. Orsi (Cambridge: Cambridge University Press, 2012), 338.

7. Eliade, *The Quest*, 6.

8. Shaw, "Feminist Anthropology and the Gendering of Religious Studies," 104–113.

9. "Religious categories must always form part of any psychological analysis of the religious experience of oppressed peoples, for in many respects so many of the power valences, the concealments, and the dynamics of repression are correlates of the social political situation." Long, *Significations*, 142.

10. Ibid., 166, 175–178, 184.

11. Clifton H. Johnson, ed., *God Struck Me Dead: Voices of Ex-Slaves* (Cleveland, Ohio: Pilgrim Press, 1993), 74.

12. Ibid., 168.

13. Ibid., 91.

14. Albert J. Raboteau, *Slave Religion: The "Invisible Institution" in the Antebellum South* (Oxford: Oxford University Press, 1980).

15. Ibid., 308.

16. Asad, *Genealogies of Religion*, 35.

17. Ibid., 43.

18. Geertz, *The Interpretation of Cultures*, 14.

19. Ibid., 144–145.

20. Ibid., 90, 96. Jason Springs and I discuss these issues in Bush, "Are Meanings the Name of the Game?," 525–533; Jason A. Springs, "Meaning vs. Power: Are Thick Description

and Power Analysis Intrinsically at Odds? Response to Interpretation, Explanation, and Clifford Geertz," *Religion Compass* 6, no. 12 (2012): 534–542.

21. "U.S. Religious Landscape Survey: Religious Beliefs and Practices: Diverse and Politically Relevant" (Pew Forum on Religion and Public Life, June 2008), 5, http://religions.pewforum.org/pdf/report2-religious-landscape-study-full.pdf.

22. Wayne Proudfoot, "Medical Materialism Revisited," *The Immanent Frame*, 2008, http://blogs.ssrc.org/tif/2008/06/30/medical-materialism-revisited/.

23. The next two pages reproduce excerpts from Bush, "Are Meanings the Name of the Game?"

24. Asad, *Genealogies of Religion*, 34–35.

25. Ibid., 33.

26. Ibid., 83.

27. Ibid., 110.

28. Katz, "Language, Epistemology, and Mysticism," 52.

29. W. T. Stace, *Mysticism and Philosophy* (Philadelphia: Lippincott, 1960), 106–107.

30. Taves, *Religious Experience Reconsidered*, xiii–xiv.

31. Sharf, "Experience," 107, 113.

32. Sharf, "Buddhist Modernism and the Rhetoric of Meditative Experience," 259–260. I discuss this at greater length in Bush, "Are Experiences Too Private to Study?," 205–211.

33. Geertz, *Available Light*, 178.

34. Suzanne Brenner, "Reconstructing Self and Society: Javanese Muslim Women and 'The Veil,'" *American Ethnologist* 23, no. 4 (November 1996): 685.

35. Ibid., 676.

36. Ibid., 672.

37. Here I follow and summarize André Droogers, "Paradoxical Views on a Paradoxical Religion: Models for the Explanation of Pentecostal Expansion in Brazil and Chile," in *More Than Opium: An Anthropological Approach to Latin American and Caribbean Pentecostal Praxis*, ed. Barbara Boudewijnse, A. F. Droogers, and Frans Kamsteeg (Lanham, Md: Scarecrow Press, 1998), 1–34.

38. Elizabeth E. Brusco, *The Reformation of Machismo: Evangelical Conversion and Gender in Colombia* (Austin: University of Texas Press, 1995), 114.

39. Ibid., 138, 144.

40. Ibid., 8–9.

41. Richard Rorty construes reductionism thus: "'Reduction' is a relation merely between linguistic items, not among ontological categories. To reduce the language of X's to the language of Y's one must show either (a) that if you can talk about Y's you do not need to talk about X's, or (b) that any given description in terms of X's applies to all and only the things to which a given description in terms of Y's applies." Richard Rorty, *Objectivity, Relativism, and Truth* (Cambridge: Cambridge University Press, 1991), 115. So to regard it as counterproductive to eliminate terminology such as "god" and "spirit" in explaining a religious practice does not entail belief in the existence of gods and spirits.

42. Brusco, *The Reformation of Machismo*, 119.

43. Ibid., 41–44, 62 ,108–110.

44. The next four paragraphs reproduce some excerpts from Bush, "Are Experiences Too Private to Study?"

45. Daniel Míguez, *Spiritual Bonfire in Argentina: Confronting Current Theories with an Ethnographic Account of Pentecostal Growth in a Buenos Aires Suburb* (Amsterdam: CEDLA, 1998), 168.

46. Ibid., 118.

47. R. Andrew Chesnut, *Born Again in Brazil: The Pentecostal Boom and the Pathogens of Poverty* (New Brunswick, N.J: Rutgers University Press, 1997), 6.

48. Griffith, *God's Daughters*, 207.

49. Ibid., 77.

50. Ibid., 81, 108.

51. Ibid., 75–76.

52. Tanya Luhrmann has important things to say on this topic in *When God Talks Back: Understanding the American Evangelical Relationship with God* (New York: Alfred A. Knopf, 2012).

53. Brenner, "Reconstructing Self and Society," 688.

54. Griffith, *God's Daughters*, 207.

55. Masuzawa, "Culture," 87.

CHAPTER 4

1. James Clifford, *The Predicament of Culture*; Vincent Crapanzano, "Hermes' Dilemma," 51–70. I discuss Clifford and Crapanzano's criticisms of Geertz and the problem of privacy and power in relation to meaning more generally in chapter 3.

2. Tomoko Masuzawa, "Culture,", 87–88.

3. Hans-Georg Gadamer, *Truth and Method*, 306.

4. Ibid., 305.

5. Paul Ricoeur, *Hermeneutics and Human Sciences: Essays on Language, Action, and Interpretation*, trans. John B. Thompson (Cambridge: Cambridge University Press, 1981), 141.

6. Ibid., 149; Paul Ricoeur, *The Conflict of Interpretations*, ed. Don Ihde (Evanston, Il.: Northwestern University Press, 1974), 298.

7. Ricoeur, *Hermeneutics and Human Sciences*, 149, 94.

8. Arun Micheelsen, "'I Don't Do Systems,'" 2–20.

9. For example, Geertz, *The Interpretation of Cultures*, 17.

10. Talal Asad, *Genealogies of Religion*, 29.

11. Lincoln makes a similar point in *Holy Terrors*, 2–3.

12. Asad, *Genealogies of Religion*, 28.

13. Clifford Geertz, *Available Light*, 171.

14. Geertz, *Interpretation of Cultures*, 10.

15. Asad, *Genealogies of Religion*, 44.

16. Ibid., 31.

17. Nancy Frankenberry and Hans Penner, "Geertz's Long-Lasting Moods, Motivations, and Metaphysical Conceptions," *Journal of Religion* 79, no. 4 (1999): 637.

18. Kevin Schilbrack, "Religion, Models of, and Reality," 438.

19. Geertz, *Interpretation of Cultures*, 92.

20. Ibid., 13.

21. Ibid., 12. Schilbrack presents and discusses these passages and other similar ones in Schilbrack, "Religion, Models of, and Reality," 438.

22. Geertz, *Interpretation of Cultures*, 12.

23. Ibid., 17.

24. Ibid., 91.

25. Ibid., 58.

26. Schilbrack, "Religion, Models of, and Reality," 445.

27. Susanne Katherina Knauth Langer, *Philosophy in a New Key; a Study in the Symbolism of Reason, Rite and Art* (Cambridge, Mass.: Harvard University Press, 1951), 89. For an account of Langer's conceptions of symbols and conceptions in *Philosophy in a New Key*, see Robert E. Innis, *Susanne Langer in Focus: The Symbolic Mind* (Bloomington: Indiana University Press, 2009), chap. 2.

28. Langer, *Philosophy in a New Key*, 98.

29. Donald Davidson, "On the Very Idea of a Conceptual Scheme," in *Inquiries into Truth and Interpretation* (Oxford: Clarendon Press, 1984).

30. Clifford Geertz, *Islam Observed*, 98. Schilbrack references several other passages in Geertz that have a similar ring to them, but he wants to read these passages in light of examples Geertz provides of religious symbols being applied to items that could be conceived in other terms, like granaries: "The religious symbols . . . add a layer of interpretation to an already interpreted situation." Schilbrack, "Religion, Models of, and Reality," 444–445. The Langer passages, however, give credence to a reading of Geertz's talk of symbols vis-à-vis experience as implying a scheme/content division.

31. Geertz, *Interpretation of Cultures*, 27.

32. Ibid., 452.

33. Ibid., 15; cf. 9.

34. This example is discussed in Bell, *Ritual Theory, Ritual Practice*, 101–104.

35. Iris Marion Young, "Throwing Like a Girl: A Phenomenology of Feminine Body Comportment, Motility, and Spatiality," in *On Female Body Experience: "Throwing Like a Girl" and Other Essays* (New York: Oxford University Press, 2005), 27–45.

36. I am indebted to Jason Springs for several of the points in this paragraph, which he has communicated to me in a formal response to a paper that I delivered at the 2010 annual conference of the American Academy of Religion and in personal conversation. Several paragraphs in this section are reprinted from Bush, "Are Meanings the Name of the Game?," 525–533.

37. Clifford Geertz, *Local Knowledge: Further Essays in Interpretive Anthropology*, 3rd ed. (New York: Basic Books, 1985), 57.

38. Ibid., 58.

39. Geertz, *Interpretation of Cultures*, 138.

40. Ibid., 9.

41. Ibid., 14.

42. Ibid., 144–145.

43. Geertz, *Interpretation of Cultures*, 90.

44. Pierre Bourdieu, *Outline of a Theory of Practice*, trans. Richard Nice (Cambridge: Cambridge University Press, 1977), 11; *Esquisse d'une Théorie de la Pratique* (Paris: Seuil, 2000), 233.

45. Arthur P. Wolf, "Gods, Ghosts, and Ancestors," in *Religion and Ritual in Chinese Society*, ed. Arthur P. Wolf (Stanford, Calif.: Stanford University Press, 1974), 155.

46. In what follows, I present the key ideas of Robert Brandom and Wilfrid Sellars. See especially Brandom, *Making It Explicit*; Sellars, *Empiricism and the Philosophy of Mind*.

47. "§140. . . . We are taught *judgments* and their connexion with other judgments. *A totality* of judgments is made plausible to us. §141. When we first begin to *believe* anything, what we believe is not a single proposition, it is a whole system of propositions. (Light dawns gradually over the whole.) §142. It is not single axioms that strike me as obvious, it is a system in which consequences and premises give one another *mutual* support." Ludwig Wittgenstein, *On Certainty*, ed. G. E. M. Anscombe and G. H. von Wright, trans. G. E. M. Anscombe and Denis Paul, 1st Harper Torchbook ed. (New York: Harper & Row, 1972).

48. "For a *large* class of cases—though not for all—in which we employ the word 'meaning' it can be defined thus: the meaning of a word is its use in the language." Wittgenstein, *Philosophical Investigations*, sec. 43.

49. Hilary Putnam, "The Meaning of 'Meaning,'" in *The Twin Earth Chronicles: Twenty Years of Reflection on Hilary Putnam's "The Meaning of 'Meaning,'"* ed. Andrew Pessin and Sanford Goldberg (Armonk, N.Y: M. E. Sharpe, 1996), 13.

50. Lopez, "Belief," 34.

51. See, for example, Donald Davidson, *Inquiries into Truth and Interpretation* (Oxford: Clarendon Press, 1984), chaps. 9, 10, 13. See also Davis, *Believing and Acting*.

52. Godlove, "Saving Belief," 10–24.

53. Robert Brandom, "From a Critique of Cognitive Internalism to a Conception of Objective Spirit: Reflections on Descombes' Anthropological Holism," *Inquiry* 47(2004): 240. The fuller account of beliefs, or commitments, as Brandom prefers, is found in Brandom, *Making It Explicit*.

54. For Brandom's discussion of his own and Rorty's views on representation, see Robert B. Brandom, *Perspectives on Pragmatism: Classical, Recent, and Contemporary* (Cambridge, Mass.: Harvard University Press, 2011), chap. 4.

55. On the significance for interpretation of the divergent purposes interpreters bring to their task, see Jeffrey Stout, "The Relativity of Interpretation," *The Monist* 69, no. 1 (1986): 103–118.

56. "A wheel that can be turned though nothing else moves with it, is not part of the mechanism," Wittgenstein says about interiority. Wittgenstein, *Philosophical Investigations*, sec. 271.

57. Brandom presents his philosophy of language as capable of accounting for various "gadamerian platitudes": "The denial of certain sorts of authority to the author of a text (what Foucault called 'fetishizing the segmentation of discourse by signatures'), the relativization of meaning to context in a very broad sense, the model of dialogue, meaning pluralism, the openendedness and mutability of semantic perspectives." Robert Brandom, *Tales of the Mighty Dead: Historical Essays in the Metaphysics of Intentionality* (Cambridge, Mass.: Harvard University Press, 2002), 93–94.

58. Foucault, *Discipline & Punish*, 27.

59. Jacques Derrida, *Margins of Philosophy*, trans. Alan Bass (Chicago: University of Chicago Press, 1982), 23.

60. Jacques Derrida, *Of Grammatology*, trans. Gayatri Chakravorty Spivak, Corrected ed. (Baltimore: Johns Hopkins University Press, 1998), 62.

61. Stephen S. Bush, "Nothing Outside the Text: Derrida and Brandom on Language and World," *Contemporary Pragmatism* 6, no. 2 (2009): 45–69.

62. Brandom, *Tales of the Mighty Dead*, 93.

63. Philip Pettit, *Republicanism: A Theory of Freedom and Government* (Oxford: Clarendon Press, 1997), 79.

64. Asad, *Genealogies of Religion*, chaps. 1 and 3.

65. Robert Brandom, *Articulating Reasons: An Introduction to Inferentialism* (Cambridge, Mass: Harvard University Press, 2000), 69–72.

66. Chidester, *Savage Systems*, 14.

67. Kevin Hector, *Theology without Metaphysics: God, Language, and the Spirit of Recognition* (Cambridge: Cambridge University Press, 2011), 266–291.

68. Elizabeth A. Johnson, *She Who Is: The Mystery of God in a Feminist Theological Discourse* (New York: Crossroad, 1992), 26–27; quoted in Hector, *Theology without Metaphysics*, 267.

69. Miranda Fricker, *Epistemic Injustice: Power and the Ethics of Knowing* (New York: Oxford University Press, 2009).

70. For an overview, see chapters 1–3, by Linda Alcoff and Elizabeth Potter, Lorraine Code, and Sandra Harding, respectively, in Linda Alcoff and Elizabeth Potter, eds., *Feminist Epistemologies* (New York: Routledge, 1993).

71. According to Fricker, hermeneutical injustice is "the injustice of having some significant area of one's social experience obscured from collective understanding owing to a structural identity prejudice in the collective hermeneutical resource." Fricker, *Epistemic Injustice*, 155.

72. Nancy Fraser, "From Irony to Prophecy to Politics: A Reply to Richard Rorty," in *Feminist Interpretations of Richard Rorty*, ed. Marianne Janack (University Park, Pa.: Pennsylvania State University Press, 2010), 54.

73. Bourdieu, *Outline of a Theory of Practice*, 171–197.

74. Ibid., 171.

75. Ibid., 79.

76. Ibid., 143.

77. Mahmood, *Politics of Piety*, 188.

78. Terry Eagleton, *Ideology: An Introduction*, New and updated ed. (London: Verso, 2007), 45.

79. Ibid., 45–61.

80. Thomas A. Tweed, *Our Lady of the Exile: Diasporic Religion at a Cuban Catholic Shrine in Miami* (New York: Oxford University Press, 2002).

81. Geertz, *Interpretation of Cultures*, 443–444.

82. Janice Patricia Boddy, *Wombs and Alien Spirits: Women, Men, and the Zār Cult in Northern Sudan* (Madison: University of Wisconsin Press, 1989), 304–305.

CHAPTER 5

1. Otto, *The Idea of the Holy*, 8.

2. Ibid., 7.

3. The asymmetry between the experiencer and the third party is also an important topic in what theorists of religion refer to as the insider/outsider problem in the study of religion. For an

overview, see Russell T. McCutcheon, ed., *The Insider/Outsider Problem in the Study of Religion: A Reader* (London; New York: Cassell, 1999).

4. James, *The Varieties of Religious Experience*, 332.

5. Eliade, *A History of Religious Ideas*, 1: xiii.

6. For defenses of perennialism, see Robert K. C. Forman, *Mysticism, Mind, Consciousness* (Albany, NY: State University of New York Press, 1999); Robert K. C. Forman, ed., *The Problem of Pure Consciousness: Mysticism and Philosophy* (New York: Oxford University Press, 1990).

7. Proudfoot, *Religious Experience*; Katz, "Language, Epistemology, and Mysticism," 22–74.

8. Jensine Andresen and Robert K. C. Forman, "Methodological Pluralism in the Study of Religion: How the Study of Consciousness and Mapping Spiritual Experiences Can Reshape Religious Methodology," in *Cognitive Models and Spiritual Maps*, ed. Jensine Andresen and Robert K. C. Forman (Bowling Green, Ohio: Academic Imprint, 2000), 7–8.

9. A point that Donald Rothberg makes in "Contemporary Epistemology and the Study of Mysticism," in *The Problem of Pure Consciousness: Mysticism and Philosophy*, ed. Robert K. C. Forman (New York: Oxford University Press, 1990), 167.

10. Katz, "Language, Epistemology, and Mysticism," 26.

11. Ibid., 66.

12. Ibid., 64–65.

13. Wayne Proudfoot, "Response," *Journal of the American Academy of Religion* 61, no. 4 (1993): 808.

14. Proudfoot, *Religious Experience*, 114. I take up the issues of the conceptual and the non-conceptual aspects of experience in *Religious Experience* in more detail in Stephen S. Bush, "Concepts and Religious Experiences: Wayne Proudfoot on the Cultural Construction of Experiences," *Religious Studies* 48, no. 1 (2012): 101–117.

15. Stace, *Mysticism and Philosophy*, 31.

16. William P. Alston, *Perceiving God*.

17. Ibid., 39n29.

18. Ibid., 38.

19. Ibid., 62.

20. Wittgenstein, *Philosophical Investigations*, secs. 43, 241. Wittgenstein has an extended legacy in the philosophy of religion, one that originates in his own reflection on religion. Brandom and Sellars's recent influence in the philosophy of religion and religious ethics is evident in several works, including Jeffrey Stout, *Democracy and Tradition* (Princeton, N.J.: Princeton University Press, 2005); Jeffrey Stout, "Davidson, Rorty, and Brandom on Truth," in *Radical Interpretation in Religion*, ed. Nancy Frankenberry (Cambridge: Cambridge University Press, 2002), 25–52; Richard Rorty, "Cultural Politics and the Question of the Existence of God," in *Radical Interpretation in Religion*, ed. Nancy Frankenberry (Cambridge: Cambridge University Press, 2002), 53–77; Jason A. Springs, *Toward a Generous Orthodoxy: Prospects for Hans Frei's Postliberal Theology* (New York: Oxford University Press, 2010); Hector, *Theology without Metaphysics*. Before these, Cornel West employs Sellars against Schleiermacher in "Schleiermacher's Hermeneutics and the Myth of the Given," *Union Seminary Quarterly Review* 34, no. 2 (1979): 71–84.

21. Sellars, *Empiricism and the Philosophy of Mind*.

22. Brandom describes the myth of the given like this: "The older empiricism thought of the unit of experience as self-contained, self-intimating events: episodes that constitute knowings

just in virtue of their brute occurrence. These primordial acts of awareness are then taken to be available to provide the raw materials that make any sort of learning possible." Robert Brandom, "The Pragmatist Enlightenment (and Its Problematic Semantics)," *European Journal of Philosophy* 12, no. 1 (2004): 4. Another, fuller statement of the myth of the given: "The Myth of the Given is the claim that there is some kind of experience the having of which does not presuppose grasp of concepts, such that merely *having* the experience counts as *knowing* something, or can serve as *evidence* for beliefs, judgments, claims, and so on, that such a non-conceptual experience can *rationally ground*, and not just causally occasion, belief." Brandom says that Sellars effectively demonstrates that "the project of making intelligible a concept of experience that is in this way amphibious between the non-conceptual world and our conceptually structured thought is a hopeless one." Robert Brandom, "Non-Inferential Knowledge, Perceptual Experience, and Secondary Qualities: Placing McDowell's Empiricism," in *Reading McDowell: On Mind and World*, ed. Nicholas H. Smith (London: Routledge, 2002), 93.

23. Brandom, "Non-Inferential Knowledge," 105n13.

24. Brandom, *Tales of the Mighty Dead*, 13.

25. Indeed, Richard Moran says that one of the primary criteria for a successful account of self-knowledge is to account for the immediacy, in the sense of not inferred from anything, of judgments of self-knowledge. Richard Moran, *Authority and Estrangement: An Essay on Self-Knowledge* (Princeton, N.J: Princeton University Press, 2001).

26. Katz, "Language, Epistemology, and Mysticism," 26; McCutcheon, *The Insider/Outsider Problem*, 257.

27. Donald Davidson, "On the Very Idea of a Conceptual Scheme," in *Inquiries into Truth and Interpretation* (Oxford: Clarendon Press, 1984), 183, 192.

28. For examples, see Daniel Clement Dennett, *Consciousness Explained* (Boston: Little, Brown and Co, 1991); Eric Schwitzgebel, "The Unreliability of Naive Introspection," *Philosophical Review* 117, no. 2 (2008): 245–273.

29. If we analyze perception as a matter of causal processes and conceptual responses, is there any room to speak of phenomenal qualities? Perhaps. This is no part of Brandom's philosophy, but Sellars does want to say something about such interior states as thoughts and sense impressions in *Empiricism and the Philosophy of Mind*, as when he says, "It is clear that the experience of seeing that something is green is not *merely* the occurrence of the propositional claim 'this is green'—not even if we add, as we must, that this claim is, so to speak, evoked or wrung from the perceiver by the object perceived. Here Nature . . . puts us to question. The something more is clearly what philosophers have in mind when they speak of 'visual impressions' or 'immediate visual experiences.'" Sellars, *Empiricism and the Philosophy of Mind*, 40. Brandom does not speak in such terms on his own initiative, but in his "Study Guide" to *Empiricism and the Philosophy of Mind*, he seems willing to grant the language of sense impressions. He distinguishes a very different role for sense impressions from the priority that those subscribing to the myth of the given accord them. For Brandom and Sellars, our speech about "sense impressions" is "essentially derivative and parasitic," derivative from and parasitic on our speech about physical objects and their properties, whereas Cartesians and others who embrace the myth want to prioritize our epistemic access to private mental episodes over our access to physical objects. As for the ontological status of such sense impressions, for Sellars, they are a theoretical entity that we use to explain two cases that are indistinguishable in how they appear to a viewer, like looking at a red triangle and an illusion of a red triangle that is indistinguishable from the veridical case.

For Brandom, "Neurophysiology or dualistic mind science might further specify for us" the nature of sense impressions. Robert Brandom, "Study Guide," in *Empiricism and the Philosophy of Mind*, by Wilfrid Sellars (Cambridge, Mass.: Harvard University Press, 1997).

30. Robert K. C. Forman, "Introduction: Mysticism, Constructivism, and Forgetting," in *The Problem of Pure Consciousness: Mysticism and Philosophy*, ed. Robert K. C. Forman (New York: Oxford University Press, 1990), 23.

31. Forman, *Mysticism, Mind, Consciousness*, 123.

32. Ibid., chap. 7.

33. Sellars, *Empiricism and the Philosophy of Mind*, 36–42.

34. Forman, *Mysticism, Mind, Consciousness*, 172.

35. John Hick, *An Interpretation of Religion: Human Responses to the Transcendent* (New Haven, Conn.: Yale University Press, 1989), chap. 14.

36. Proudfoot, *Religious Experience*, 121–122.

37. Frank Jackson, "Epiphenomenal Qualia," in *There's Something about Mary: Essays on Phenomenal Consciousness and Frank Jackson's Knowledge Argument*, ed. Peter Ludlow, Yujin Nagasawa, and Daniel Stoljar (Cambridge, Mass.: MIT Press, 2004), 39–50; Frank Jackson, "What Mary Didn't Know," in *There's Something about Mary: Essays on Phenomenal Consciousness and Frank Jackson's Knowledge Argument*, ed. Peter Ludlow, Yujin Nagasawa, and Daniel Stoljar (Cambridge, Mass.: MIT Press, 2004), 51–56.

38. I am inclined, following Mark Johnston, to regard hallucination as a special case of illusion, but I will retain it as its own category since it will have special explanatory value for visionary, auditory, and tactile religious experiences. See Mark Johnston, "The Obscure Object of Hallucination," *Philosophical Studies* 120 (2004): 113–183.

39. Sharf, "Experience," 108–110.

40. Ibid., 113–114.

41. Taves, *Religious Experience Reconsidered*.

42. Ibid., 25.

43. Ibid., 165.

44. Ibid., 31.

45. "We can locate 'things set apart and forbidden' at one end of a continuum that runs from the ordinary to the special." Ibid., 27.

46. Barbara G. Myerhoff, *Number Our Days* (New York: Dutton, 1978), 235.

47. Robert Orsi, "Everyday Miracles: The Study of Lived Religion," in *Lived Religion in America: Toward a History of Practice*, ed. David D. Hall (Princeton, N.J.: Princeton University Press, 1997), 4–6. Taves aligns herself with the study of lived religion in Bender and Taves, "Introduction," 12–13.

48. Taves, *Religious Experience Reconsidered*, 35.

49. Ibid., 15.

50. Ibid., 46.

51. Ibid., 12.

52. Ibid., 30.

53. Ibid., 62.

54. Ibid., 64.

55. Ibid., 99.

56. I benefited throughout this section from an unpublished paper of Lori Veilleux on cognitive science and social practice theory.

57. Richard Rorty, *Philosophy and the Mirror of Nature*, 30th anniversary ed. (Princeton, N.J: Princeton University Press, 2009).

58. Donald Davidson, "Thought and Talk," in *Inquiries into Truth and Interpretation* (Oxford: Clarendon, 1984), 155–170.

59. Tim Van Gelder, "What Might Cognition Be, If Not Computation?," *Journal of Philosophy* 92, no. 7 (1995): 345–381. See also Andy Clark, "An Embodied Cognitive Science?," *Trends in Cognitive Science* 3, no. 9 (1999): 349.

60. Brandom, *Perspectives on Pragmatism*, 12.

61. Ibid., 12–13.

CHAPTER 6

1. Myerhoff, *Number Our Days*, 259–261.

2. Eliade, *The Quest*, 6.

3. Jantzen, *Power, Gender and Christian Mysticism*, 346; Charles Taylor, *Varieties of Religion Today: William James Revisited* (Cambridge, Mass.: Harvard University Press, 2002). I will try to complicate this impression of James later in this chapter.

4. Jantzen, *Power, Gender and Christian Mysticism*; Sharf, "Experience"; Hollywood, *Sensible Ecstasy*.

5. Eagleton, *Ideology*, 45. On page 29, Eagleton gives another helpful formulation: "A discursive field in which self-promoting social powers conflict and collide over questions central to the reproduction of social power as a whole."

6. Scott, "The Evidence of Experience," 797.

7. Proudfoot, *Religious Experience*, xiv–xvi. Andrew Dole has recently challenged this reading of Schleiermacher, claiming that Schleiermacher does not want to put religion outside the reach of science but just the opposite. He wants to give science full reign to investigate religion. Schleiermacher, according to Dole, conceives of religion and science as compatible and so sees no need to protect religion from naturalistic assumptions. Dole, *Schleiermacher on Religion and the Natural Order*, chap. 5. Even if Dole is correct about Schleiermacher, however, it is still the case that the concept of experience has served protective purposes in the experiential approach to religion.

8. McCutcheon, *Manufacturing Religion*, chap. 2.

9. Jantzen, Power, *Gender and Christian Mysticism*, 322.

10. Ibid., 334.

11. Ibid., 330.

12. Ibid., 346.

13. Grace Jantzen, *Becoming Divine: Toward a Feminist Philosophy of Religion* (Bloomington, Ind.: Indiana University Press, 1999), especially chaps. 2 and 11.

14. Sharf, "Experience," 107.

15. Sharf, "The Zen of Japanese Nationalism."

16. Sharf, "Experience," 98.

17. Ibid., 111.

18. Ibid., 103.

19. See chapters 3 and 4 and Bush, "Are Experiences Too Private to Study?," 199–223.

20. I. M. Lewis, *Ecstatic Religion: A Study of Shamanism and Spirit Possession*, 2nd ed. (London; New York: Routledge, 1989), 28–29.

21. Griffith, *God's Daughters*, 158.

22. Weber, *Economy and Society*, 1:241.

23. Max Weber, *The Sociology of Religion*, 4th ed., trans. Ephraim Fischoff (Boston: Beacon Press, 1993), 46–48.

24. Weber, *Economy and Society*, 2:1115.

25. Karl Marx, "A Contribution to the Critique of Hegel's Philosophy of Right: Introduction," in *Marx: Early Political Writings*, trans. and ed. Joseph J. O'Malley and Richard A. Davis (Cambridge: Cambridge University Press, 1994), 57.

26. E. P. Thompson, *The Making of the English Working Class*, First Vintage ed. (New York: Vintage, 1966), 368.

27. Lewis, *Ecstatic Religion*.

28. Aihwa Ong, *Spirits of Resistance and Capitalist Discipline: Factory Women in Malaysia* (Albany: State University of New York Press, 1987), 207.

29. Brusco, *The Reformation of Machismo*.

30. Griffith, *God's Daughters*, 178.

31. Ibid., 172.

32. Ibid., 161.

33. Lee A. Kirkpatrick, *Attachment, Evolution, and the Psychology of Religion* (New York: Guilford Press, 2005), 28–29. Philip Tite brought attachment theory to my attention. For an application of attachment theory to the Nag Hammadi texts, see Philip L. Tite, "Theoretical Challenges in Studying Religious Experience in Gnosticism: A Prolegomena for Social Analysis," *Bulletin for the Study of Religion* 42, no. 1 (2013): 8–18.

34. Kirkpatrick, *Attachment, Evolution, and the Psychology of Religion*, chap. 3.

35. C. R. Chandra Shekar, "Possession Syndrome in India," in *Altered States of Consciousness and Mental Health: A Cross-Cultural Perspective*, ed. Colleen A. Ward (Newbury Park, Calif.: SAGE, 1989), 88.

36. Robert A. Orsi, *Between Heaven and Earth,* 4.

37. Griffith, *God's Daughters*, 207.

38. Lewis, *Ecstatic Religion*, 26.

39. Ibid., 18.

40. Jon Elster, *Making Sense of Marx* (Cambridge: Cambridge University Press, 1985), 27–28.

41. John L. Comaroff and Jean Comaroff, "Of Totemism and Ethnicity," in *Ethnography and the Historical Imagination*, ed. John L. Comaroff and Jean Comaroff (Boulder, Colo.: Westview Press, 1992), 60–61.

42. Sallie B. King, *Socially Engaged Buddhism* (Honolulu: University of Hawai'i Press, 2009), 40–50.

43. Grace M. Jantzen, "Mysticism and Experience," *Religious Studies* 25, no. 3 (September 1989): 398.

44. Grace M. Jantzen, "Feminists, Philosophers, and Mystics," *Hypatia* 9, no. 4 (1994): 203–204.

45. Jantzen, *Power, Gender and Christian Mysticism*, 347.

46. James, *The Varieties of Religious Experience*, 45.

47. Ibid., 48.

48. William James, "The Moral Philosopher and the Moral Life," in *The Will to Believe and Other Essays in Popular Philosophy*, by William James, ed. Frederick Burkhardt, Fredson Bowers, and Ignas K. Skrupskelis (Cambridge, Mass: Harvard University Press, 1979), 141–162.

49. Sarah Coakley, *Powers and Submissions: Spirituality, Philosophy and Gender* (Malden, Mass.: Blackwell, 2002), 34.

50. Ibid., 37–38.

51. Jantzen, *Power, Gender and Christian Mysticism*, 346.

52. Émile Durkheim, *The Elementary Forms of Religious Life*, trans. Karen E. Fields (New York: Free Press, 1995), 217–218.

53. Ibid., 220–222.

54. Ibid., 420–421.

55. Ibid., 429.

56. Karen E. Fields, "Translator's Introduction," in *The Elementary Forms of Religious Life*, by Émile Durkheim (New York: Free Press, 1995), xl.

57. Mauss and Brunschvicg are quoted in Steven Lukes, *Émile Durkheim: His Life and Work: A Historical and Critical Study* (Stanford, Calif.: Stanford University Press, 1985), 339n71.

58. René Girard, "Mimesis and Violence," in *The Girard Reader*, ed. James G. Williams (New York: Crossroad, 1996), 10–11.

59. Lincoln, *Holy Terrors*, 7.

60. In personal conversation, Griffith confirmed that this seems correct to her.

61. Edward L. Cleary, "Introduction: Pentecostals, Prominence, and Politics," in *Power, Politics, and Pentecostals in Latin America*, ed. Edward L. Cleary and Hannah W. Stewart-Gambino (Boulder, Colo.: Westview Press, 1997), 14–15.

62. Mary Daly, *Beyond God the Father: Toward a Philosophy of Women's Liberation* (Boston: Beacon Press, 1973); Johnson, *She Who Is*; Sallie McFague, *Metaphorical Theology: Models of God in Religious Language* (Philadelphia: Fortress Press, 1982); Judith Plaskow, *Standing Again at Sinai: Judaism from a Feminist Perspective*, 1st ed. (New York: Harper & Row, 1990); Rosemary Radford Ruether, *Sexism and God-Talk: Toward a Feminist Theology*, 10th anniversary ed. (Boston: Beacon Press, 1993).

63. Bernard Spilka, Ralph W. Hood, and Richard L. Gorsuch, *The Psychology of Religion: An Empirical Approach*, 3rd ed. (New York: Guilford, 2003), 310.

64. Quoted and translated in Ross S. Kraemer, ed., *Maenads, Martyrs, Matrons, Monastics: A Sourcebook on Women's Religions in the Greco-Roman World* (Philadelphia: Fortress Press, 1988), 226.

65. Elisabeth of Schönau, *Third Book of Visions*, in *Complete Works*, trans. Anne L. Clark (New York: Paulist Press, 2000).

66. See, for example, the essays in Sarah Coakley, ed., *Religion and the Body* (Cambridge: Cambridge University Press, 1997).

67. Amy Hollywood, "Practice, Belief, and Feminist Philosophy of Religion," in *Feminist Philosophy of Religion: Critical Readings*, ed. Pamela Sue Anderson and Beverley Clack (London: Routledge, 2004), 225–240.

68. See Stephen S. Bush, "The Ethics of Ecstasy: Georges Bataille and Amy Hollywood on Mysticism, Morality, and Violence," *Journal of Religious Ethics* 39, no. 2 (June 2011): 299–320.

69. Marcel Mauss, "Body Techniques," in *Sociology and Psychology: Essays*, trans. Ben Brewster (London: Routledge & K. Paul, 1979), 122.

70. Asad, *Genealogies of Religion*, 76–77.

71. Hollywood, "Practice, Belief, and Feminist Philosophy of Religion," 230.

72. Ibid., 234.

73. Ibid., 237.

74. For a helpful discussion of the historical and international context of the Islamic renewal movement as it relates to veiling, see Leila Ahmed, *A Quiet Revolution: The Veil's Resurgence, from the Middle East to America* (New Haven, Conn.: Yale University Press, 2011).

75. Mahmood, *Politics of Piety*, 123.

76. Ibid., 157.

77. Brenner, "Reconstructing Self and Society," 685. This example is discussed at greater length in chapter 3.

78. Griffith, *God's Daughters*, 140.

79. Hollywood, "Practice, Belief, and Feminist Philosophy of Religion," 236.

CHAPTER 7

1. These rituals are discussed in Catherine Bell, "Performance," in *Critical Terms for Religious Studies*, ed. Mark C. Taylor (Chicago: University of Chicago Press, 1998), 212–218; Wolf, "Gods, Ghosts, and Ancestors," 131–182.

2. Alasdair MacIntyre, *After Virtue: A Study in Moral Theory*, 3rd ed. (Notre Dame, Ind.: University of Notre Dame Press, 2007), 187. I say that I am appropriating MacIntyre's definition selectively because it is less important to me than to MacIntyre to maintain the distinction between forms of cooperative human activity that systematically extend "human powers to achieve excellence" and "human conceptions of the ends and goods involved" from those that do not. I do think that religions are practices in his sense, but whether or not bricklaying fails to achieve the status of a practice, like MacIntyre says, is not important to my account.

3. Michaelsen, "'I Don't Do Systems,'" 9.

4. Foucault, *Discipline & Punish*, 27.

5. This model of social criticism is drawn from Stout, *Democracy and Tradition*, and Terry P. Pinkard, *Hegel's Phenomenology: The Sociality of Reason* (Cambridge: Cambridge University Press, 1994).

6. Geertz, *The Interpretation of Cultures*, 21.

7. Ibid., 10.

8. Anne S. Brown and David D. Hall, "Family Strategies and Religious Practice: Baptism and the Lord's Supper in Early New England," in *Lived Religion in America: Toward a History of Practice*, ed. David D. Hall (Princeton, N.J.: Princeton University Press, 1997), 61.

9. David Decosimo, "Comparison and the Ubiquity of Resemblance," *Journal of the American Academy of Religion* 78, no. 1 (2010): 226–258. Decosimo helpfully quotes a relevant insight from Nelson Goodman: "Similarity is relative, variable and context-dependent . . . anything is in some way like anything else . . . every two things have some property in common" (227).

10. Lewis, *Ecstatic Religion*.

11. Boddy, *Wombs and Alien Spirits*.

12. Geertz, *Local Knowledge*, chap. 3.

13. Masuzawa, "Culture," 88.

14. Ibid., 91.

15. "Practical logic" is a Bourdieuan term. Pierre Bourdieu, *The Logic of Practice*, trans. Richard Nice (Stanford, Calif.: Stanford University Press, 1990).

16. Masuzawa, "Culture," 82–88.

17. A helpful resource on these matters is Davis, *Believing and Acting*.

18. Orsi, *Between Heaven and Earth*, 158.

19. R. Marie Griffith, "Submissive Wives, Wounded Daughters, and Female Soldiers: Prayer and Christian Womanhood in Women's Aglow Fellowship," in *Lived Religion in America: Toward a History of Practice*, ed. David D. Hall (Princeton, N.J.: Princeton University Press, 1997), 160–195; Orsi, "Everyday Miracles," 3–21.

20. On Geertz and practice and lived religion, see David D. Hall, "Introduction," in *Lived Religion in America: Toward a History of Practice*, ed. David D. Hall (Princeton, N.J.: Princeton University Press, 1997), ix, xi. Orsi refers to the study of lived religion as a sort of phenomenology of religion, a "materialist phenomenology of religion." Orsi, "Everyday Miracles," 8.

21. Hall, "Introduction," ix.

22. Orsi, *Between Heaven and Earth*, 5.

23. Ibid., 2.

24. Ibid., 4.

25. Masuzawa, "Culture," 89.

26. Jeffrey Stout, "What Is the Meaning of a Text?" *New Literary History* 14, no. 1 (1982): 3. See also Stout, "The Relativity of Interpretation," 103–118. In addition to these two essays by Stout, my reflections on interpretation in these paragraphs have been significantly informed by Brandom, *Tales of the Mighty Dead*, chap. 3.

27. Hollywood, "Practice, Belief, and Feminist Philosophy of Religion," 225–240.

28. Jantzen, *Power, Gender and Christian Mysticism*.

29. For similar criticisms of philosophy of religion, see also chapters 5 and 6 in Coakley, *Powers and Submissions*.

30. For a fuller discussion of this topic, see Schilbrack, *Philosophy and the Study of Religions*, 189–197. Some people describe these issues about religious ethics and theology as a question of normativity in distinction from the nonnormative subfields. But this attempt to limit normativity to ethics and theology is problematic. See Thomas A. Lewis, "On the Role of Normativity in Religious Studies," in *The Cambridge Companion to Religious Studies*, ed. Robert A. Orsi (Cambridge; New York: Cambridge University Press, 2012), 168–185.

31. Michelle Alexander, *The New Jim Crow: Mass Incarceration in the Age of Colorblindness* (New York: New Press, 2010).

32. Nicholas Wolterstorff, *Justice: Rights and Wrongs* (Princeton, N.J.: Princeton University Press, 2008), xi.

33. George A. Lindbeck, *The Nature of Doctrine: Religion and Theology in a Postliberal Age*, 1st ed. (Philadelphia: Westminster Press, 1984). On the experiential-expressivist model of theology and Lindbeck's cultural-linguistic alternative, see chapter 2.

34. Hans W. Frei, *Types of Christian Theology* (New Haven, Conn.: Yale University Press, 1992), 11–14.

35. Hector, *Theology without Metaphysics*. See also Jason A. Spring's important book on Hans Frei, *Toward a Generous Orthodoxy*.

36. Hector, *Theology without Metaphysics,* chap. 6.

BIBLIOGRAPHY

Ahmed, Leila. *A Quiet Revolution: The Veil's Resurgence, from the Middle East to America*. New Haven, Conn.: Yale University Press, 2011.

Alcoff, Linda, and Elizabeth Potter, eds. *Feminist Epistemologies*. New York: Routledge, 1993.

Alexander, Michelle. *The New Jim Crow: Mass Incarceration in the Age of Colorblindness*. New York: New Press, 2010.

Alexander, Jeffrey C., and Philip Smith. "Introduction: The Rise and Fall of Clifford Geertz." In *Interpreting Clifford Geertz: Cultural Investigation in the Social Sciences*, edited by Jeffrey C. Alexander, Philip Smith, and Matthew Norton. New York: Palgrave Macmillan, 2011.

Alston, William P. *Perceiving God: The Epistemology of Religious Experience*. Ithaca, N.Y.: Cornell University Press, 1991.

Andresen, Jensine, and Robert K. C. Forman. "Methodological Pluralism in the Study of Religion: How the Study of Consciousness and Mapping Spiritual Experiences Can Reshape Religious Methodology." In *Cognitive Models and Spiritual Maps*, edited by Jensine Andresen and Robert K. C. Forman. Bowling Green, Ohio: Academic Imprint, 2000.

Asad, Talal. *Genealogies of Religion: Discipline and Reasons of Power in Christianity and Islam*. Baltimore: Johns Hopkins University Press, 1993.

———. "Thinking about Religion, Belief, and Politics." In *The Cambridge Companion to Religious Studies*, edited by Robert A. Orsi, 36–58. Cambridge: Cambridge University Press, 2012.

Bell, Catherine. "Performance." In *Critical Terms for Religious Studies*, edited by Mark C. Taylor, 205–224. Chicago: University of Chicago Press, 1998.

———. *Ritual Theory, Ritual Practice*. New York: Oxford University Press, 1992.

Bender, Courtney. *The New Metaphysicals: Spirituality and the American Religious Imagination*. Chicago: University of Chicago Press, 2010.

Bender, Courtney, and Ann Taves. "Introduction: Things of Value." In *What Matters?: Ethnographies of Value in a Not So Secular Age*, edited by Courtney Bender and Ann Taves, 1–33. New York: Columbia University Press, 2012.

Benhabib, Seyla. *Situating the Self: Gender, Community, and Postmodernism in Contemporary Ethics*. Cambridge: Polity Press, 1992.

Boddy, Janice Patricia. *Wombs and Alien Spirits: Women, Men, and the Zār Cult in Northern Sudan*. Madison: University of Wisconsin Press, 1989.

Bourdieu, Pierre. *Esquisse d'une Théorie de la Pratique*. Paris: Seuil, 2000.

———. *The Logic of Practice*. Translated by Richard Nice. Stanford, Calif.: Stanford University Press, 1990.

———. *Outline of a Theory of Practice*. Translated by Richard Nice. Cambridge: Cambridge University Press, 1977.

Brandom, Robert. *Articulating Reasons: An Introduction to Inferentialism*. Cambridge, Mass: Harvard University Press, 2000.

———. "From a Critique of Cognitive Internalism to a Conception of Objective Spirit: Reflections on Descombes' Anthropological Holism." *Inquiry* 47 (2004): 236–253.

———. *Making It Explicit: Reasoning, Representing, and Discursive Commitment*. Cambridge, Mass.: Harvard University Press, 1994.

———. "Non-Inferential Knowledge, Perceptual Experience, and Secondary Qualities: Placing McDowell's Empiricism." In *Reading McDowell: On Mind and World*, edited by Nicholas H. Smith. London; New York: Routledge, 2002.

———. *Perspectives on Pragmatism: Classical, Recent, and Contemporary*. Cambridge, Mass.: Harvard University Press, 2011.

———. "The Pragmatist Enlightenment (and Its Problematic Semantics)." *European Journal of Philosophy* 12, no. 1 (2004): 1–16.

———. "Study Guide." In *Empiricism and the Philosophy of Mind*, by Wilfrid Sellars. Cambridge, Mass.: Harvard University Press, 1997.

———. *Tales of the Mighty Dead: Historical Essays in the Metaphysics of Intentionality*. Cambridge, Mass.: Harvard University Press, 2002.

Brenner, Suzanne. "Reconstructing Self and Society: Javanese Muslim Women and 'The Veil.'" *American Ethnologist* 23, no. 4 (November 1996): 673–697.

Brown, Anne S., and David D. Hall. "Family Strategies and Religious Practice: Baptism and the Lord's Supper in Early New England." In *Lived Religion in America: Toward a History of Practice*, edited by David D. Hall, 41–68. Princeton, N.J.: Princeton University Press, 1997.

Brusco, Elizabeth E. *The Reformation of Machismo: Evangelical Conversion and Gender in Colombia*. Austin: University of Texas Press, 1995.

Bush, Stephen S. "Are Experiences Too Private to Study?" *Journal of Religion* 92, no. 2 (April 2012): 199–223.

———. "Are Meanings the Name of the Game? Religion as Symbolic Meaning and Religion as Power." *Religion Compass* 6, no. 12 (2012): 525–533.

———. "Concepts and Religious Experiences: Wayne Proudfoot on the Cultural Construction of Experiences." *Religious Studies* 48, no. 1 (2012): 101–117.

———. "The Ethics of Ecstasy: Georges Bataille and Amy Hollywood on Mysticism, Morality, and Violence." *Journal of Religious Ethics* 39, no. 2 (June 2011): 299–320.

———. "Nothing Outside the Text: Derrida and Brandom on Language and World." *Contemporary Pragmatism* 6, no. 2 (2009): 45–69.

Carnes, Mark C. *Secret Ritual and Manhood in Victorian America*. New Haven, Conn.: Yale University Press, 1989.

Chandra Shekar, C. R. "Possession Syndrome in India." In *Altered States of Consciousness and Mental Health: A Cross-Cultural Perspective*, edited by Colleen A. Ward, 79–95. Newbury Park, Calif.: SAGE Publications, 1989.

Chesnut, R. Andrew. *Born Again in Brazil: The Pentecostal Boom and the Pathogens of Poverty*. New Brunswick, N.J.: Rutgers University Press, 1997.

Chidester, David. "Material Terms for the Study of Religion." *Journal of the American Academy of Religion* 68, no. 2 (2000): 367–380.

———. *Savage Systems: Colonialism and Comparative Religion in Southern Africa*. Charlottesville: University Press of Virginia, 1996.

Christ, Carol P. "Mircea Eliade and the Feminist Paradigm Shift." *Journal of Feminist Studies in Religion* 7, no. 2 (Fall 1991): 75–94.

Clark, Andy. "An Embodied Cognitive Science?" *Trends in Cognitive Science* 3, no. 9 (1999): 345–351.

Cleary, Edward L. "Introduction: Pentecostals, Prominence, and Politics." In *Power, Politics, and Pentecostals in Latin America*, edited by Edward L. Cleary and Hannah W. Stewart-Gambino, 1–24. Boulder, Colo.: Westview Press, 1997.

Clifford, James. *The Predicament of Culture: Twentieth-Century Ethnography, Literature, and Art*. Cambridge, Mass.: Harvard University Press, 1988.

Coakley, Sarah. *Powers and Submissions: Spirituality, Philosophy and Gender*. Malden, Mass.: Blackwell Publishers, 2002.

———., ed. *Religion and the Body*. Cambridge: Cambridge University Press, 1997.

Comaroff, John L., and Jean Comaroff. "Of Totemism and Ethnicity." In *Ethnography and the Historical Imagination*, edited by John L. Comaroff and Jean Comaroff, 3–48. Boulder, Colo.: Westview Press, 1992.

Crapanzano, Vincent. "Hermes' Dilemma: The Masking of Subversion in Ethnographic Description." In *Writing Culture: The Poetics and Politics of Ethnography: A School of American Research Advanced Seminar*, edited by James Clifford and George E. Marcus, 51–70. 25th anniversary ed. Berkeley: University of California Press, 2010.

Daly, Mary. *Beyond God the Father: Toward a Philosophy of Women's Liberation*. Boston: Beacon Press, 1973.

Davidson, Donald. *Inquiries into Truth and Interpretation*. Oxford: Clarendon Press, 1984.

———. "On the Very Idea of a Conceptual Scheme." In *Inquiries into Truth and Interpretation*. Oxford: Clarendon Press, 1984.

———. "Thought and Talk." In *Inquiries into Truth and Interpretation*, 155–170. Oxford: Clarendon, 1984.

Davis, G. Scott. *Believing and Acting: The Pragmatic Turn in Comparative Religion and Ethics*. Oxford: Oxford University Press, 2012.

Decosimo, David. "Comparison and the Ubiquity of Resemblance." *Journal of the American Academy of Religion* 78, no. 1 (2010): 226–258.

Dennett, Daniel Clement. *Consciousness Explained*. Boston: Little, Brown and Co, 1991.

Derrida, Jacques. *Margins of Philosophy*. Translated by Alan Bass. Chicago: University of Chicago Press, 1982.

———. *Of Grammatology*. Translated by Gayatri Chakravorty Spivak. Corrected ed. Baltimore: Johns Hopkins University Press, 1998.

Dole, Andrew. "Schleiermacher and Otto on Religion." *Religious Studies* 40, no. 4 (2004): 389–413.

———. *Schleiermacher on Religion and the Natural Order*. New York: Oxford University Press, 2010.

Dreyfus, Hubert L. *Being-in-the-World: A Commentary on Heidegger's* Being and Time, *Division I*. Cambridge, Mass.: MIT Press, 1991.

Droogers, André. "Paradoxical Views on a Paradoxical Religion: Models for the Explanation of Pentecostal Expansion in Brazil and Chile." In *More Than Opium: An Anthropological Approach to Latin American and Caribbean Pentecostal Praxis*, edited by Barbara Boudewijnse, A. F. Droogers, and Frans Kamsteeg, 1–34. Lanham, Md.: Scarecrow Press, 1998.

Durkheim, Émile. *The Elementary Forms of Religious Life*. Translated by Karen E. Fields. New York: Free Press, 1995.

Eagleton, Terry. *Ideology: An Introduction*. New and Updated ed. London: Verso, 2007.

Eliade, Mircea. *A History of Religious Ideas*. Translated by Willard R. Trask. 3 vols. Chicago: University of Chicago Press, 1978–1985.

———. *The Quest: History and Meaning in Religion*. Chicago: University of Chicago Press, 1969.

———. *Rites and Symbols of Initiation: The Mysteries of Birth and Rebirth*. New York: Harper & Row, 1965.

———. *The Sacred and the Profane: The Nature of Religion*. Translated by Willard R. Trask. New York: Harcourt, 1959.

Elisabeth of Schönau. *Third Book of Visions*. In *Complete Works*, translated by Anne L. Clark. New York: Paulist Press, 2000.

Elster, Jon. *Making Sense of Marx*. Cambridge: Cambridge University Press, 1985.

Fanon, Frantz. *The Wretched of the Earth*. Translated by Richard Philcox. New York: Grove, 2004.

Fields, Karen E. "Translator's Introduction." In *The Elementary Forms of Religious Life*, by Émile Durkheim, xvii–lxxiii. New York: Free Press, 1995.

Fitzgerald, Timothy. *The Ideology of Religious Studies*. New York: Oxford University Press, 2000.

Forman, Robert K. C. "Introduction: Mysticism, Constructivism, and Forgetting." In *The Problem of Pure Consciousness: Mysticism and Philosophy*, edited by Robert K. C. Forman, 3–48. New York: Oxford University Press, 1990.

———. *Mysticism, Mind, Consciousness*. Albany: State University of New York Press, 1999.

———., ed. *The Problem of Pure Consciousness: Mysticism and Philosophy*. New York: Oxford University Press, 1990.

Foucault, Michel. *The Birth of the Clinic: An Archaeology of Medical Perception*. Translated by A. M. Sheridan Smith. 1st American ed. New York: Pantheon Books, 1973.

———. *Discipline & Punish: The Birth of the Prison*. Translated by Alan Sheridan. 2nd Vintage ed. New York: Vintage, 1995.

———. *The History of Sexuality*. Translated by Robert Hurley. Vintage Books ed. New York: Vintage Books, 1990.

————. *Madness and Civilization: A History of Insanity in the Age of Reason.* Translated by Richard Howard. New York: Vintage Books, 1988.

————. *The Order of Things: An Archaeology of the Human Sciences.* London: Routledge, 2002.

————. "Truth and Power." In *Power/Knowledge: Selected Interviews and Other Writings, 1972–1977,* edited by Colin Gordon, 109–133. 1st American ed. New York: Pantheon Books, 1980.

Frankenberry, Nancy, and Hans Penner. "Geertz's Long-Lasting Moods, Motivations, and Metaphysical Conceptions." *Journal of Religion* 79, no. 4 (1999): 617–640.

Fraser, Nancy. "From Irony to Prophecy to Politics: A Reply to Richard Rorty." In *Feminist Interpretations of Richard Rorty,* edited by Marianne Janack, 47–54. University Park: Pennsylvania State University Press, 2010.

Frei, Hans W. *Types of Christian Theology.* New Haven, Conn.: Yale University Press, 1992.

Fricker, Miranda. *Epistemic Injustice: Power and the Ethics of Knowing.* New York: Oxford University Press, 2009.

Gadamer, Hans-Georg. *Truth and Method.* Translated by Joel Weinsheimer and Donald G. Marshall. 2nd ed. London: Continuum, 2004.

Geertz, Clifford. *Available Light: Anthropological Reflections on Philosophical Topics.* Princeton, N.J.: Princeton University Press, 2001.

————. *The Interpretation of Cultures.* New York: Basic Books, 1973.

————. *Islam Observed: Religious Development in Morocco and Indonesia.* Phoenix ed. Chicago: University of Chicago Press, 1971.

————. *Local Knowledge: Further Essays In Interpretive Anthropology.* 3rd ed. New York: Basic Books, 2000.

————. *Person, Time, and Conduct in Bali: An Essay in Cultural Analysis.* New Haven, Conn.: Southeast Asia Studies, Yale University, 1966.

Girard, René. "Mimesis and Violence." In *The Girard Reader,* edited by James G. Williams, 9–19. New York: Crossroad, 1996.

Glaude, Eddie S. *Exodus!: Religion, Race, and Nation in Early Nineteenth-Century Black America.* Chicago: University of Chicago Press, 2000.

Godlove, Terry F., Jr., "Saving Belief: On the New Materialism in Religious Studies." In *Radical Interpretation in Religion,* edited by Nancy Frankenberry, 10–24. Cambridge: Cambridge University Press, 2002.

Griffith, R. Marie. *God's Daughters: Evangelical Women and the Power of Submission.* Berkeley: University of California Press, 1997.

————. "Sexing Religion." In *The Cambridge Companion to Religious Studies,* edited by Robert A. Orsi, 338–359. Cambridge: Cambridge University Press, 2012.

————. "Submissive Wives, Wounded Daughters, and Female Soldiers: Prayer and Christian Womanhood in Women's Aglow Fellowship." In *Lived Religion in America: Toward a History of Practice,* edited by David D. Hall, 160–195. Princeton, N.J.: Princeton University Press, 1997.

Griffiths, Paul. "The Very Idea of Religion." *First Things* 103, no. 1 (2000): 30–35.

Hall, David D. "Introduction." In *Lived Religion in America: Toward a History of Practice,* edited by David D. Hall, vii–xiii. Princeton, N.J.: Princeton University Press, 1997.

Hart, D. G. *The University Gets Religion: Religious Studies in American Higher Education.* Baltimore: Johns Hopkins University Press, 1999.

Hector, Kevin. *Theology without Metaphysics: God, Language, and the Spirit of Recognition.* Cambridge: Cambridge University Press, 2011.

Heidegger, Martin. *Being and Time.* Translated by Joan Stambaugh. Albany: State University of New York Press, 1996.

Hick, John. *An Interpretation of Religion: Human Responses to the Transcendent.* New Haven, Conn.: Yale University Press, 1989.

Higginbotham, Evelyn Brooks. *Righteous Discontent: The Women's Movement in the Black Baptist Church, 1880–1920.* Cambridge, Mass.: Harvard University Press, 1993.

Hollywood, Amy. "Practice, Belief, and Feminist Philosophy of Religion." In *Feminist Philosophy of Religion: Critical Readings*, edited by Pamela Sue Anderson and Beverley Clack, 225–240. London: Routledge, 2004.

———. *Sensible Ecstasy: Mysticism, Sexual Difference, and the Demands of History.* Chicago: University of Chicago Press, 2002.

Huxley, Aldous. *The Perennial Philosophy.* 1st ed. New York: Harper, 1945.

Inglis, Fred. *Clifford Geertz: Culture, Custom and Ethics.* Cambridge: Polity Press, 2000.

Innis, Robert E. *Susanne Langer in Focus: The Symbolic Mind.* Bloomington: Indiana University Press, 2009.

Jackson, Frank. "Epiphenomenal Qualia." In *There's Something about Mary: Essays on Phenomenal Consciousness and Frank Jackson's Knowledge Argument*, edited by Peter Ludlow, Yujin Nagasawa, and Daniel Stoljar, 39–50. Cambridge, Mass.: MIT Press, 2004.

———. "What Mary Didn't Know." In *There's Something about Mary: Essays on Phenomenal Consciousness and Frank Jackson's Knowledge Argument*, edited by Peter Ludlow, Yujin Nagasawa, and Daniel Stoljar, 51–56. Cambridge, Mass.: MIT Press, 2004.

James, William. "The Moral Philosopher and the Moral Life." In *The Will to Believe and Other Essays in Popular Philosophy*, by William James, edited by Frederick Burkhardt, Fredson Bowers, and Ignas K. Skrupskelis, 141–162. Cambridge, Mass.: Harvard University Press, 1979.

———. *The Varieties of Religious Experience.* Cambridge, Mass.: Harvard University Press, 1985.

Jantzen, Grace M. *Becoming Divine: Toward a Feminist Philosophy of Religion.* Bloomington: Indiana University Press, 1999.

———. "Could There Be a Mystical Core of Religion?" *Religious Studies* 26, no. 1 (1990): 59–71.

———. "Feminists, Philosophers, and Mystics." *Hypatia* 9, no. 4 (1994): 186–206.

———. "Mysticism and Experience." *Religious Studies* 25, no. 3 (September 1989): 295–315.

———. *Power, Gender and Christian Mysticism.* Cambridge: Cambridge University Press, 1995.

Jay, Martin. *Songs of Experience: Modern American and European Variations on a Universal Theme.* Berkeley: University of California Press, 2005.

Jay, Nancy B. *Throughout Your Generations Forever: Sacrifice, Religion, and Paternity.* Chicago: University of Chicago Press, 1992.

Johnson, Clifton H., ed. *God Struck Me Dead: Voices of Ex-Slaves.* Cleveland, Ohio: Pilgrim Press, 1993.

Johnson, Elizabeth A. *She Who Is: The Mystery of God in a Feminist Theological Discourse.* New York: Crossroad, 1992.

Johnston, Mark. "The Obscure Object of Hallucination." *Philosophical Studies* 120 (2004): 118–183.

Jordan, Mark D. *The Invention of Sodomy in Christian Theology.* Chicago: University of Chicago Press, 1997.

Katz, Steven T. "Language, Epistemology, and Mysticism." In *Mysticism and Philosophical Analysis*, edited by Steven T. Katz, 22–74. London: Sheldon Press, 1978.

King, Richard. *Orientalism and Religion: Postcolonial Theory, India and "the Mystic East."* London: Routledge, 1999.

King, Sallie B. *Socially Engaged Buddhism*. Honolulu: University of Hawai'i Press, 2009.

Kirkpatrick, Lee A. *Attachment, Evolution, and the Psychology of Religion*. New York: Guilford Press, 2005.

Kraemer, Ross Shepard, ed., *Maenads, Martyrs, Matrons, Monastics: A Sourcebook on Women's Religions in the Greco-Roman World*. Philadelphia: Fortress Press, 1988.

Kripal, Jeffrey J. *Kali's Child: The Mystical and the Erotic in the Life and Teachings of Ramakrishna*. Chicago: University of Chicago Press, 1995.

Langer, Susanne Katherina Knauth. *Philosophy in a New Key: A Study in the Symbolism of Reason, Rite and Art*. Cambridge, Mass.: Harvard University Press, 1951.

Leeuw, G. van der. *Religion in Essence & Manifestation: A Study in Phenomenology*. Translated by John Evan Turner. London: G. Allen & Unwin, 1938.

Lewis, I. M. *Ecstatic Religion: A Study of Shamanism and Spirit Possession*. 2nd ed. London: Routledge, 1989.

Lewis, Thomas A. "On the Role of Normativity in Religious Studies." In *The Cambridge Companion to Religious Studies*, edited by Robert A. Orsi, 168–185. Cambridge: Cambridge University Press, 2012.

Lincoln, Bruce. *Holy Terrors: Thinking about Religion after September 11*. Chicago: University of Chicago Press, 2003.

———. *Theorizing Myth: Narrative, Ideology, and Scholarship*. Chicago: University of Chicago Press, 1999.

Lindbeck, George A. *The Nature of Doctrine: Religion and Theology in a Postliberal Age*. 1st ed. Philadelphia: Westminster Press, 1984.

Long, Charles H. *Significations: Signs, Symbols, and Images in the Interpretation of Religion*. Philadelphia: Fortress Press, 1986.

Lopez Jr., Donald S. "Belief." In *Critical Terms for Religious Studies*, edited by Mark C. Taylor. Chicago: University of Chicago Press, 1998.

Luhrmann, Tanya. *When God Talks Back: Understanding the American Evangelical Relationship with God*. New York: Alfred A. Knopf, 2012.

Lukes, Steven. *Émile Durkheim: His Life and Work: A Historical and Critical Study*. Stanford, Calif.: Stanford University Press, 1985.

MacIntyre, Alasdair. *After Virtue: A Study in Moral Theory*. 3rd ed. Notre Dame, Ind.: University of Notre Dame Press, 2007.

Mahmood, Saba. *Politics of Piety: The Islamic Revival and the Feminist Subject*. Princeton, N.J.: Princeton University Press, 2005.

Marx, Karl. "A Contribution to the Critique of Hegel's Philosophy of Right: Introduction." In *Marx: Early Political Writings*, edited and translated by Joseph J. O'Malley and Richard A. Davis, 57–70. Cambridge: Cambridge University Press, 1994.

Masuzawa, Tomoko. "Culture." In *Critical Terms for Religious Studies*, edited by Mark C. Taylor, 70–93. Chicago: University of Chicago Press, 1998.

———. *The Invention of World Religions, Or, How European Universalism Was Preserved in the Language of Pluralism*. Chicago: University of Chicago Press, 2005.

Mauss, Marcel. "Body Techniques." In *Sociology and Psychology: Essays*, translated by Ben Brewster, 95–123. London: Routledge & K. Paul, 1979.

McCutcheon, Russell T. *Critics Not Caretakers: Redescribing the Public Study of Religion*. Albany: State University of New York Press, 2001.

———., ed. *The Insider/Outsider Problem in the Study of Religion: A Reader*. London: Cassell, 1999.

———. *Manufacturing Religion: The Discourse on Sui Generis Religion and the Politics of Nostalgia*. New York: Oxford University Press, 2003.

McFague, Sallie. *Metaphorical Theology: Models of God in Religious Language*. Philadelphia: Fortress Press, 1982.

Micheelsen, Arun. "'I Don't Do Systems': An Interview with Clifford Geertz." *Method & Theory in the Study of Religion* 14, no. 1 (2002): 2–20.

Míguez, Daniel. *Spiritual Bonfire in Argentina: Confronting Current Theories with an Ethnographic Account of Pentecostal Growth in a Buenos Aires Suburb*. Amsterdam: CEDLA, 1998.

Moran, Richard. *Authority and Estrangement: An Essay on Self-Knowledge*. Princeton, N.J.: Princeton University Press, 2001.

Myerhoff, Barbara G. *Number Our Days*. New York: Dutton, 1978.

Ong, Aihwa. *Spirits of Resistance and Capitalist Discipline: Factory Women in Malaysia*. Albany: State University of New York Press, 1987.

Orsi, Robert. "Belief." *Material Religion: The Journal of Objects, Art and Belief* 7, no. 1 (2011): 10–16.

———. *Between Heaven and Earth: The Religious Worlds People Make and the Scholars Who Study Them*. Princeton, N.J.: Princeton University Press, 2005.

———., ed. *The Cambridge Companion to Religious Studies*. Cambridge: Cambridge University Press, 2012.

———. "Everyday Miracles: The Study of Lived Religion." In *Lived Religion in America: Toward a History of Practice*, edited by David D. Hall, 3–21. Princeton, N.J.: Princeton University Press, 1997.

Otto, Rudolf. *The Idea of the Holy: An Inquiry into the Non-Rational Factor in the Idea of the Divine and Its Relation to the Rational*. Translated by John W. Harvey. 2nd ed. New York: Oxford University Press, 1958.

Pettit, Philip. *Republicanism: A Theory of Freedom and Government*. Oxford: Clarendon Press, 1997.

Pinkard, Terry P. *Hegel's Phenomenology: The Sociality of Reason*. Cambridge: Cambridge University Press, 1994.

Pinn, Anthony B. *The African American Religious Experience in America*. Westport, Conn.: Greenwood Press, 2006.

Plaskow, Judith. *Standing Again at Sinai: Judaism from a Feminist Perspective*. 1st ed. New York: Harper & Row, 1990.

Proudfoot, Wayne. "Medical Materialism Revisited." *The Immanent Frame*, 2008. http://blogs.ssrc.org/tif/2008/06/30/medical-materialism-revisited/.

———. *Religious Experience*. Berkeley: University of California Press, 1985.

———. "Response." *Journal of the American Academy of Religion* 61, no. 4 (1993): 793–803.

Putnam, Hilary. "The Meaning of 'Meaning.'" In *The Twin Earth Chronicles: Twenty Years of Reflection on Hilary Putnam's "The Meaning of 'Meaning,'"* edited by Andrew Pessin and Sanford Goldberg, 3–52. Armonk, N.Y.: M. E. Sharpe, 1996.

Raboteau, Albert J. *Slave Religion: The "Invisible Institution" in the Antebellum South.* Oxford: Oxford University Press, 1980.

Richardson, Robert D. "Schleiermacher and the Transcendentalists." In *Transient and Permanent: The Transcendentalist Movement and Its Contexts*, edited by Charles Capper and Conrad Edick Wright, 121–147. Boston: Massachusetts Historical Society, 1999.

Ricoeur, Paul. *The Conflict of Interpretations.* Edited by Don Ihde. Evanston, Ill.: Northwestern University Press, 1974.

———. *Freud and Philosophy: An Essay on Interpretation.* Translated by Denis Savage. New Haven, Conn.: Yale University Press, 1970.

———. *Hermeneutics and Human Sciences: Essays on Language, Action, and Interpretation.* Translated by John B. Thompson. Cambridge: Cambridge University Press, 1981.

———. "The Model of the Text: Meaningful Action Considered as a Text." In *From Text to Action*, translated by Kathleen Blamey and John B. Thompson, 144–167. Evanston, Ill.: Northwestern University Press, 1991.

———. *The Symbolism of Evil.* Translated by Emerson Buchanan. 1st ed. New York: Harper & Row, 1967.

Rorty, Richard. "Cultural Politics and the Question of the Existence of God." In *Radical Interpretation in Religion*, edited by Nancy Frankenberry, 53–77. Cambridge: Cambridge University Press, 2002.

———. *Objectivity, Relativism, and Truth.* Cambridge: Cambridge University Press, 1991.

———. *Philosophy and the Mirror of Nature.* 30th anniversary ed. Princeton, N.J.: Princeton University Press, 2009.

Roth, Harold D. "Against Cognitive Imperialism: A Call for a Non-Ethnocentric Approach to Cognitive Science and Religious Studies." *Religion East & West* 8 (2008): 1–26.

Rothberg, Donald. "Contemporary Epistemology and the Study of Mysticism." In *The Problem of Pure Consciousness: Mysticism and Philosophy*, edited by Robert K. C. Forman, 163–210. New York: Oxford University Press, 1990.

Ruether, Rosemary Radford. *Sexism and God-Talk: Toward a Feminist Theology.* 10th anniversary ed. Boston: Beacon Press, 1993.

Said, Edward W. *Orientalism.* 25th Anniversary ed. New York: Vintage Books, 2003.

Saiving, Valerie. "Androcentrism in Religious Studies." *Journal of Religion* 56, no. 2 (1976): 177–197.

Schilbrack, Kevin. *Philosophy and the Study of Religions: A Manifesto.* Malden, Mass.: Wiley Blackwell, 2014.

———. "Religion, Models of, and Reality: Are We Through with Geertz?" *Journal of the American Academy of Religion* 73, no. 2 (2005): 429–452.

———. "The Social Construction of 'Religion' and Its Limits: A Critical Reading of Timothy Fitzgerald." *Method and Theory in the Study of Religion* 24 (2012): 97–117.

Schleiermacher, Friedrich. *The Christian Faith.* Edited by H. R. Mackintosh and James Stuart Stewart. 2nd ed. Edinburgh: T & T Clark, 1999.

———. *Hermeneutics: The Handwritten Manuscripts.* Edited by Heinz Kimmerle. Translated by James Duke and James Forstman. Missoula, Mont.: Scholars Press, 1977.

———. *On Religion: Speeches to Its Cultured Despisers.* Translated by Richard Crouter. New York: Cambridge University Press, 1996.

Schmidt, Leigh Eric. "The Making of Modern 'Mysticism.'" *Journal of the American Academy of Religion* 71, no. 2 (June 2003): 273–302.

Schwitzgebel, Eric. "The Unreliability of Naive Introspection." *Philosophical Review* 117, no. 2 (2008): 245–273.

Scott, James C. *Weapons of the Weak: Everyday Forms of Peasant Resistance*. New Haven, Conn.: Yale University Press, 1985.

Scott, Joan W. "The Evidence of Experience." *Critical Inquiry* 17, no. 4 (1991): 773–797.

Sellars, Wilfrid. *Empiricism and the Philosophy of Mind*. Cambridge, Mass.: Harvard University Press, 1997.

Sharf, Robert H. "Buddhist Modernism and the Rhetoric of Meditative Experience." *Numen* 42, no. 3 (1995): 228–283.

———. "Experience." In *Critical Terms for Religious Studies*, edited by Mark C. Taylor, 94–116. Chicago: University of Chicago Press, 1998.

———. "Ritual." In *Critical Terms for the Study of Buddhism*, edited by Donald S. Lopez Jr. Chicago: University of Chicago Press, 2005.

———. "Whose Zen? Zen Nationalism Revisited." In *Rude Awakenings: Zen, the Kyoto School, and the Question of Nationalism*, edited by James W. Heisig and John C. Maraldo. Honolulu: University of Hawai'i Press, 1995.

———. "Zen and Japanese Nationalism." *History of Religions* 33, no. 1 (1993): 1–43.

———. "The Zen of Japanese Nationalism." In *Curators of the Buddha: The Study of Buddhism under Colonialism*, edited by Donald S. Lopez Jr. Chicago: University of Chicago Press, 1995.

Shaw, Rosalind. "Feminist Anthropology and the Gendering of Religious Studies." In *The Insider/Outsider Problem in the Study of Religion*, edited by Russell T. McCutcheon, 104–113. New York: Cassell, 1999.

Smart, Ninian. *The Phenomenon of Religion*. New York: Herder and Herder, 1973.

Smith, Jonathan Z. "Religion, Religions, Religious." In *Critical Terms for Religious Studies*, edited by Mark C. Taylor, 269–284. Chicago: University of Chicago Press, 1998.

Smith, Wilfred Cantwell. *The Meaning and End of Religion*. San Francisco: Harper & Row, 1978.

Spilka, Bernard, Ralph W. Hood, and Richard L. Gorsuch. *The Psychology of Religion: An Empirical Approach*. 3rd ed. New York: Guilford, 2003.

Spivak, Gayatri Chakravorty. "Can the Subaltern Speak?" In *Marxism and the Interpretation of Culture*, edited by Cary Nelson and Lawrence Grossberg, 271–313. Urbana: University of Illinois Press, 1988.

Springs, Jason A. "Meaning vs. Power: Are Thick Description and Power Analysis Intrinsically at Odds? Response to Interpretation, Explanation, and Clifford Geertz." *Religion Compass* 6, no. 12 (2012): 534–542.

———. *Toward a Generous Orthodoxy: Prospects for Hans Frei's Postliberal Theology*. New York: Oxford University Press, 2010.

Stace, W. T. *Mysticism and Philosophy*. Philadelphia: Lippincott, 1960.

Stanton, Elizabeth Cady. *The Woman's Bible*. Boston: Northeastern University Press, 1993.

Stout, Jeffrey. "Davidson, Rorty, and Brandom on Truth." In *Radical Interpretation in Religion*, edited by Nancy Frankenberry, 25–52. Cambridge: Cambridge University Press, 2002.

———. *Democracy and Tradition*. Princeton, N.J.: Princeton University Press, 2005.

———. "The Relativity of Interpretation." *The Monist* 69, no. 1 (1986): 103–118.

———. "What Is the Meaning of a Text?" *New Literary History* 14, no. 1 (1982): 1–12.

Taves, Ann. *Religious Experience Reconsidered: A Building-Block Approach to the Study of Religion and Other Special Things*. Princeton, N.J.: Princeton University Press, 2009.

Taylor, Charles. *Varieties of Religion Today: William James Revisited*. Cambridge, Mass.: Harvard University Press, 2002.

Thompson, E. P. *The Making of the English Working Class*. First Vintage ed. New York: Vintage, 1966.

Tite, Philip L. "Theoretical Challenges in Studying Religious Experience in Gnosticism: A Prolegomena for Social Analysis." *Bulletin for the Study of Religion* 42, no. 1 (2013): 8–18.

Turner, Denys. "Doing Theology in the University." In *Fields of Faith: Theology and Religious Studies for the Twenty-First Century*, edited by David Ford, Ben Quash, and Janet Martin Soskice 25–38. Cambridge: Cambridge University Press, 2005.

Tweed, Thomas A. *Our Lady of the Exile: Diasporic Religion at a Cuban Catholic Shrine in Miami*. New York: Oxford University Press, 2002.

Twiss, Sumner B., and Walter H. Conser. "Introduction." In *Experience of the Sacred: Readings in the Phenomenology of Religion*, edited by Sumner B. Twiss and Walter H. Conser, 1–74. Hanover, N.H.: University Press of New England, 1992.

"U. S. Religious Landscape Survey: Religious Beliefs and Practices: Diverse and Politically Relevant." Pew Forum on Religion and Public Life, June 2008. http://religions.pewforum.org/pdf/report2-religious-landscape-study-full.pdf.

Van Gelder, Tim. "What Might Cognition Be, If Not Computation?" *Journal of Philosophy* 92, no. 7 (1995): 345–381.

Weber, Max. *Economy and Society: An Outline of Interpretive Sociology*. Edited by Guenther Roth and Claus Wittich. Translated by Ephraim Fischoff et al. 2 vols. Berkeley: University of California Press, 1978.

———. *The Sociology of Religion*. Translated by Ephraim Fischoff. 4th ed. Boston: Beacon Press, 1993.

———. *Sociological Writings*. Edited by Wolf V. Heydebrand. New York: Continuum, 1994.

West, Cornel. "Schleiermacher's Hermeneutics and the Myth of the Given." *Union Seminary Quarterly Review* 34, no. 2 (1979): 71–84.

Whitehead, Alfred North. *Religion in the Making*. Cambridge: Cambridge University Press, 2011.

Wittgenstein, Ludwig. *On Certainty*. Edited by G. E. M. Anscombe and G. H. von Wright. Translated by G. E. M. Anscombe and Denis Paul. 1st Harper Torchbook ed. New York: Harper & Row, 1972.

———. *Philosophical Investigations: The German Text, with a Revised English Translation*. Translated by G. E. M. Anscombe. 3rd ed. Oxford: Blackwell, 2001.

Wolf, Arthur P. "Gods, Ghosts, and Ancestors." In *Religion and Ritual in Chinese Society*, edited by Arthur P. Wolf, 131–182. Stanford, Calif.: Stanford University Press, 1974.

Wolterstorff, Nicholas. *Justice: Rights and Wrongs*. Princeton, N.J.: Princeton University Press, 2008.

Young, Iris Marion. *On Female Body Experience: "Throwing Like a Girl" and Other Essays*. New York: Oxford University Press, 2005.

Young, Robert. *White Mythologies: Writing History and the West*. London: Routledge, 1990.

INDEX

African Americans, 50, 69

Alexander, Michelle, 215

Alston, William, 136, 137, 140, 151–152

Anti-representationalism, 113

Anti-Semitism, 51

Asad, Talal, 1–2, 12, 48–49, 53, 54, 62–63, 66, 69–70, 72–74, 94, 96, 130, 185–187, 225n37

Asceticism, 74

Attachment theory, 173, 237n33

Augustine, 49

Aung San Suu Kyi, 176

Authorial intent, 212

Authority, 170–171

Barnard, G. William, 134, 165

Beauvoir, Simone de, 46

Beliefs
  culture and, 140
  Geertz's appeal to, 48
  meaning and, 110–112, 121–122, 194–195
  perceptual experiences and, 140
  power and, 52, 225n37

Bell, Catherine, 49

Bender, Courtney, 62

Benhabib, Seyla, 4, 30, 41

Bernard of Clairvaux, 56, 177, 182

Boddy, Janice, 130–131, 206, 209

Bourdieu, Pierre, 3, 7, 10–13, 17, 43, 44, 99, 103–104, 127–129, 159–160, 185

Bracketing, 29

Brandom, Robert, 7, 10, 14–16, 107, 110, 113, 118, 119–120, 138, 141, 161, 231n54, 233n20, 234n22

Brazil, Pentecostalism in, 82–83

Brenner, Suzanne, 78–79, 84, 187

Brown, Anne S., 205

Brunschvicg, Leon, 180

Brusco, Elizabeth E., 80, 81, 172, 174, 175

Bureaucratic power, 171

Burke, Kenneth, 93

Butler, Judith, 3, 11, 12, 43, 44, 129, 185

Carnes, Mark C., 50

Cartesianism, 3–7, 147

Carus, Paul, 59

Catholicism, 82

Charismatic Christianity, 80, 83

Charismatic power, 171

Chesnut, R. Andrew, 82, 84, 181

Chidester, David, 12, 50, 51, 123

Chinese domestic rituals, 105, 189–190

Christ, Carol, 61